Economic Policy Reforms

Going for Growth

OECD

ORGANISATION FOR ECONOMIC CO-OPERATION AND DEVELOPMENT

ORGANISATION FOR ECONOMIC CO-OPERATION AND DEVELOPMENT

The OECD is a unique forum where the governments of 30 democracies work together to address the economic, social and environmental challenges of globalisation. The OECD is also at the forefront of efforts to understand and to help governments respond to new developments and concerns, such as corporate governance, the information economy and the challenges of an ageing population. The Organisation provides a setting where governments can compare policy experiences, seek answers to common problems, identify good practice and work to co-ordinate domestic and international policies.

The OECD member countries are: Australia, Austria, Belgium, Canada, the Czech Republic, Denmark, Finland, France, Germany, Greece, Hungary, Iceland, Ireland, Italy, Japan, Korea, Luxembourg, Mexico, the Netherlands, New Zealand, Norway, Poland, Portugal, the Slovak Republic, Spain, Sweden, Switzerland, Turkey, the United Kingdom and the United States. The Commission of the European Communities takes part in the work of the OECD.

OECD Publishing disseminates widely the results of the Organisation's statistics gathering and research on economic, social and environmental issues, as well as the conventions, guidelines and standards agreed by its members.

This work is published on the responsibility of the Secretary-General of the OECD. The opinions expressed and arguments employed herein do not necessarily reflect the official views of the Organisation or of the governments of its member countries.

Publié en français sous le titre :
Objectif croissance
Réformes économiques

Reprinted 2005

Foreword

This new OECD publication, *Economic Policy Reforms: Going for Growth,* is designed to help policy makers as they look for ways to achieve improved standards of living for citizens. It also aims to bring the debate on the important issues of economic reforms and their consequences to a wider public. Drawing on in-depth knowledge of economic circumstances and policy objectives in individual countries, it develops a benchmarking system based on a set of policy indicators. It then proposes a number of policy priorities for each country that would help promote stronger economic growth.

Although more than 50 000 delegates register for OECD meetings each year, many of these delegates and others primarily see the Organisation's work through the prism of their own area of interest – as I know from my own personal experience as a Ministerial delegate and from the testimony of others. As such, in presenting this publication, I am aware that its scope may surprise many readers, by showing that the OECD has a wealth of experience to draw on, and conducts structural policy analysis and surveillance in its member countries in almost every area of public policy.

To do this, the OECD uses a process based on mutual accountability and peer pressure. In addition to monitoring the performance of individual countries, structural surveillance at the OECD also includes cross-country monitoring focusing on a broad range of specific fields, including work and family life, ageing and employment policies, national education systems, and regulatory reform. Naturally enough, recommendations in these various fields often reflect objectives that go beyond growth or income maximisation and relate to wider dimensions of welfare. Policy recommendations in the field of labour and social affairs, for example, need to find a balance between equity and efficiency in their policy recommendations. The surveillance processes for education tend to stress the importance of equitable access to education in addition to the goal of increasing human capital.

Different areas of government may give differing weights to the respective importance of wealth and income maximisation on the one hand and broader equity issues on the other. How these differences are resolved affects, of course, the thrust of policy priorities. In *Economic Policy Reforms,* the main objective targeted is stronger economic growth. Its underlying premise is that growth is essential to create the additional resources needed to address a number of broader social and equity concerns, and therefore is key to the search for improving standards of living for all citizens.

As policy makers and others grapple with the challenges posed by the increasing interdependence of our economies, growth has to be at the top of our agenda. I wish to acknowledge the OECD-wide contribution that has enabled this project to benefit from inputs from many parts of the Organisation, and to thank the team led by Jean-Philippe Cotis, OECD's Chief Economist, for suggesting the idea and bringing it to fruition.

Donald J. Johnston
OECD Secretary-General

ECONOMIC POLICY REFORMS – ISBN 92-64-00836-5 – © OECD 2005

Table of Contents

The codes for country names and currencies used in this volume are those attributed to them by the International Organization for Standardization (ISO). These are listed below in alphabetical order by country code.

ISO Country Code	Country Name	ISO Currency Code
AUS	Australia	AUD
AUT	Austria	EUR
BEL	Belgium	EUR
CAN	Canada	CAD
CHE	Switzerland	CHF
CZE	Czech Republic	CZK
DEU	Germany	EUR
DNK	Denmark	DKK
ESP	Spain	EUR
EU	European Union (15 members prior to 2004 enlargement)	n/a
FIN	Finland	EUR
FRA	France	EUR
GBR	United Kingdom	GBP
GRC	Greece	EUR
HUN	Hungary	HUF
IRL	Ireland	EUR
ISL	Iceland	ISK
ITA	Italy	EUR
JPN	Japan	JPY
KOR	Republic of Korea	KRW
LUX	Luxembourg	EUR
MEX	Mexico	MXN
NLD	Netherlands	EUR
NOR	Norway	NOK
NZL	New Zealand	NZD
POL	Poland	PLN
PRT	Portugal	EUR
SVK	Slovak Republic	SKK
SWE	Sweden	SEK
TUR	Turkey	TRL
USA	United States	USD

Preface

Growth is back at the centre-stage of public attention throughout the OECD. This renewed focus is not accidental. Disappointment with long-term economic performance has been increasingly noticeable in many OECD countries. At the same time, it is widely felt that regaining growth momentum is key to preserving standards of living at a time of rapidly ageing societies.

Achieving stronger growth presents national policy makers with serious challenges. Learning from past mistakes and strengthening even successful policies will be important. But learning by doing, in isolation, may not be enough. Learning from others may be equally or even more important to raising national performance.

In large part, this is why the OECD was created, at a time of widespread confidence in the capacity of less advanced member countries to achieve full economic convergence with the best performers. Learning from others has often been impeded however by the sense that one's own circumstances are too singular to allow for meaningful transposition from abroad. Indeed, many signs are suggesting that economic convergence among industrialised countries has stalled or even backtracked since the 1980s, indicating that adaptation of OECD surveillance may be needed.

Surveillance processes at the OECD already include country-specific and sector-specific surveys that cover all member countries. What they do not yet include, however, is cross-country surveillance of growth, based on systematic benchmarking and with a view to advising member countries on national priorities. In the context of stalling convergence, benchmarking may help expose more clearly the areas where countries are lagging.

Successful benchmarking may also be easier to accomplish at a time when substantial progress has been made in cross-country data availability and econometric analysis. Methodological progress has made it possible to go beyond what may be described as "superficial benchmarking", where one makes international comparisons of GDP per capita, labour productivity or employment rates without knowing what lies behind apparent differences in performance. For example, a relatively low level of GDP per capita may have strikingly different welfare implications depending on whether it reflects the prevalence of public policies inhibiting economic initiative or a genuinely stronger preference for leisure. In the latter case, higher GDP per capita does not translate into higher quality of life, which is nonetheless the ultimate objective of national policies.

Our new publication, *Economic Policy Reforms*, is an attempt at "deep benchmarking" involving carefully constructed structural policy indicators with a proven, econometric link to economic performance. This should help assess the extent to which divergence in performance reflects differences in the effectiveness of public policies, rather than differences in tastes and societal choices.

The main aim of this new publication is therefore to facilitate the transfer of successful national experiences while avoiding the pitfalls of "one-size-fits-all" policy prescriptions that would impinge on legitimate international diversity.

To illustrate the usefulness of "deep benchmarking", it is instructive to consider the extreme variability of employment rates of persons aged 55 or over across OECD member countries. Analysis suggests that this diversity was mainly caused by disincentives embedded in public policies rather than different attitudes towards retirement age. For those countries which currently suffer from low rates of employment of ageing workers, there may thus be hope that better policies can tap an important source of growth. This example also highlights that growth surveillance may serve to increase not only standards of living, but welfare in a wider sense by promoting fuller participation in economic and social life.

Because this publication addresses complex issues, considerable efforts have been made to ensure it is transparent and self-contained. All the indicators are documented with graphs and their construction made as clear as possible to the reader. A special thematic chapter is devoted to our indicators of product market regulation. The link between some key policy indicators and performance are explored in two thematic chapters dealing with the impact of public policies on the supply of labour from ageing workers and women. This analytical material is intended to provide clear justifications for our assessment of OECD-wide progress achieved in the field of growth-oriented structural reforms. It is also central to understanding the motivation behind the selection of five policy priorities for each member country.

When dealing with national priorities, it is important to also leave room for individual considerations. However well designed, a set of comparable indicators will never fully capture national circumstances. Here the expertise of our country specialists has been used to tailor two policy priorities for each country that may or may not be reflected in the standardised indicators.

For all its many contributors, representing various OECD Directorates, there is a clear recognition that the launch of *Economic Policy Reforms* is only the starting point of a long process leading to further learning along the way. Wider coverage of potential sources of growth, such as financial markets and innovation policies, will be sought in the future, as will methodological and presentational improvements. We also hope that interested readers will help us, through their constructive remarks and critiques, to make this publication increasingly useful, relevant, and, hopefully, interesting.

Jean-Philippe Cotis
OECD Chief Economist

PART I

Taking Stock of Structural Policies in OECD Countries

The cut-off date for information used in Part I is end-November 2004.

ISBN 92-64-00836-5
Economic Policy Reforms
© OECD 2005

Chapter 1

Structural Policy Priorities

Over the past decade, the gap in GDP per capita relative to the United States has widened in a number of countries, including the large continental European economies and Japan. The gap is linked to lower hours worked per capita, lower output levels per hour worked, or both. This chapter describes broad trends in economic performance since the mid-1990s and summarises structural policy priorities for all member countries to enhance GDP per capita. The policy priorities are identified on the basis of cross-country comparisons of performance and policy settings.

Introduction

Over the past decade, trends in GDP per capita and productivity have diverged across major OECD countries. In Japan and some of the largest EU member states, growth rates have declined, contrasting with the acceleration observed in the United States and a few other countries. This diverging performance across the major economies and the concurrent widening of income gaps have brought renewed attention to the influence of institutions and structural policy settings on productivity and GDP growth, and have highlighted the need for reforms to improve growth performance.

In order to support the corresponding reform efforts, the OECD has developed a set of indicators to evaluate the economic performance and the effectiveness of structural policies of member countries. These indicators are used to identify policy priorities for each country to enhance long-term growth. This work builds on the structural surveillance already carried out in the OECD, both the general monitoring reported in the *OECD Economic Surveys* and reviews of specific areas of structural policy (Box 1.1).

For each country, a total of five policy priorities have been identified, mostly in the areas of labour and product markets and, to a lesser extent, education. In all cases, the selection of policy indicators and priorities is made with an overall view to raise GDP per capita. Increasing GDP per capita is obviously not the only objective of governments, who strive to improve living standards and welfare more generally, but higher output increases their scope to attain other goals (Annex 1.A.1). Identifying the same number of priorities for well – and less well-performing countries alike has obvious implications. On the one hand, in countries with weak performance and policy settings that deviate from best practice in many areas, important policy priorities may be left out. On the other hand, in countries with very good performance and policies close to best practice, the priorities identified may not always be seen as having a high degree of urgency.

Box 1.1. **Structural surveillance in the OECD**

This stocktaking of structural reforms aims at providing member countries and interested readers with a cross-country report surveying the wide array of factors and policies that drive long-term growth, in order ultimately to improve performance. This exercise builds on the various structural surveillance processes that are part of the regular work of the OECD. These include general surveillance on a country-by-country basis that is reported in the *Economic Surveys* and cross-country surveillance focused on more specific fields that is reported in a variety of OECD publications.

Box 1.1. **Structural surveillance in the OECD** (cont.)

The general surveillance reported in the OECD Economic Surveys involves the monitoring of long-term economic performance and structural-policy settings, in addition to policy recommendations to improve performance. While cross-country comparisons of performance and policies are used extensively in this work, policy recommendations are often arrived at without international benchmarking, and are instead based on in-depth knowledge of country circumstances and policy objectives. By contrast, the present report makes much more systematic use of benchmarking in deriving policy priorities.

The structural surveillance work in the OECD that focuses on more specific issues is organised along the following lines:

- Labour market performance and social conditions are monitored on a regular basis, and this often involves a review of policies on the basis of internationally-comparable indicators (e.g. benefit replacement rates, the intensity of employment protection legislation and various aspects of active labour market policies). The results of this surveillance are reported in the OECD Employment Outlook and Benefits and Wages, and in country reports on the public employment service, work and family life, and ageing and employment policies.

- The extent and the quality of education of the young and of the population at large, and related policies, are reviewed on a regular basis. The reviews are published in Education at a Glance, reports from the Programme for International Student Assessment (PISA), and country reviews on national policies for education.

- Developments in taxation of labour income are examined on a yearly basis, and this includes the construction of standardised indicators of average and marginal tax rates for all member countries. The indicators are published in Taxing Wages.

- Support to agriculture and the different forms of such assistance is monitored on an annual basis and published in Agricultural Policies in OECD Countries.

- Performance and policies with respect to science, technology and industry is reviewed regularly and published in Science, Technology and Industry: Outlook, the OECD Information Technology Outlook, the OECD Communications Outlook and the OECD SME and Entrepreneurship Outlook.

- Policies that have an impact on high quality regulation, competition and market openness in product markets are regularly reviewed and published in the series of OECD Reviews of Regulatory Reforms.

In some cases, the monitoring of performance and policies is accompanied by country-specific recommendations. This has been the case in e.g. reviews of public employment services, work and family life, ageing and employment policies, national education systems, and regulatory reforms.

The policy recommendations that emerge from the surveillance of these various fields may sometimes give emphasis to objectives that go beyond growth or income maximisation and relate to wider dimensions of welfare. Thus, for example, the surveillance processes for labour and social affairs emphasise the need to find a balance between equity and efficiency in their policy recommendations, and the surveillance processes for education tend to stress the importance of equitable access to education in addition to the goal of increasing human capital.

Broad trends in performance

Looking at trend performances over the past decade or so, many countries have managed to pursue or resume convergence of living standards on that of the leading country (United States) despite the particularly strong performance observed in the latter over the period (Figure 1.1).[1] Since 1993, GDP per capita rose relative to that in the United States in over half of member countries: English-speaking and Nordic countries, as well as Central European countries, Greece, Korea and Spain. The countries that grew fastest relative to the United States are mainly those where GDP per capita remains comparatively low (Hungary, Korea, Poland and Slovakia). A notable exception is Ireland, which after more than 15 years of the fastest growth in GDP per capita in the OECD area is close to par with living standards in the United States.[2]

In contrast, the gap in GDP per capita has either remained unchanged or widened in several continental European countries over the same period (Austria, Belgium, France, Germany, Italy and Switzerland) as well as in Japan. For the European Union and Japan, the level of GDP per capita remains between 25 and 30% below that in the United States. While the size of the gap varies quite significantly across EU countries, differences are relatively small among the largest member states (with gaps also between 25 and 30%). The most disappointing performance over the past decade in the OECD area has been registered in Mexico and Turkey, which combined the weakest (after Switzerland) growth rate and the lowest levels of GDP per capita.

The gap in GDP per capita can be broken down into labour-utilisation and labour-productivity gaps (Figure 1.2). Lower total hours worked per person of working age account for the main part of the GDP per capita gap in many continental European countries

Figure 1.1. **GDP per capita levels and growth rates:**
Gap *vis-à-vis* the United States[1]

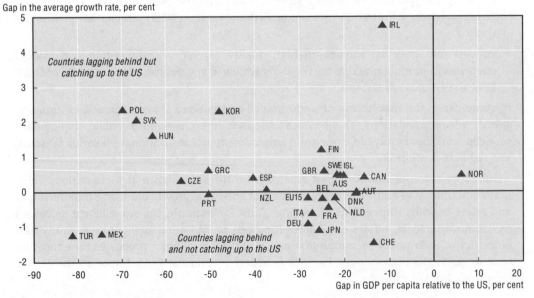

Note: EU15, excluding Luxembourg.

1. The average growth rate of GDP per capita is calculated over the period 1994-2003 on the basis of volumes data from national accounts sources. The level of GDP per capita is for 2002 on the basis of 2000 PPPs.

Source: OECD, *National Accounts of OECD Countries*, 2004 and *OECD Economic Outlook*, No. 76.

Figure 1.2. **The sources of real income differences, 2002**

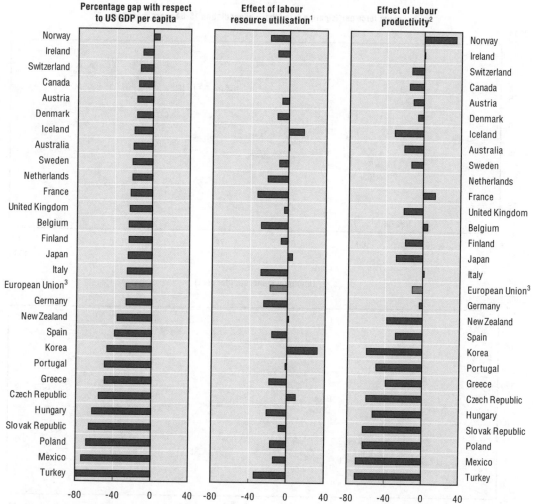

1. Labour resource utilisation is measured as total number of hours worked divided by population.
2. Labour productivity is measured as GDP per hour worked.
3. Excluding Luxembourg.

Source: OECD, *National Accounts of OECD Countries*, 2004; *OECD Labour Force Statistics*, 2004 and *OECD Economic Outlook*, No. 76.

(Belgium, France, Germany, Italy and the Netherlands). This is due to low participation of people of working age in the labour market and high unemployment (Figure 1.3). This effect is typically reinforced by fewer hours worked per employee, as part-time work is more prevalent and annual working hours for full-time workers are lower. Since 1995, labour utilisation in continental Europe has been affected by two opposite trends: relatively strong gains in employment ratios have been offset to varying degrees by a continuing decline in average hours worked per employee. This development often reflects an increasing share of women in the labour force, as women are more likely to work part-time. However, in some countries the decline in average hours has gone beyond what can be accounted for by an increase in voluntary part-time work.

Lower productivity levels per hour worked account for the bulk of the gap in GDP per capita in Japan and most non-US English-speaking countries, as well as in Iceland, Switzerland and most lower-income member countries (Czech Republic, Korea, Mexico, Portugal and

Figure 1.3. **Sources of change in labour resource utilisation**

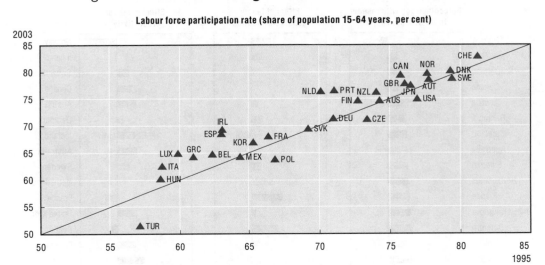

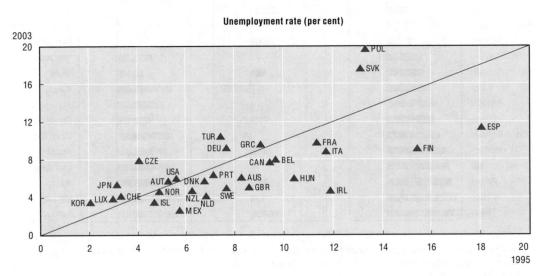

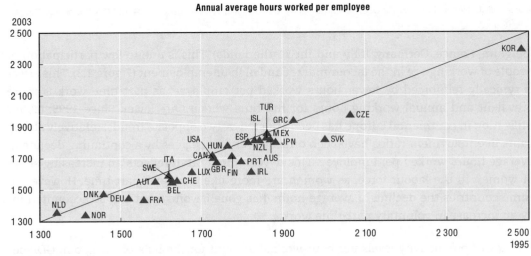

Source: OECD Economic Outlook, No. 76 and OECD Labour Force Statistics, 2004.

Figure 1.4. **Labour productivity**[1]

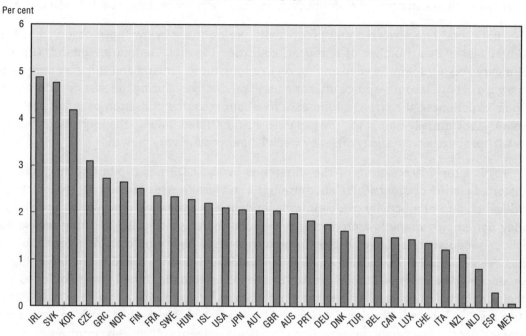

A. Labour productivity, average growth rates 1994-2003[2]

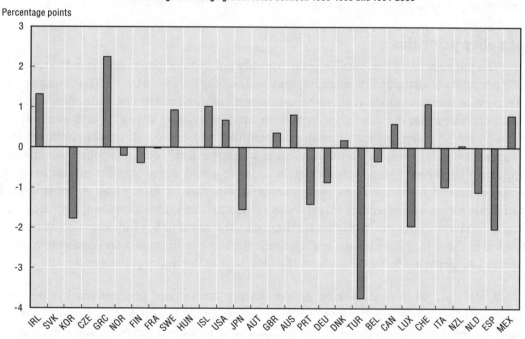

B. Change in average growth rates between 1985-1993 and 1994-2003[3]

1. Measured as GDP per hour worked.
2. Labour productivity is not reported for Poland due to missing hours data. Slovak Republic covers 1995-2003. For Luxembourg, labour productivity is derived by using domestic employment (including cross-border workers).
3. The change in labour productivity is not reported for Austria; Czech Republic, Hungary and Slovak Republic due to short hours data series.

Source: OECD, National Accounts of OECD Countries, 2004; OECD Labour Force Statistics, 2004 and OECD Economic Outlook, No. 76.

Slovak Republic). Of these, only the Czech Republic, Korea and the Slovak Republic have managed to obtain productivity growth rates well in excess of those in the United States (Figure 1.4), thus narrowing the productivity gap significantly over the past ten years.

Both total hours worked and productivity per hour are below those observed in the United States in a number of European countries (Austria, Denmark, Finland, Greece, Hungary, Poland, Spain, Sweden and Turkey). Among these, Finland and Hungary narrowed the gaps in both labour resource utilisation and productivity during the past decade. While Spain experienced the strongest increase in labour resource utilisation over the past ten years – substantially narrowing the gap *vis-à-vis* the United States – the impact on the gap in GDP per capita was largely offset by weak labour productivity growth.

This simple accounting of the difference in the GDP per capita gap may give a distorted picture of countries' relative strengths and weaknesses because aggregate labour utilisation and productivity can be interdependent. Countries with low labour utilisation may not employ many low productivity workers, thereby artificially boosting measured labour productivity relative to that in countries with high employment rates. Thus, it has been estimated that raising employment rates and hours worked in the large "high-productivity" continental European countries to the level in the United States could reduce their productivity levels relative to the United States by up to 15% (Artus and Cette, 2004). As a result, a labour-utilisation deficit could become a sizeable productivity gap. Increased employment of low-productivity workers in a few continental European countries over the past decade is also estimated to have slowed productivity growth in these countries, but cannot fully account for the very low growth in output per hour worked.

Areas of policy priorities

The purpose of this stocktaking is to identify policy priorities most likely to stimulate GDP per capita in all individual member countries and the European Union. The starting point is the preceding examination of labour utilisation and productivity performance, which is expanded in further detail to uncover specific areas of relative strengths and weaknesses. A broad set of policy indicators is then assembled and compared across countries (see Chapter 2) with the aim of identifying cases where performance and policy weaknesses appear to be linked.[3] More specifically, in order to avoid a one-size-fits-all approach to policy reform, a deviation from best-practice in a particular policy area is considered a candidate for priority selection only if a weak performance is also identified in an area that is affected by the policy in question. Furthermore, the set of policy indicators considered is limited to those that have been shown empirically to have an impact on economic growth. Annex 1.A2 provides further details on the selection of the policy priorities.

At this stage, the stocktaking covers mainly labour and product market policies, supplemented by a few policy/performance indicators for health and education.[4] On the basis of these indicators, three policy priorities are identified for each member country and the European Union (Table 1.1), and are discussed in the country notes in Chapter 3. The table and the country notes also include two additional policy priorities identified for each country that are not necessarily based on cross-country comparison of policy indicators, thereby allowing for important policy requirements in areas not yet covered by quantitative indicators.[5] Considering the potential synergies between the individual policies, the priorities are best seen as a package, as the benefit from taking action on several fronts simultaneously is likely to be greater than the sum of the benefits obtained from acting on individual policy recommendations in isolation.

Policies to improve labour productivity performance

There is broad evidence that policies and institutional settings that foster product market competition play a key role in influencing firms to seek efficiency gains, through adopting either technological or organisational best practices. Growing recognition of this has contributed to widespread reform of product market regulation, leading to a more pro-competitive climate in most OECD countries (see Chapter 4). However, while a certain degree of convergence towards best practice in product market regulation has been observed since the late 1990s, significant scope for improvement remains in virtually all areas: state control of economic activities; barriers to entrepreneurial activity (administrative burdens or restrictions on market access); and barriers to trade (mainly in agriculture and services) and foreign direct investment.

In Europe, progress towards the completion of the EU single market for goods and services has helped boost competitive pressures arising from cross-border activities, even though important non-trade barriers remain. The process of EU integration has also contributed to significant reforms in network services (albeit at different paces across industries and countries), including through privatisation and opening of market access to potential competitors in sectors traditionally dominated by monopolies. Nonetheless, it is a priority for many European countries (including non-EU members) to strengthen competitive pressures in network and other industries:

- Barriers to entry in network industries (such as electricity, telecommunication and railways) and/or professional services should be further reduced in Denmark, France, Germany, Greece, Iceland and Switzerland.

- Administrative burdens on start-ups should be lowered (Austria, Czech Republic, Greece, Hungary and Turkey).

- The burdens of regulation on business operations arising from price controls or administrative procedures should be eased (Belgium, Ireland and the Netherlands).

- The extent of public ownership should be reduced (Finland, Hungary, Italy, Norway, Poland, Portugal, Sweden and Turkey).

Considering, in addition, that fully taking advantage of new technological opportunities may require significant labour re-allocation in many industries, efforts to seek efficiency gains may be hampered in some countries by excessively strict employment protection legislation (EPL).

Outside Europe, the productivity gap relative to the United States either widened further or has remained large during the past ten years. While product market regulation is not generally seen as overly stringent, further liberalisation of specific network industries and/or services (such as retail distribution and professional services) continues to be a priority in Japan and Canada – where little reform has taken place since the 1980s – as well as in Korea and Mexico. The case for stimulating competition in service sectors is particularly compelling in Japan, where the price of services relative to that of consumer goods is the highest in OECD countries even after controlling for differences in income levels (Figure 1.5).

Figure 1.5. **Relative price of services and GDP per capita**

A. Ratio of the price level of consumer services to that of consumer goods and the level of GDP per capita[1]

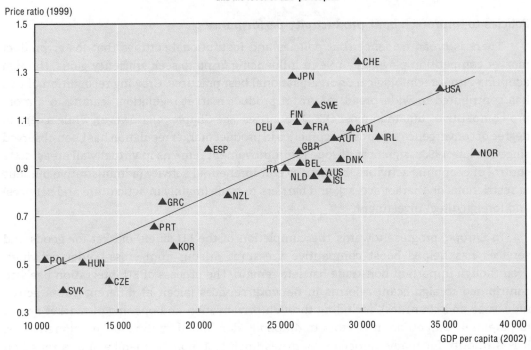

B. The relative price ratio adjusted for differences in the level of GDP per capita[2]

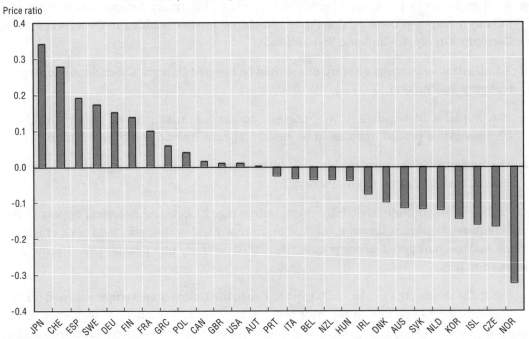

1. Consumer services are a proxy for non-tradable products and goods (semi-durables and durables) are a proxy for tradable products. The level of GDP per capita in 2002 is measured in US dollars on the basis of 2000 PPPs.
2. Measured as the difference between the actual and the fitted value of the price ratio appearing in panel A.

Source: OECD, National Accounts of OECD Countries, 2004; OECD Economic Outlook, No. 76 and Purchasing Power Parities and Real Expenditure, 2002.

Important barriers to competition still prevail in the agricultural sector of many countries, and these take various forms, such as import barriers, domestic price support for specific products and/or transfer payments to farmers. In terms of economic efficiency, high producer support to agriculture results in a misallocation of resources in most OECD countries and creates trade and price distortions in world markets for agricultural commodities, often at the expense of producers in developing countries (OECD, 2004a). While overall policy-determined transfers to agriculture have slightly risen in 2003, some efforts have been made to at least reduce their trade-distorting impact, essentially by gradually decoupling the amount of aid from the quantity of output produced or input consumed. However, reductions in trade-distorting support to agriculture should be a key priority in the European Union as a whole, as well as in Iceland, Japan, Korea, Norway, Switzerland and the United States. In this regard, the pledge to eliminate all forms of export subsidisation made in the context of the recent agreement on a framework for continuing the Doha Round should be fulfilled.

The accumulation of skills and competencies – or human capital – can raise productivity by improving the "quality" of the labour force, thereby also facilitating the adoption of new technologies and/or the innovation process. Differences in the average level of human capital across countries may reflect both variations in quantity (such as the average number of years spent in formal education) and in "quality" of schooling (OECD, 2004b). While some indicators of performance can be constructed, more direct policy indicators are difficult to develop in part due to the lack of consensus about what constitutes "best practice" in this area.

Although the percentage of population that has attained at least upper secondary education has risen in virtually all OECD countries over the past 15-20 years, productivity gains may be hampered in several countries by the significant share of the working-age population still lacking basic skills. Hence, further efforts need to be made to raise the standards of the compulsory school system (Germany, Luxembourg, Mexico, New Zealand, Portugal, Slovak Republic, Spain and the United States) and to reduce the proportion of young people leaving school without at least upper-secondary education (Australia, Iceland, Italy, and the United Kingdom). At the same time, reforms aimed at strengthening human capital investment should take into account the need in some cases to reduce undue delays in labour market entry of young people, in particular from tertiary education.

Policies to improve labour resource utilisation

Incremental changes in policies aimed at improving labour market performance have been common over the past few years, but significant reforms have been rare. The Agenda 2010 programme in Germany is a useful step in the right direction. It represents a shift in policy, especially by reducing work disincentives through the limitation of the duration of unemployment benefits and the lowering of benefit levels for those out of jobs for a long time. In return, extra resources are devoted to providing job-search assistance, such as personalised job counselling and monitoring, so as to improve matching. In addition, a few countries (Austria, France, Finland, Germany, Italy and Portugal) have introduced reforms of their pension systems and/or *de facto* early retirement schemes in the past two years that will ultimately reduce financial disincentive to work at older ages.

In some cases, reforms have also been introduced or extended in areas of labour taxation (Ireland, Netherlands and the United Kingdom), active labour market policies (Australia, Denmark and the Netherlands) and unemployment benefits (Denmark). Some countries have combined a number of measures to raise work incentives, in particular for workers with low earnings potential, so as to strengthen their attachment to labour market. For instance, in-work benefits such as earned-income tax credits have been used in some cases in combination with effective activation policies and/or targeted reductions in employers' social security contributions, (France, Ireland, United Kingdom and United States). While these packages of measures have had some success in raising participation rates among those mainly targeted, they increase effective marginal tax rates in the income range where in-work benefits are withdrawn, potentially reducing hours worked.

Notwithstanding these reforms and a general improvement in labour market outcomes since the mid-1990s, labour under-utilisation remains an area of key policy priority for most continental European countries. In some of these countries (Austria, Belgium, France and Luxembourg), labour force participation among older workers is particularly low but could be boosted by a reduction in the "implicit tax on continued work" (see Chapter 5). Strong financial disincentives to remain in the labour force after the age of 55 often arise from the design of the pension system and/or from other benefit programmes (notably those concerned with unemployment and disability). These can be used as pathways to early retirement rather than for the purposes for which the programmes were designed.

Efforts to cut work disincentives need to be supplemented by measures to stimulate employers' demand for labour. This is particularly the case in countries where unemployment is already high, especially among younger and low-skilled workers. Significant reductions in unemployment rates may be difficult to achieve without a decline in the cost of labour at low income/productivity levels (Belgium, Czech Republic, France, Germany, Hungary, Italy, Poland and Slovak Republic). While this can be attained through a cut in social security contributions on low wages, the impact of such measures would be reinforced if increases in the statutory minimum wage were kept more moderate than for wages in general. This especially applies where such wage floors are relatively high, such as in France, where they are scheduled to rise further partly as a result of introducing the 35-hour week.

Better alignment between wages and productivity at the firm level could also be achieved by changes to centralised wage bargaining processes in certain sectors, as is the case in Italy and Spain. This may in some cases be facilitated by a reduction in the extent of administrative extension of collective wage agreements applied to all firms within a sector, and by the public sector taking the lead in decentralising bargaining. The stringency of employment protection legislation, especially for regular contracts, should also be eased in some countries (Czech Republic, France, Greece and Portugal) in order to boost demand for labour and reduce the incidence of long-term unemployment. Given that such reform to employment protection legislation is likely to raise both job creation and job losses, it should be accompanied by a re-enforcement of measures to assist laid-off workers to find a new job.

Even in countries where aggregate employment rates are less of a problem, targeted reforms could bring about further improvements. For example, the relatively low hours worked per capita and per employee observed in Denmark, Norway and Sweden may result from a combination of greater use of disability and sickness benefits, and higher labour income taxation than in other countries. High labour costs, together with high net replacement rates for the long-term unemployed may contribute to prevent structural unemployment in Finland from falling back to levels before the large negative shocks of the early 1990s and to a level more comparable with that observed in other Nordic countries, despite similarities in other labour market institutions and policy settings.

Canada and, to a lesser extent, New Zealand could achieve further improvements in labour-market performance by reforming specific features of their income support system. Australia and the United Kingdom could boost participation rates by limiting entry into disability benefit schemes to those that are unable to work, given the sharp increase in recent years in the proportion of disability benefit recipients among the non-employed. Finally, although participation and employment rates are relatively high in Japan, overall labour resource utilisation has clearly fallen on average over the past ten years. In order to reverse the trend, priority should be given to easing employment protection legislation which impedes firms' willingness to hire, and thus hampers their restructuring effort.

Challenges ahead

With performance diverging across geographical zones, it is not surprising that the same can be observed for policy priorities. More specifically:

- Low utilisation of potential labour resources in continental European countries is reflected in a large number of policy priorities aimed at boosting labour supply and demand. Nonetheless, higher employment may come at a price of lower average productivity, and a number of priorities for these countries also concern liberalisation of product markets and improvements in education systems.

- For countries with low levels of income per capita, but also for Japan, productivity is the main gap in performance, and important policy priorities relate to liberalisation of product markets.

- English-speaking countries generally have high utilisation of potential labour resources but variable productivity performance and strengthening the performance of education systems is a recurrent priority for these countries.

Looking at the distribution of indicator-based priorities across main policy areas, labour and product market policies each account for about 45% of total priorities with most of the rest being accounted for by recommendations in the field of education. Concerning the labour market, the priorities are evenly split between recommendations to reform the income-support system (including the pension system so as to lower financial disincentives to continue work for older people), to reduce tax wedges on labour income and to review labour market regulation, in particular regarding employment protection legislation and statutory minimum wages. With respect to the product market, a similar number of priorities has been identified for each of the broad areas, namely state control over business operation (public ownership and price controls), barriers to entrepreneurship, and barriers to foreign trade and investment.

Table 1.1. **Structural policies and performance: proposed priorities**

	Performance areas	
	Labour utilisation	Labour productivity
Australia	Refocus disability benefit schemes to encourage work by those with substantial work capacity. Increase the weight of employability in the setting of minimum wages ("award wages"). Strengthen employment prospects for lower-skilled workers by improving vocational education. *Reduce tax wedge on low-income workers to improve work incentives for this group.*	*Accelerate reforms aimed at lowering barriers to entry in network industries.*
Austria	Reduce implicit tax on continued work to cut disincentives to work at older ages. *Reform child support benefit system to weaken inactivity traps.*	Raise overall human capital by improving graduation rates from tertiary education. Reduce administrative costs for start-ups and ease entry regulations in professional services. *Strengthen competition law and enforcement by giving more powers to the competition authority.*
Belgium	Strengthen work incentives by reducing the tax wedge on labour income. Reduce disincentives to work at older ages by limiting early retirement through unemployment. *Reduce the incidence of long-term unemployment by strengthening job-search requirements and improving skills of the unemployed.*	Ease sectoral regulations and subject all new regulations to an efficiency test. *Improve educational outcomes for students from ethnic backgrounds.*
Canada	Strengthen incentives to move from welfare to work via stricter job search and activation requirements. *Restrain growth in public health care costs to limit increases in taxation and labour costs.*	Switch from foreign ownership barriers to other means to pursue cultural goals, etc. Further liberalise professional services by removing inter-provincial trade restrictions. *Reduce effective taxation on capital to encourage business investment.*
Czech Republic	Stimulate hiring by cutting the costs of EPL for regular workers. Reduce tax wedge on low-income workers to strengthen work incentives for this group. *Further liberalise the rental housing market to increase labour mobility.*	Implement intended reform of bankruptcy laws and simplify business registration. *Reform system of taxes and benefits to reduce poverty traps for non-employed households.*
Denmark	Strengthen work incentives by reducing the tax wedge on labour income. Assist disabled beneficiaries to rejoin the labour force part time, and introduce a waiting period and stronger certification for sickness benefit. *Reduce implicit tax on continued work embedded in the early retirement scheme.*	Reduce barriers to entry in industries to strengthen competition in product markets. *Improve educational achievements to raise the efficiency of the work force.*
Finland	Strengthen work incentives by reducing the tax wedge on labour income. Reduce implicit tax on continued work at older ages by reforming early retirement pathways. *Promote greater flexibility in centralised wage agreements to expand employment opportunities.* *Reduce the incidence of long-term unemployment by tapering unemployment benefits with duration.*	Reduce the scale of public ownership, especially raising private provision of publicly-funded services.

ECONOMIC POLICY REFORMS – ISBN 92-64-00836-5 – © OECD 2005

Table 1.1. **Structural policies and performance: proposed priorities** (cont.)

	Performance areas	
	Labour utilisation	Labour productivity
France	Stimulate hiring by cutting the costs of EPL for regular workers.	*Accelerate reforms aimed at lowering barriers to entry in network industries.*
	Stimulate labour demand for youth and low-skilled by allowing for a relative decline in the minimum cost of labour.	*Promote greater competition in retail distribution by reviewing regulation concerning retail outlet locations and pricing rules.*
	Reduce implicit tax on continued work at older ages by reforming early retirement pathways.	
Germany	Strengthen work incentives by reducing the tax wedge on labour income.	Improve secondary education achievements to raise efficiency of the workforce.
	Reduce disincentives to work at older ages by removing preferential unemployment benefit eligibility conditions for older workers.	Liberalise professional services by phasing-out binding fee schedules in specific professions.
		Raise competition in government procurement to increase public spending efficiency.
Greece	Reduce age/gender imbalances in unemployment by easing the most stringent provisions of EPL.	Accelerate reforms aimed at lowering barriers to entry in network industries.
	Reduce disincentives to work at older ages by linking pension to lifetime earnings.	Promote greater domestic competition by reducing administrative costs for start-ups.
		Simplify the tax code to reduce compliance costs for businesses and to boost private investment.
Hungary	Reduce the tax wedge for low-income workers to improve their incentives to work in the formal economy.	Reduce state control on the operations of network industries to allow prices to better reflect market signals and to facilitate entry.
	Refocus disability benefit schemes to encourage work by those with substantial work capacity.	Promote greater domestic competition by reducing administrative costs for start-ups.
	Downsize the housing loan subsidy programme to reduce housing market distortions and facilitate labour mobility.	
Iceland		Lower barriers to entry for domestic and foreign firms especially in the energy and fisheries sectors.
	Reduce government backing of bonds issued by the Housing Finance Fund to reduce housing market distortions and facilitate labour mobility.	Raise overall human capital by improving enrolment and graduation rates from upper-secondary education.
		Reduce producer support to agriculture, especially the most trade-distorting type.
		Raise public-sector efficiency by accelerating performance measurement and management.
Ireland	Strengthen work incentives for lower-skilled second earners via a tax credit or a subsidy for child care.	Ease regulatory burden on business operations to reduce compliance costs.
	Phase-out tax deductibility of mortgage payments to reduce housing market distortions and facilitate labour mobility.	Promote greater competition in network industries and retail distribution by facilitating entry.
		Strengthen enforcement of competition law by giving the competition authority more power.
Italy	Strengthen work incentives by reducing the tax wedge on labour income.	Reduce the scope of public ownership by allowing for more competition in the provision of public local services.
	Promote greater flexibility in wage bargaining by decentralising wage-setting arrangements in the public sector.	Raise overall human capital by improving access to, and graduation rates from, upper-secondary and tertiary education.
		Improve corporate governance by strengthening directors' independence and minority shareholder rights.

Table 1.1. **Structural policies and performance: proposed priorities** (*cont.*)

	Performance areas	
	Labour utilisation	Labour productivity
Japan	Stimulate hiring by cutting the costs of EPL for regular workers.	Promote greater competition in network industries and professional services by facilitating entry. Reduce producer support to agriculture, especially the most trade-distorting type. *Improve the soundness and functioning of financial system by resolving the non-performing loan problem.* *Reduce barriers to foreign direct investment to enhance technological transfers from abroad.*
Korea	Stimulate hiring by cutting the costs of EPL for regular workers.	Promote greater competition in network industries and professional services by facilitating entry. Reduce producer support to agriculture, especially the most trade-distorting type. *Improve the soundness and functioning of the financial system by extending privatisation and strengthening financial supervision.* *Reduce barriers to foreign direct investment to enhance technological transfers from abroad.*
Luxembourg	Reduce implicit tax on continued work at older ages by reforming early retirement pathways. Strengthen incentives to move from welfare to work by raising in-work benefits at low wages relative to unemployment benefits.	Improve primary and secondary education achievements to raise efficiency of the work force. *Raise public-sector efficiency by expanding the role of e-government and simplifying administrative procedures.* *Reduce barriers to competition in telecommunications to reap further benefits from liberalisation.*
Mexico	*Shift burden of taxation towards consumption by broadening the value-added tax base.*	Improve secondary education achievements to raise efficiency of the workforce. Promote greater competition in product markets by reducing barriers to entry in industries. Reduce barriers to foreign ownership to enhance technological transfers from abroad. *Strengthen investors' confidence by improving the enforceability of contracts.*
Netherlands	Strengthen work incentives by reducing the tax wedge on labour income. Refocus disability benefit schemes to encourage work by those with substantial work capacity. *Stimulate labour mobility by reforming residential zoning restrictions.*	Reduce compliance costs for businesses by simplifying administrative procedures. *Promote greater competition in network industries and retail distribution by facilitating entry.*
New Zealand	Strengthen incentives to move from welfare to work via activation requirements and back-to-work bonuses. *Stimulate labour demand by reconsidering recent measures that have raised labour costs.*	Reduce barriers to foreign ownership and use other means to protect sensitive land. Improve educational achievement, in particular among ethnic minorities. *Improve the regulatory framework for addressing infrastructure bottlenecks.*
Norway	Refocus disability and sickness benefit schemes to encourage work by those with substantial work capacity. *Use direct transfers rather than provisions of labour market and natural resource policies to achieve regional objectives.* *Reduce future pension contributions by using the Petroleum Fund to pre-fund part of pension liabilities.*	Reduce the scope of public ownership by pursuing privatisation of competitive activities in network industries. Reduce producer support to agriculture, especially the most trade-distorting type.

ECONOMIC POLICY REFORMS – ISBN 92-64-00836-5 – © OECD 2005

Table 1.1. **Structural policies and performance: proposed priorities** (*cont.*)

	Performance areas	
	Labour utilisation	Labour productivity
Poland	Refocus disability benefit schemes to encourage work by those with substantial work capacity. *Increase labour mobility by improving transport and housing infrastructure.* *Stimulate labour demand for youth and low-skilled by allowing for a relative decline in the minimum cost of labour.*	Intensify competitive pressures in a number of sectors by strengthening the privatisation programme. Reduce barriers to foreign ownership to enhance technological transfers from abroad.
Portugal	Stimulate hiring of regular workers and facilitate labour mobility by cutting the costs of EPL.	Improve secondary education achievements to raise efficiency of the workforce. Reduce state control in certain network industries to promote effective competition. *Raise public-sector efficiency by accelerating the reform of public administration.* *Simplify the tax system to reduce compliance costs for businesses.*
Slovak Republic	Reduce the tax wedge for low-income workers to improve their incentives to work in the formal economy. *Promote a rules-based business environment by strengthening the governance of the judicial and enforcement systems law.* *Reduce future pension contributions by raising standard retirement age.*	Reduce state control in certains network industries to promote effective competition. Raise overall level of human capital by improving secondary education achievements and access to tertiary education.
Spain	Promote greater flexibility in wage determination by limiting the extent of administrative extension of collective agreements. Stimulate hiring of regular workers by cutting the costs of EPL for this group. *Reduce future pension contributions by making the public pension system actuarially fair.* *Phase out tax advantages for home ownership to reduce housing market distortions and facilitate labour mobility.*	Raise overall level of human capital by improving upper-secondary and tertiary education achievements.
Sweden	Refocus sickness and disability benefit schemes to encourage work by those with substantial work capacity. Strengthen work incentives by reducing the tax wedge on labour income. *Reduce work disincentives by reconsidering measures that would result in lower working hours.* *Improve labour mobility by reducing housing market distortions.*	Reduce the scope of public ownership by allowing for more competition in the provision of public local services.
Switzerland	*Refocus invalidity pension schemes to encourage work by those with substantial work capacity and to stem rises in tax burden.* *Promote competition in the provision of medical products and services to contain increases in health care costs.*	Further liberalise professional services by removing inter-cantonal trade restrictions. Promote greater competition in product markets by reducing barriers to entry in network industries. Reduce producer support to agriculture, especially the most trade-distorting type.

Table 1.1. **Structural policies and performance: proposed priorities** (cont.)

	Performance areas	
	Labour utilisation	Labour productivity
Turkey	Strengthen incentives to work in formal activities by reducing the tax wedge on labour income.	Promote greater domestic competition by reducing administrative costs for start-ups. Reduce the scope of public ownership to allow for more competition in network industries. *Raise public-sector efficiency by implementing results-oriented budgeting in core public activities.* *Reduce genders imbalances in education by raising educational enrolments by women.*
United Kingdom	Refocus invalidity pension schemes to encourage work by those with substantial work capacity. Strengthen employment prospects for low-skilled workers by improving vocational education at the upper-secondary level.	Improve public infrastructure, especially for transport to further reduce bottlenecks. *Raise public-sector efficiency by strengthening incentives to pursue performance targets in publicly-funded services.* *Enhance competition in some service sectors by reviewing planning restrictions.*
United States	Limit increases in labour costs by reforming Medicare to restrain health care costs. *Encourage private saving by shifting the burden of taxation towards consumption.*	Improve primary and secondary education achievements to raise efficiency of the workforce. Reduce producer support to agriculture, especially the most trade-distorting type. *Stand firm on promoting transparency and accountability in corporate governance.*
European Union	*Improve intra-EU labour mobility by enhancing portability of pension and other benefit entitlements.*	Ease internal regulatory obstacles to cross-border trade and entry to strengthen competition. Promote greater competition in product markets by further reducing barriers to market contestability in network industries. Reduce producer support to agriculture, especially the most trade-distorting type. *Enhance competition in financial services by ensuring full implementation of Financial Services Action Plan.*

Notes

1. Given that the high ranking of Norway partly reflects the contribution from exploiting its oil reserves, the United States is considered as the leading country in terms of GDP per capita.

2. However, GDP per capita overstates the level of living standards in Ireland because of large income transfers to abroad from foreign subsidiaries (see Annex 1.A.1).

3. The indicators displayed in Chapter 2 are generally comparable across countries and over time. However, movements in some of the indicators may also reflect changes in the methodology used for the calculation.

4. The efficiency of the health sector is considered even though the link with growth performance is perhaps not as obvious as in the case of education. The reason is that fast-rising health care costs, as have been observed in many countries in recent years, can have an adverse influence on employment rates by putting upward pressures on indirect labour costs. In countries where health care is provided by the public sector, the associated costs are reflected in social security contribution rates and hence the tax wedge. And, in countries where health care is, to a large extent, provided by the private sector, the cost increases will not show up in the measured tax wedge, but will nonetheless be reflected in labour costs.

5. The policy areas covered by indicators will be expanded in the future as planned special studies on particular policy-performance linkages will enrich the indicator set used for surveillance.

ANNEX 1.A.1

Cross-country Comparison of Economic Performance and Living Standards: Some Caveats

In this report, GDP per capita is used as the proxy for living standards mainly for reasons of simplicity and timely availability of data that are measured in a broadly comparable way across countries. Yet, it may in some cases provide a misleading picture of underlying living standards for a number of reasons. First, GDP measures the flow of domestic output, whereas a more accurate measure of living standards would be the sum of consumption and changes in the net stock of wealth, both held at home and abroad. While reliable measures of wealth are virtually non-existent for many countries, net national income per capita would, in this regard, constitute a better measure than GDP per capita as it takes into account both the net flow of income on foreign investment and the depreciation of the capital stock. However, even this measure is not available for all OECD countries and, with a few notable exceptions such as Ireland, Luxembourg and Switzerland, country comparisons would not be altered substantially by the inclusion of these elements.

Second, even though the standardisation of national accounts conventions has made the measurement of GDP broadly comparable across countries, some distortion may be introduced in the conversion of country-specific measures into a common currency. The approach taken in this exercise, which consists in using Purchasing Power Parity (PPP) conversion rates, has become fairly standard in studies involving international comparisons of economic variables measured and expressed in domestic currencies.[1] However, differences in levels of GDP per capita across countries can be sensitive to the base year chosen for the PPP conversion. These limitations notwithstanding, it is unlikely that the broad comparison would change significantly on the basis of a more accurate measure of living standards and in any case, sustained increases in the latter are difficult to imagine without rising GDP per capita.

Third, countries are concerned not only with average living standards but also with their distribution across populations. Trade-offs may exist between levels and distribution of income and, in these cases, policies may be set so as to sacrifice some gains in average living standards in return for greater equity. However, the trade-offs may frequently be less stark than perceived, particularly in a longer term perspective. Some countries (e.g. Denmark, the Netherlands and Sweden) have indeed managed to achieve high levels of employment and living standards while maintaining a relatively low degree of income inequality.

More generally, even the best measure of material living standards would not necessarily accurately reflect differences in welfare across countries as the latter depend also on non-material aspects. Furthermore, welfare differences would reflect hard-to-measure differences in preferences of citizens, including with respect to the decision to allocate productivity gains between leisure and income. Viewed from a different angle, to the extent that it seems natural for people to demand more leisure as they become richer, a rise in GDP per capita stemming from an increased use of labour resources, both in terms of employment rates and hours worked does not necessarily imply a welfare improvement. In this regard, various studies have noted that a significant proportion of the gap in GDP per capita in Europe vis-à-vis the United States may well reflect a higher preference for leisure in the former and for material consumption in the latter.[2] Even so, it is likely that large discrepancies observed in cross-country employment rates and hours worked have a lot to do with the pervasive influence of different structural policies.[3]

Notes

1. For instance, Chapter 3 shows, for each country, the degree of convergence achieved over time in GDP per capita vis-à-vis the United States. There is a question as to whether the comparison should in such cases be made on the basis of constant or time-varying PPPs. For the figures shown in Chapter 3, the constant PPP approach was chosen. However, for most countries, using time-varying PPPs would not significantly after the outcome.

2. For a recent discussion of the welfare aspects of the comparison between the United States and Europe, see Gordon (2004) and Blanchard (2004).

3. For recent evidence on the effect of policies on labour force participation and hours worked, see Chapters 5 and 6, and Nickell (2003).

ANNEX 1.A.2

Selection of Policy Priorities

This annex provides further details on the process of selecting policy priorities that are listed in Table 1.1 and discussed in the country notes. As mentioned in the main text, the first stage of the selection process is the identification of performance weaknesses vis-à-vis the best performing countries. The second stage involves the identification of policy measures that can help to address the observed performance weaknesses. The following discusses the two different processes under separate headings.

In a nutshell, the vast majority of policy recommendations were based on:

● Identified weaknesses in performance at an aggregate level and/or at a disaggregate level based on international benchmarking.

● Associated identified weaknesses in policy settings based on cross-country comparisons.

The identification of performance weaknesses

The top-level indicator of performance is the comparative level of GDP per capita vis-à-vis the United States, which has traditionally led the OECD countries in terms of material living standards. Gaps in GDP per capita can in turn be disaggregated into labour utilisation gaps, i.e. differences in hours worked per capita, and labour productivity gaps, i.e. differences in GDP per hour worked. As shown in Figure 1.2 in the main text, the broad-brush picture that emerges from such a decomposition is that the key performance weaknesses relate to low labour utilisation in Europe and low productivity levels in non-European countries.

The proximate determinants of GDP per capita can be further disaggregated. For example, the source of labour utilisation gaps can be explored by using the following decomposition:

● Hours worked per employed person.

● Aggregate structural unemployment rate.

● Aggregate trend labour force participation rate.

● Population of working age relative to total population.

If the overall labour utilisation gap is due to the aggregate unemployment and/or labour force participation rates, a further dis-aggregation can determine if this is due to high incidence of youth, women and persons over 55 in these two measures. For example, the labour utilisation deficit in Europe is typically linked to high unemployment and low participation rates, the latter often concentrated on low participation of older workers.

While benchmarking of performance on the leading countries is useful to identify weaknesses for laggards, it is less useful for identifying problems for successful economies. This is most obvious for the leading country, with the United States combining high productivity levels, high hours worked per employed person, low unemployment rates and high labour force participation rates. Many other relatively high GDP-per-capita countries also score high on most performance indicators. To the extent that this is not the case in some areas, it is an indication of opportunities to improve on an already good overall performance. Also, recent large movements away from good performance can signal a weakness that needs to be addressed, examples being the increase in structural unemployment in Japan since the early 1990s and the rise in the number of disability benefit recipients in a number of countries over the recent decade.

Identification of policy priorities

To address the identified performance weaknesses, five policy priorities are selected for all countries, irrespective of whether their performance is clearly bad or relatively good. Of those five priorities, three are selected on the basis of cross-country comparison of indicators of the stance of policies, whereas the other two are based on the judgement and experience of country experts. Setting the same arbitrary number of policy priorities for all countries has been motivated by the desire to help improve everyone's performance, the best performing economies included. It may also ensure a certain degree of simplicity and equality of treatment across member countries.

The implication of an identical number of priorities for all countries

Choosing the same number of priorities in each country has also certain implications. While every country can improve specific aspects of performance, some will need far deeper and widespread reforms in order to catch up with the leading countries or to prevent from falling further behind. A fixed number of priorities imply, therefore, that for some member states, policy recommendations that would seem important to implement will be left out. Conversely, for the best performing countries, and where areas of absolute weaknesses are more difficult to identify, the set of priorities may include policy recommendations that may not appear strikingly pressing. Likewise, it may also include policy recommendations that are not selected in less well-performing countries even if the same policy area in the latter is even further away from best practice. These points are illustrated below with some graphic examples.

The selection of indicator-based policy priorities
The selection process

In order to help identify areas of policy priorities in each country, a broad set of policy indicators has been assembled, with a view to allow for direct cross-country comparison. The indicators included in the set are those that have been found to have a significant impact on a specific aspect of performance on the basis of previous empirical work. For the most part, the current set of indicators covers broad aspects of product and labour market policies, reflecting the intensive research efforts conducted in these fields at the OECD. These have been supplemented by a few indicators related to education and health. However, for future exercises more indicators are likely to be added, especially in the areas not sufficiently covered by the current set, such as technology, innovation and access to financial services.

By their nature, these indicators are intended to provide a quantitative summary of the stance of a policy in a particular area. As such, they do not necessarily fully capture all the dimensions of a policy setting, nor the extent to which policies are enforced in each country. For example, the impact on work incentives of high income support for long-term unemployed may be in some cases offset by stringent conditions limiting the access to benefits. This calls for caution and judgment in using indicators of replacement rates to select priorities. The same is true for indicators of product and labour market regulations, where the application of similar rules can vary across countries depending, *inter alia*, on court interpretation of specific provisions. In this regard, selecting a policy priority on the basis of a previously-identified performance weakness contributes to minimising the problem of potentially misleading indicators.

The OECD average is used as a benchmark for policies. Hence, when a country finds itself below average both in a particular performance area and in one or more of the policy settings having an impact on the specific performance area, policy priorities can be selected. In fact, most of the policy recommendations identified as priorities in this exercise reflect a matching between a sub-par performance and an inadequate policy setting. However, there are exceptions which can be illustrated with some examples, which *inter alia* shows how judgement and local knowledge is brought to bear on the selection as opposed to pure mechanical application of indicators.

Some examples:

In each example, the performance of OECD countries in a particular area is plotted against one of the relevant policy indicators, with the horizontal and vertical axis representing the OECD average performance and policy setting, respectively. Countries lying below the horizontal axis are seen as having a weak performance in the specific area under consideration whereas countries located to the right of the vertical axis are identified as having a weakness in a policy setting relevant to the performance area. Hence, countries appearing in the lower-right (or south-east) quadrant of each scatter plot can be seen as natural candidates for a priority in the policy setting examined.

For instance, panels A and B of Figure 1.A2.1 plot the participation rate of older workers against two related policy areas, the implicit tax on continued work (panel A) and the share of working-age population receiving disability benefit (panel B). In both cases, a number of countries can be found in the lower-right quadrant, indicating that in these countries participation rates for older workers are below the OECD average and, according to empirical studies, one of the reasons is that these workers face relatively strong financial disincentives to stay longer in the labour market and/or can use the disability benefit programme as an early route to early retirement.

Figure 1.A2.1. **Relating performance to policy: some examples**

Percentage points gap *vis-à-vis* OECD average

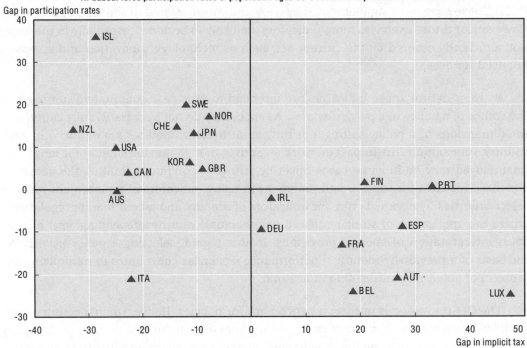

A. Labour force participation rates of population aged 55-64 and the implicit tax on continued work[1]

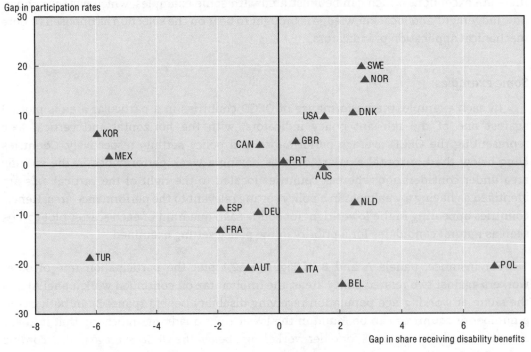

B. Labour force participation rates of population aged 55-64 and the share of working-age population not working and receiving disability benefits

1. Average of implicit tax on continued work in early retirement route, for 55 and 60 years old.

Source: OECD Labour Force Statistics; OECD Transforming Disability into Ability, 2003 and Chapter 5 in this publication.

In principle, a policy priority could be selected each time a country appears in the lower-right quadrant. However, the limit on the overall number of priorities selected for each country implies that some are being left out. For instance, reducing the implicit tax on continued work was selected as a priority in the case of Austria, Belgium, France and Luxembourg, but not Germany and Spain where other priorities were seen as more pressing in light of performance in other areas such as productivity. As for reforming the disability benefit programme, among the countries lying clearly in the lower-right quadrant, it was chosen as a priority for the Netherlands and Poland. It was not selected for Italy and Belgium given that for both countries, reducing the tax wedge was seen as more important given the low overall participation rates.

On the other hand, a reform of the disability benefit system was chosen as a priority for Australia and the United Kingdom even though participation of older workers in these countries is either around or slightly above OECD average. The reason is that for both countries, areas of absolute weaknesses – as defined as performance below OECD average – are not so easy to identify. In such a case, a performance that is close to the OECD average is taken as a relative weakness. However, that alone would not have been sufficient. The priority was selected also because in both countries the share of working-age population receiving disability benefit has been rising markedly since the early 1990s.

Although not shown in the figure, another difficulty occurs in the cases of countries having a performance problem in a specific area but no clear weaknesses in the relevant policy setting. For instance, even though the level of productivity in New Zealand remains below the OECD average, it is not easy to find a problem with the relevant policies. Hence the selected priorities may not seem as pressing.

It should be noted that these caveats concern a small number of recommendations that is likely to diminish as the set of performance and policy indicators is refined and extended to areas not covered in this exercise.

Other key priorities

Notwithstanding future improvements in the set of indicators, there will always remain important policy areas that can not be assessed on the basis of a quantitative indicator. In order to ensure that the exercise does not neglect key policy issues that are not covered by indicators, two additional priorities are thus selected for each country, mostly drawing on the vast and detailed expertise from various OECD working committees; these will normally be issues that have also been addressed by the Economic and Development Review Committee. Hence, details regarding the context and motivation for these additional priorities are usually found in the *Economic Survey* of a particular country. In many cases, these priorities may be supported by a policy indicator but in the cases where they are not, judgment is used as regards their impact on specific area of economic performance.

References

ARTUS, P. and G. CETTE (2004), *Productivité et croissance*, Conseil d'analyse économique.

BLANCHARD, O.J. (2004), "The economic future of Europe", *Journal of Economic Perspectives*, Vol. 18, No. 4.

GORDON, R.J. (2004), "Two centuries of economic growth: Europe chasing the American frontier", *NBER Working Paper* No. 10662.

NICKELL, S. (2003), "Employment and taxes", *CES IFO Working Paper* No. 1109.

OECD (2004a), *Agricultural Policies in OECD Countries: At a Glance*, Paris.

OECD (2004b), *Education at a Glance: OECD Indicators 2004*, Paris.

ISBN 92-64-00836-5
Economic Policy Reforms
© OECD 2005

Chapter 2

Structural Policy Indicators

This chapter contains comparative OECD indicators for labour costs and labour taxation; unemployment, disability and sickness income support; labour market and product market regulation; barriers to competition, trade and investment, sectoral regulation, educational attainment and achievement; health expenditure; and public investment. These indicators have been used to identify the policy priorities that are discussed in this report.

Figure 2.1. **Cost of labour**

A. Minimum wages[1]
Percentage of median wage

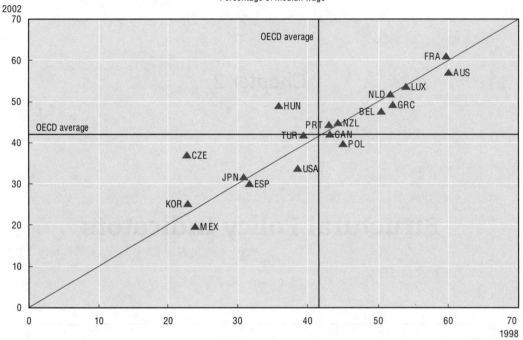

B. Minimum cost of labour, 2002[2]
Percentage of labour cost of average worker

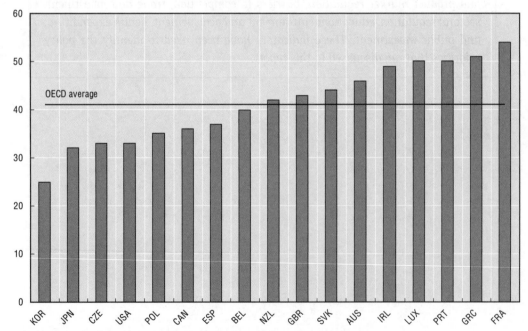

1. Missing countries do not have statutory minimum wage.
2. The cost of labour is the sum of the wage level and the corresponding social security contribution paid by employers.

Source: Chart A: OECD Labour Force Statistics, 2004; Chart B: OECD Employment Outlook, 2004 and OECD Taxing Wages, 2003/2004.

ECONOMIC POLICY REFORMS – ISBN 92-64-00836-5 – © OECD 2005

Figure 2.2. **Net income replacement rates for unemployment**[1,2]

Percentage of earnings

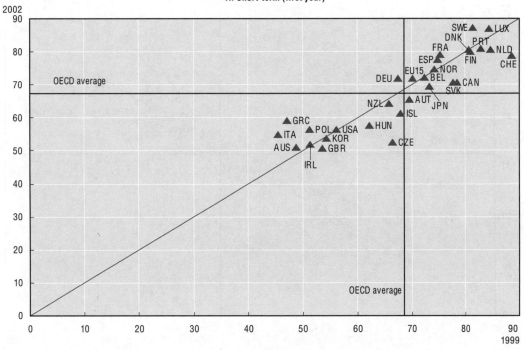

A. Short-term (first year)

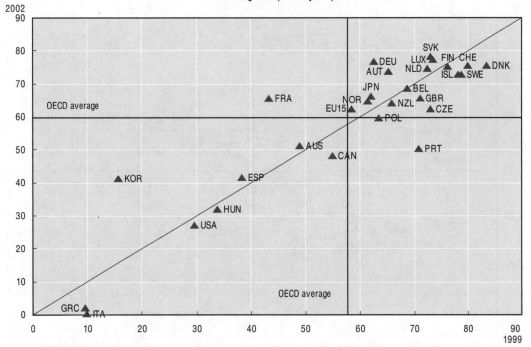

B. Long-term (after 5 years)

1. Average of replacement rates for unemployed who earned 67% and 100% of average worker earnings at the time of losing job.
2. The comparability of net replacement rates between two points in time may be affected by methodological or definitional changes.

Source: OECD Benefits and Wages: OECD Indicators, 2004.

Figure 2.3. **Average tax wedge on labour**[1]

Percentage of total labour compensation

A. At 67% of average worker earnings[2]

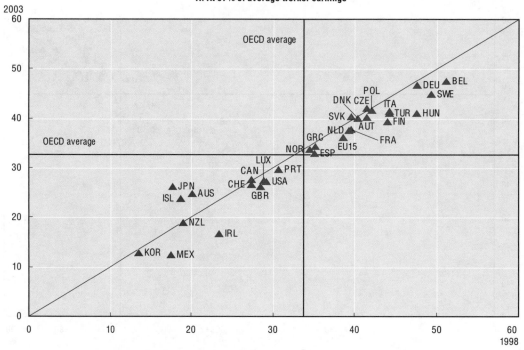

B. At 100% of average worker earnings[3]

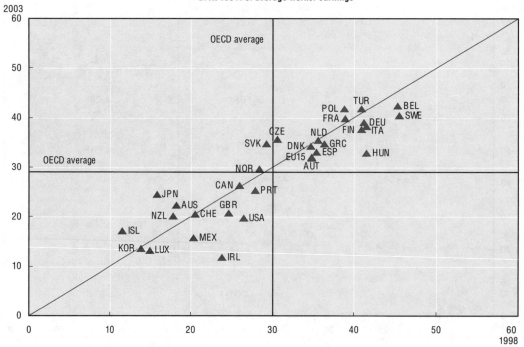

1. Measured as the difference between total labour compensation paid by the employer and the net take-home pay of employees, as a ratio of total labour compensation. It therefore includes both employer's and employee's social security contributions.
2. Single person with no child.
3. Couple with 2 children, average of 3 family situations.

Source: OECD Taxing Wages, 2003/2004.

Figure 2.4. **Labour taxation**

Percentage of average worker earnings

A. Implicit tax on continued work: early retirement[1,2]

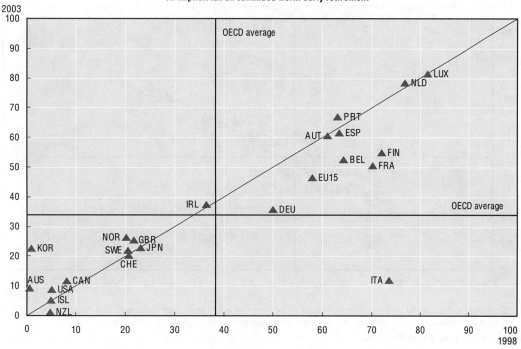

B. Implicit tax on continued work: old-age pension[2,3]

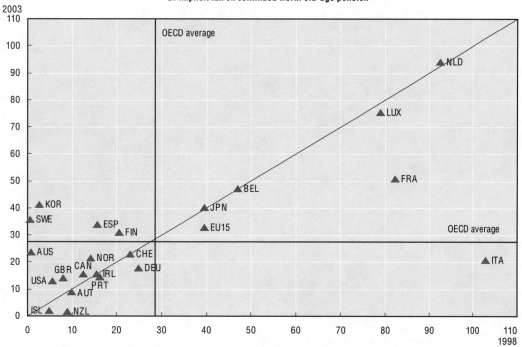

1. Average of implicit tax on continued work in early retirement route, for 55 and 60 years old.
2. EU15, excluding Denmark and Greece.
3. Implicit tax on continued work in regular old-age pension, for 60 years old.

Source: Chapter 5 in this publication.

Figure 2.4. **Labour taxation** (*cont.*)

C. Ratio of average tax rate on second earner relative to a single earner[1]

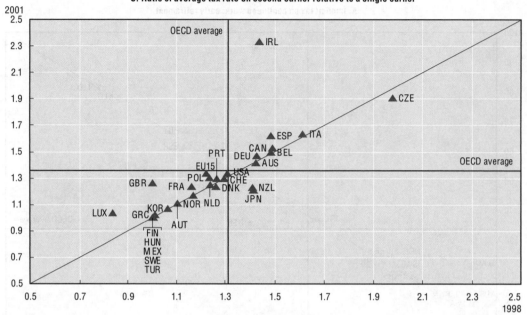

1. This ratio is calculated at an earnings level of 67 per cent of average worker earnings. The spouse of the second earner is assumed to earn 100% of average worker earnings in a family with two children.

Source: OECD Taxing Wages, 2003/2004.

ECONOMIC POLICY REFORMS – ISBN 92-64-00836-5 – © OECD 2005

Figure 2.5. **Income support for disability and sickness**

A. Per cent of working age population non-employed and receiving disability benefits[1]

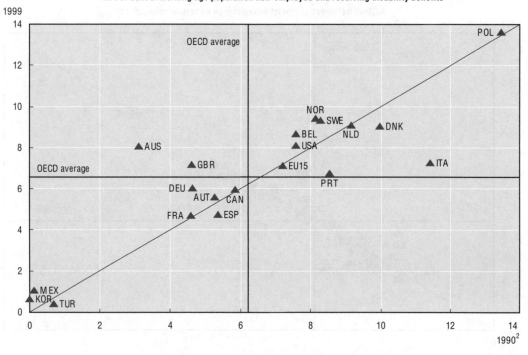

B. Number of weeks lost due to sickness leave in 1999[3]

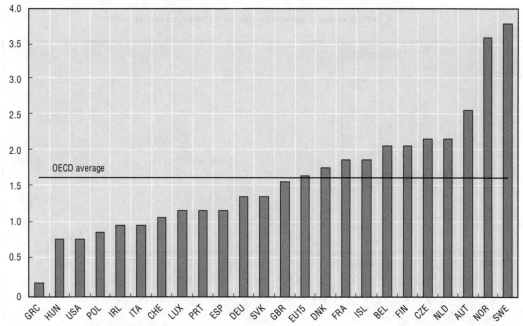

1. EU15, excluding Finland, Greece, Ireland and Luxembourg.
2. 1995 for Austria, Mexico and Poland.
3. The number for the United States may not be strictly comparable as it comes from a different source and refers to 2003.

Source: Chart A: OECD *Transforming Disability into Ability*, 2003 and National Compensation Survey (for the United States); Chart B: OECD *Employment Outlook*, 2004.

Figure 2.6. **Employment Protection Legislation (EPL)**
Index scale of 0-6 from least to most restrictive

A. Restrictiveness of protection legislation on regular employment[1]

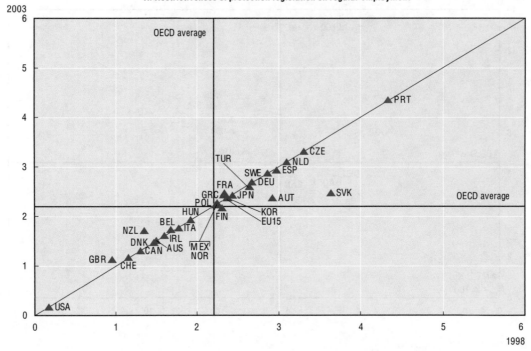

B. Restrictiveness of protection legislation on temporary employment[1,2]

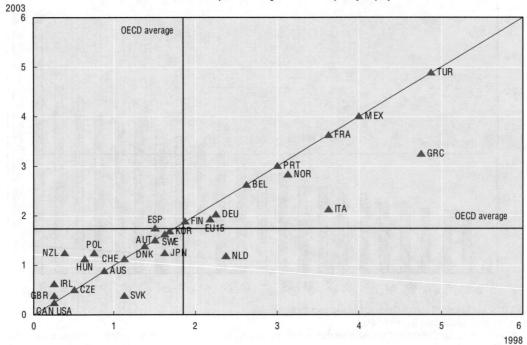

1. EU15, excluding Luxembourg.
2. The figure for Spain is different from the one reported in *Employment Outlook* (2004) due to a re-assessment of regulation in this area.

Source: OECD Employment Outlook, 2004.

Figure 2.7. **Difference between coverage rates of collective bargaining agreements and trade union density rates**[1, 2]

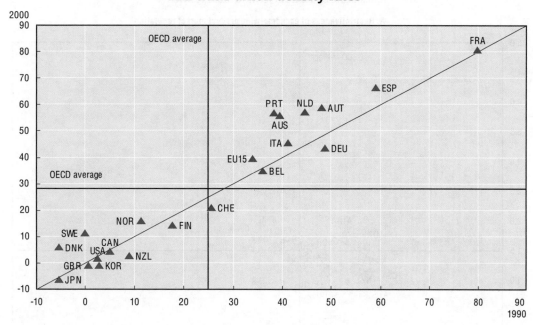

1. The coverage rate is measured as the percentage of workers who are covered by collective bargaining agreements, regardless of whether or not they belong to a trade union. The union density rate is the percentage of workers belonging to a trade union. Each data point on the figure is calculated as the simple arithmetic difference between the two rates.
2. The 2000 data point for trade union density is 1998 for Spain and 2001 for Switzerland.

Source: OECD Employment Outlook, 2004.

Figure 2.8. **Product market regulation**

Index scale of 0-6 from least to most restrictive

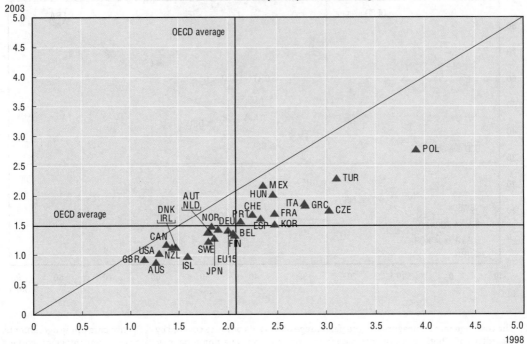

A. Restrictiveness of economy-wide product market regulation[1]

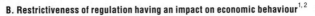

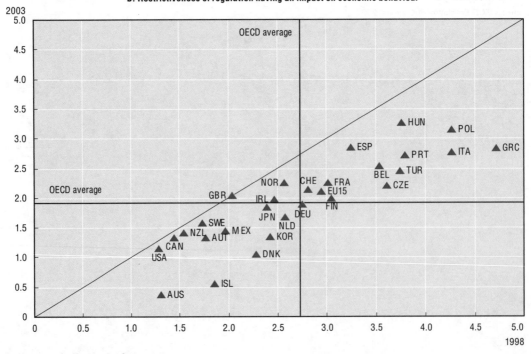

B. Restrictiveness of regulation having an impact on economic behaviour[1,2]

1. EU15, excluding Luxembourg.
2. Economic regulation includes all domestic regulatory provisions affecting private governance and product market competition such as state control and legal barriers to entry in competitive market.

Source: Chapter 4 in this publication.

ECONOMIC POLICY REFORMS – ISBN 92-64-00836-5 – © OECD 2005

Figure 2.9. **State control of business operations**

Index scale of 0-6 from least to most restrictive

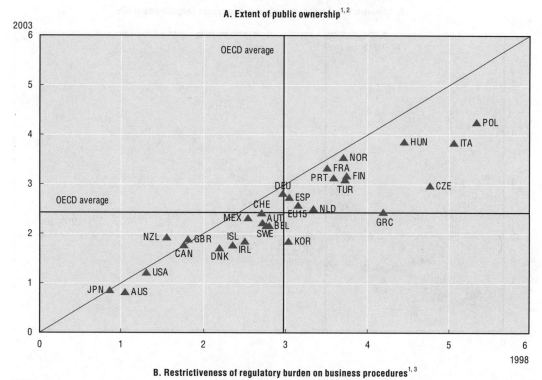

A. Extent of public ownership[1,2]

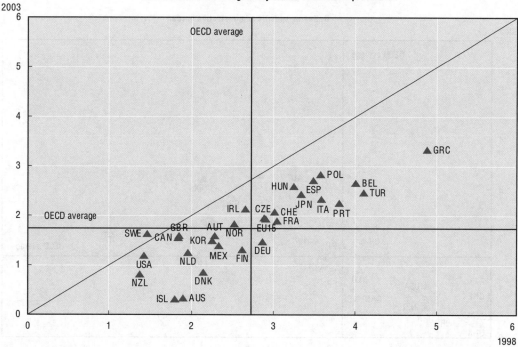

B. Restrictiveness of regulatory burden on business procedures[1,3]

1. EU15, excluding Luxembourg.
2. Covers scope and size of public entreprise as well as the direct state control over business enterprise (via voting rights or legislative bodies). Even though a policy priority was selected for Slovak Republic on the basis of this indicator, it is missing from the chart due to lack of data for 1998. The value of the index for 2003 is 1.9.
3. Concerns the involvement of the state in business operations via price controls or the use of command and control regulation.
Source: Chapter 4 in this publication.

Figure 2.10. **Barriers to entrepreneurship**

Index scale of 0-6 from least to most restrictive

A. Administrative burdens on corporations and sole proprietor start-ups

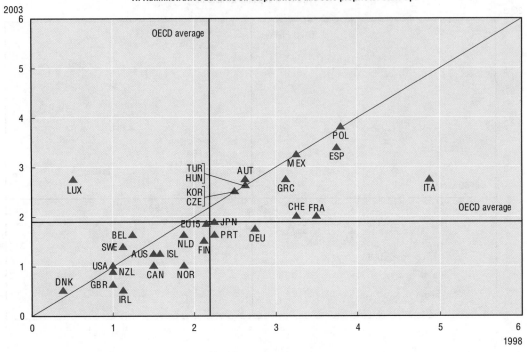

B. Sector-specific administrative burden

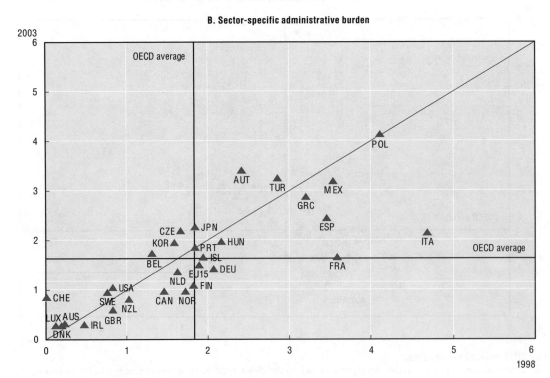

Source: Chapter 4 in this publication.

ECONOMIC POLICY REFORMS – ISBN 92-64-00836-5 – © OECD 2005

Figure 2.11. **Barriers to entry**[1]

Index scale of 0-6 from least to most restrictive

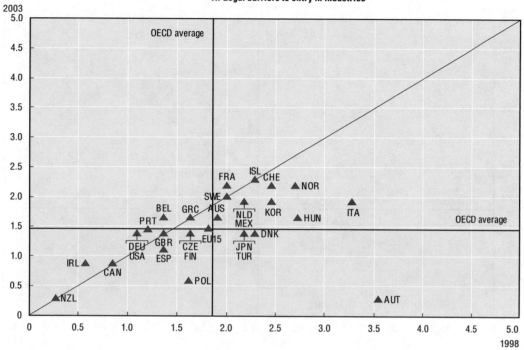

A. Legal barriers to entry in industries

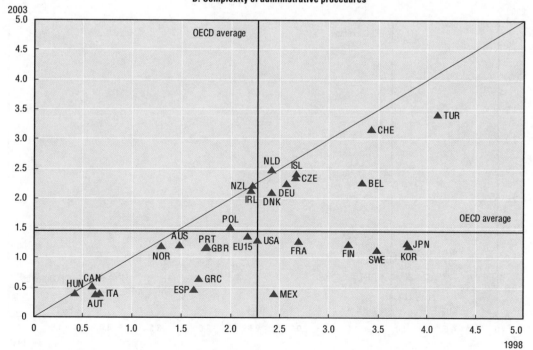

B. Complexity of administrative procedures[2]

1. EU15, excluding Luxembourg.
2. Concerns complexity of government communication of rules and procedures as well as of licences and permit systems. Corresponds to the indicator of regulatory and administrative opacity in Chapter 4.

Source: Chapter 4 in this publication.

Figure 2.12. **Barriers to foreign direct investment**

Index scale of 0-6 from least to most restrictive

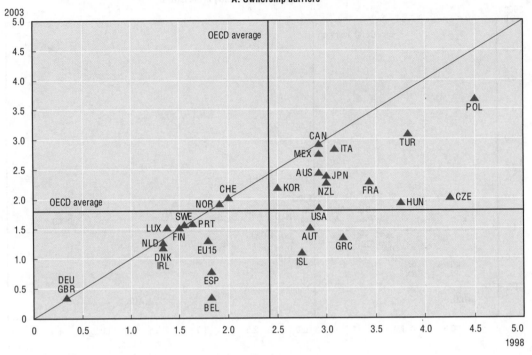

A. Ownership barriers

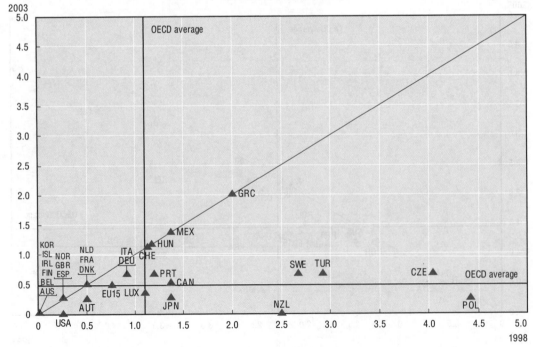

B. Discriminatory procedures

Source: Chapter 4 in this publication.

ECONOMIC POLICY REFORMS – ISBN 92-64-00836-5 – © OECD 2005

Figure 2.13. **Sectoral regulation**

Index scale of 0-6 from least to most restrictive

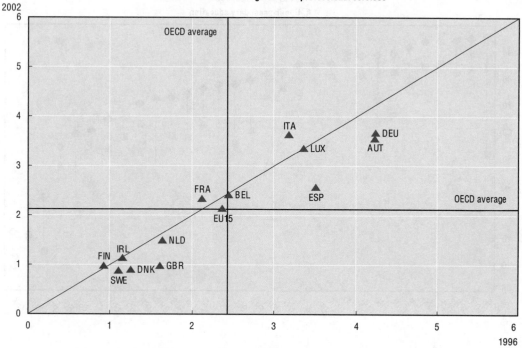

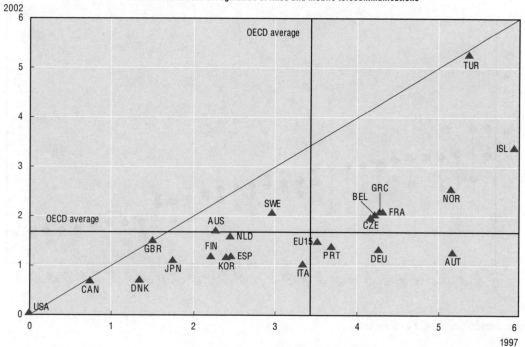

1. Index of regulations in professional services (accounting, law, engineering and architecture). Even though a policy priority was selected for Canada and Japan on the basis of this indicator, they are missing from the chart due to lack of data for 2002. The value of the index for Canada and Japan for 1996 is 2.6 and 3.2 respectively.

Source: European Commission and OECD.

Figure 2.14. **Educational attainment, 2002**
Percentage of population aged 25-34 and 45-54

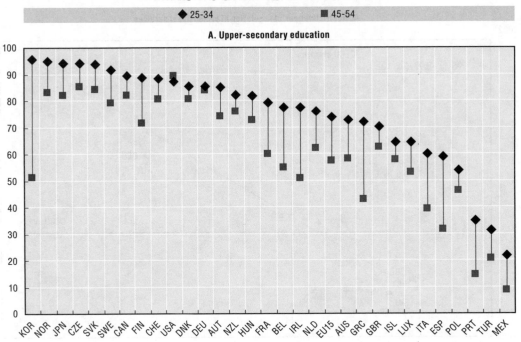

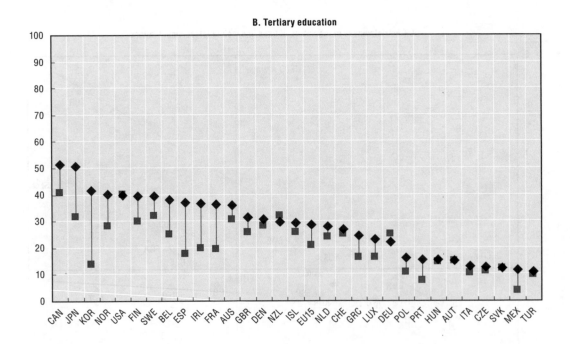

Source: OECD Education at a Glance, 2004.

Figure 2.15. **Educational achievement**

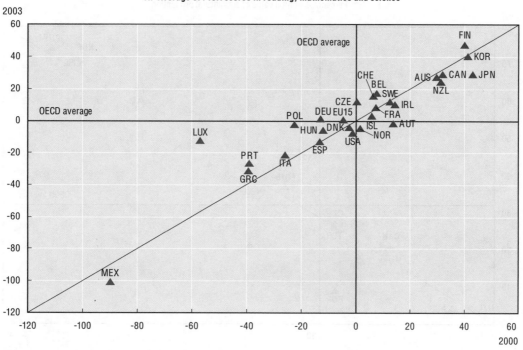

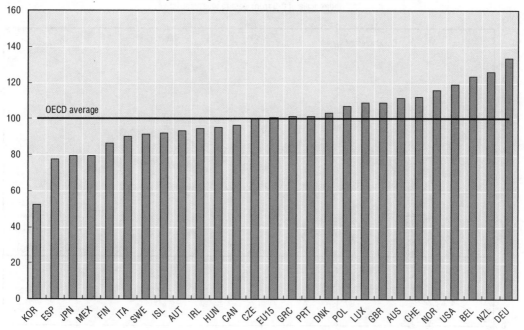

1. PISA stands for Programme for International Student Assessment.

Source: Chart A: *OECD Learning for Tomorrow's World*, PISA 2003; Chart B: *OECD Knowledge and Skills for Life*, PISA 2000.

Figure 2.16. **Barriers to external trade**

A. Producer support estimate to agriculture[1]
Percentage of total value of agricultural production

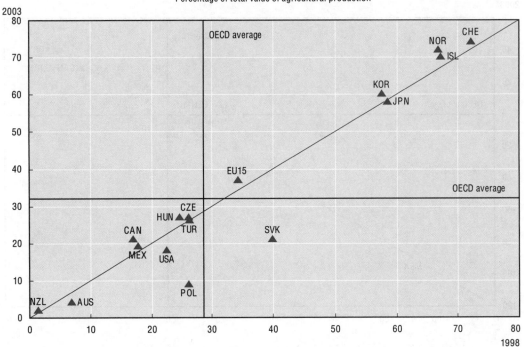

B. Importance of external trade tariffs
Index scale of 0-6 from least to most restrictive

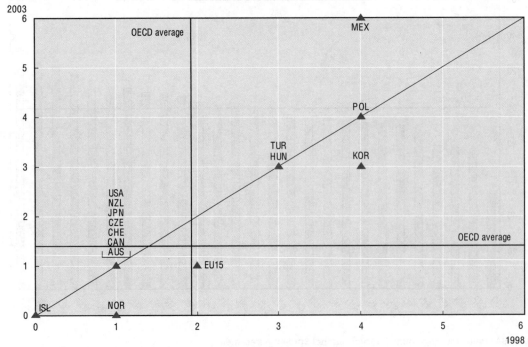

1. A single producer support estimate is calculated for EU countries.

Source: Chart A: OECD Producer and consumer support estimates database; Chart B: Chapter 4 in this publication.

Figure 2.17. **Health expenditure, 2002**[1]
Percentage of GDP

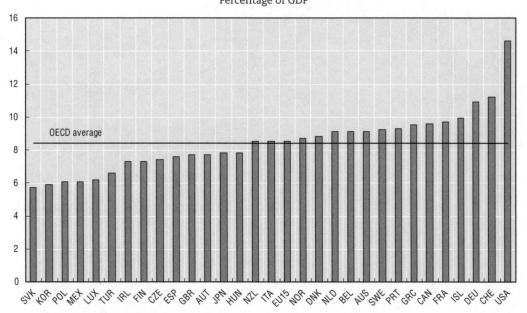

1. 2001 for Australia, Japan and Korea; 2000 for Turkey.
Source: OECD Health database.

Figure 2.18. **Public investment**
Percentage of GDP

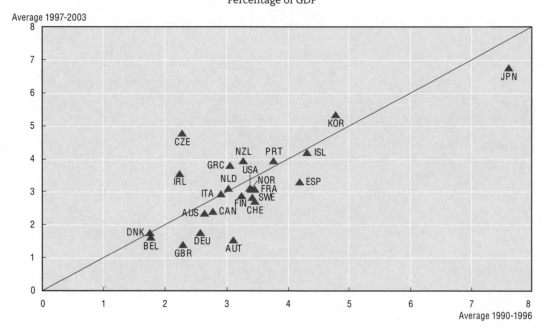

Source: OECD Economic Outlook, No. 76.

ISBN 92-64-00836-5
Economic Policy Reforms
© OECD 2005

Chapter 3

Country Notes

This chapter contains information on key policy priorities for individual OECD member countries and for the European Union.

AUSTRALIA

Growth has been steady and brisk, but the income gap with leading countries remains significant. Employment rates for the low-skilled and for older workers are still relatively low.

Priorities supported by indicators

Reduce minimum cost of labour

"Award wages" (the *de-facto* minimum wages) are more than half of median earnings – thus relatively higher than in most OECD countries – and may therefore impede employment of the low-skilled.

Actions taken: Continued reforms of the previously rigid industrial relations system have greatly increased workplace flexibility which has raised labour productivity and thus had a dampening effect on unit labour cost.

Recommendations: Yearly adjustments to award wages should take better account of the employability of award-wage earners.

Reform disability benefit schemes

The sharp rise in recent years in the number of people receiving the Disability Support Pension has contributed to the relatively low labour force participation rate for persons aged 55 and over.

Actions taken: To assist people with disabilities to develop and improve their work capacity, new places in employment assistance, vocational education and training and rehabilitation services have been created since mid-2003.

Recommendations: Tighten eligibility criteria for the Disability Support Pension, aiming to encourage labour market engagement of people with substantial work capacity.

Strengthen vocational education at the upper-secondary level

Given the deteriorating labour market prospects for low-skilled workers, especially for early school-leavers, the upper-secondary education system's emphasis on preparation for university study is too narrow.

Actions taken: A range of recent government initiatives aims at increasing the labour market responsiveness and flexibility of the vocational education and training (VET) system.

Recommendations: The links between schools, VET and higher education should be strengthened by enhancing educational pathways for young people, and by more flexible and better-targeted funding of higher education provision.

Other key priorities

● Re-balance benefit entitlement conditions and mutual obligations strategies, and reduce marginal effective tax rates further, to encourage greater labour force participation.

● Strengthen competitive pressures in the economy via completion of the National Competition Policy Agenda and adoption of a new coordinated agenda to further advance reform in sectors such as electricity, rail, gas and water.

AUSTRALIA

Structural indicators

	1990	1995	2000	2003
Trend GDP per capita (% growth rate)	2.1	2.0	2.3	2.4
Trend employment rate	69.3	69.5	70.9	71.3
Trend participation rate	73.4	74.6	75.3	75.6
Structural unemployment rate (NAIRU)	5.7	6.8	5.9	5.6

Source: Estimates based on *OECD Economic Outlook*, No. 76.

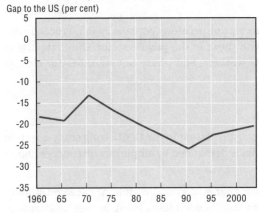

A. Convergence in GDP per capita has resumed[1]

Gap to the US (per cent)

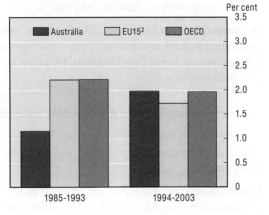

B. Annual growth in GDP per hour has risen

Per cent

Australia   EU15[2]   OECD

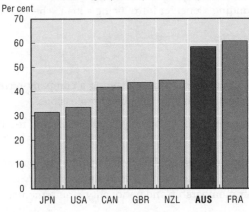

C. Minimum wages (awards) are relatively high, 2002[3]

Per cent

JPN USA CAN GBR NZL **AUS** FRA

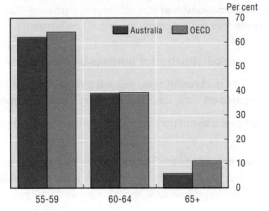

D. Participation rates for older workers are low, 2003

Per cent

Australia   OECD

55-59   60-64   65+

1. Percentage gap with respect to US GDP per capita (in constant 2000 PPPs).
2. Excluding Austria and Luxembourg.
3. Minimum wage as a percentage of the median wage.
Source: Charts A and B: *National Accounts of OECD Countries*, 2004; *OECD Labour Force Statistics*, 2004; *OECD Economic Outlook*, No. 76; Charts C and D: *OECD Labour Force Statistics*, 2004.

AUSTRIA

GDP per capita is relatively high although the gap vis-à-vis leading countries has widened in recent years, reflecting mainly weak growth in labour resource utilisation.

Priorities supported by indicators

Reduce implicit tax on continued work at older age

Low abatements on early-retirement pensions, especially for public-sector workers, high unemployment benefits and subsidised part-time employment for older workers encourage early retirement.

Actions taken: The accounting period for the pension base and abatements for early-retirement pensions have been raised. Early retirement on account of unemployment has been abolished. The duration of employment required to reach the full pension replacement rate has risen. The statutory retirement age for civil servants has been raised.

Recommendations: Make the adjustment for early receipt of pensions actuarially fair. Proceed with harmonising pension schemes in the public sector with those in the private sector. Eliminate higher unemployment benefit entitlements for older jobless workers, and phase out subsidies for old-age part-time employment.

Improve graduation rates from tertiary education

Graduation rates from tertiary education are among the lowest in the OECD. Long study duration and insufficient orientation of tertiary institutions to skills demanded by employers discourage higher education.

Actions taken: Introduction of government funding of higher-education institutions based on student enrolment. Student fees earmarked to the universities in which students enrol, as well as increased independence of universities, have strengthened incentives to offer attractive study programmes. Performance-related elements in university funding and in contracts for staff have widened.

Recommendations: Strengthen performance-based funding. Consider introducing a loan scheme for study fees with income-contingent repayments.

Reduce administrative burdens on start-ups

Firm creation rates are relatively low. High administrative costs of registering a company have weighed on start-ups, as have entry barriers in specific sectors, such as the liberal professions.

Actions taken: Entry restrictions in some sectors have been lowered, notably in wholesale and retail trade.

Recommendations: Reduce the costs of setting up companies, especially limited liability companies. Further narrow the range of trades requiring certificates of qualification. Ease regulation of entry into the liberal professions, abolishing compulsory chamber membership and nationality requirements.

Other key priorities

● Reduce inactivity traps in the benefit system by restructuring child benefits in favour of vouchers for child care, and better integrating job-placement activities with social assistance.
● Strengthen competition law and enforcement by assigning more powers and resources to the competition authority, streamlining the institutional setup, simplifying rules on vertical agreements and introducing a credible leniency programme.

ECONOMIC POLICY REFORMS – ISBN 92-64-00836-5 – © OECD 2005

AUSTRIA

Structural indicators

	1990	1995	2000	2003
Trend GDP per capita (% growth rate)	1.5	1.8	2.3	2.1
Trend employment rate	74.3	74.2	74.7	75.3
Trend participation rate	77.6	78.0	78.7	79.2
Structural unemployment rate (NAIRU)	4.3	4.9	5.0	4.9

Source: Estimates based on *OECD Economic Outlook,* No. 76.

A. Convergence in GDP per capita has stalled[1]

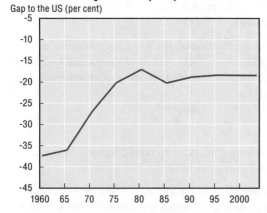

B. Annual growth in GDP per hour is relatively high

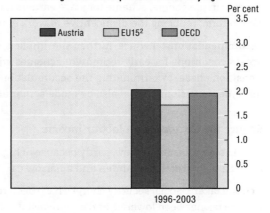

C. Participation rates for older workers are low, 2003

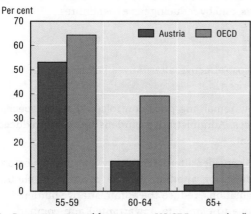

D. The share of population with tertiary education is low, 2002[3]

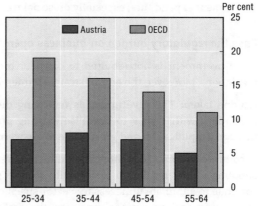

1. Percentage gap with respect to US GDP per capita (in constant 2000 PPPs).
2. Excluding Austria and Luxembourg.
3. Tertiary type A programmes, providing qualifications for advanced research or higher skill professions.
Source: Charts A and B: *National Accounts of OECD Countries,* 2004; *OECD Labour Force Statistics,* 2004; *OECD Economic Outlook,* No. 76; Chart C: *OECD Labour Force Statistics,* 2004; Chart D: *OECD Education at a Glance,* 2004.

BELGIUM

Despite increases in employment rates, labour utilisation remains low. Labour productivity growth has slowed, albeit from a relatively high rate.

Priorities supported by indicators

Reduce the implicit tax on continued work at older ages

Attractive publicly-subsidised routes to early retirement, notably unemployment insurance (UI) benefits and early retirement pensions, underpin low employment rates for the older working-age population.

Actions taken: Job-search requirements up to age 58 have been progressively introduced for new UI claimants. UI top-ups paid by employers to older workers made redundant are now subject to a (reduced) social security charge. The ceiling on wages taken into account in computing public pension benefits in the general scheme for wage earners has been indexed to wages instead of prices since the 1996 reform, reducing the disincentive to work extra years.

Recommendations: Reduce further the implicit tax on continued work by progressively aligning access conditions for early retirement schemes with those for early retirement pensions and, in the transition phase, by terminating the accumulation of pension rights for those in such schemes. Early retirement pensions should also be made actuarially fair.

Reduce the tax wedge on labour income

Labour utilisation is low, partly because of high effective tax rates on labour income. These in turn reflect a high overall tax burden and a narrow capital-income tax base.

Actions taken: Social security charges have been reduced, especially for low income earners, personal income tax has been lowered, and a non-wastable tax credit for those on low labour incomes has been introduced.

Recommendations: Room should be made for further reductions in taxes on labour income by cutting government expenditure, especially on social transfers, and by reducing tax expenditures.

Ease the regulatory burden on business operations

Government is not required to consider more cost-effective alternatives before adopting new regulations. Moreover, the administrative burden has risen.

Actions taken: The government is reviewing the few remaining price controls and sector-specific regulations with a view to liberalise existing practices. Administrative burdens are being reduced through simplification and greater use of e-government.

Recommendations: Regulators should be required to consider alternative policy instruments before adopting a new regulation and should receive guidance on alternatives. The government should continue to eliminate unnecessary sector-specific regulations, reduce the administrative burden and review laws and regulations governing the professions to eliminate unwarranted anti-competitive practices.

Other key priorities

● Improve education outcomes for students from ethnic backgrounds and strengthen the enforcement of anti-discrimination laws to enhance this group's labour-market performance.

● Make UI conditional on properly enforced job-search requirements and increase efforts to upgrade skills for unemployed people.

ECONOMIC POLICY REFORMS – ISBN 92-64-00836-5 – © OECD 2005

BELGIUM

Structural indicators

	1990	1995	2000	2003
Trend GDP per capita (% growth rate)	1.9	1.5	1.8	1.7
Trend employment rate	57.9	59.4	61.4	62.1
Trend participation rate	62.5	64.1	66.0	66.9
Structural unemployment rate (NAIRU)	7.3	7.4	7.0	7.2

Source: Estimates based on *OECD Economic Outlook*, No. 76.

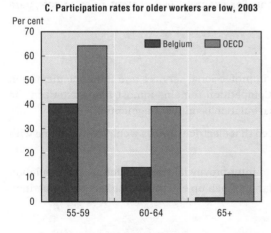

A. Convergence in GDP per capita has stalled[1]

Gap to the US (per cent)

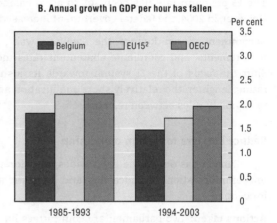

B. Annual growth in GDP per hour has fallen

Per cent

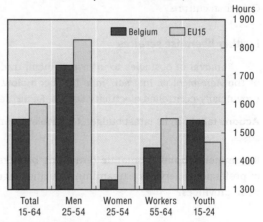

C. Participation rates for older workers are low, 2003

Per cent

D. Annual hours per worker are modest, 2002

Hours

1. Percentage gap with respect to US GDP per capita (in constant 2000 PPPs).
2. Excluding Austria and Luxembourg.
Source: Charts A and B: *National Accounts of OECD Countries*, 2004; *OECD Labour Force Statistics*, 2004; *OECD Economic Outlook*, No. 76; Chart C: *OECD Labour Force Statistics*, 2004; Chart D: *European Union Labour Force Survey*.

CANADA

GDP per capita growth since the mid 1990s has been higher than the OECD average, reflecting in part an acceleration in labour productivity. However, the latter remains below the US level, resulting in a significant income gap.

Priorities supported by indicators

Reduce work disincentives in the income support system

Provincial social assistance systems create welfare traps, and the federal Employment Insurance (EI) system reduces labour mobility and cross-subsidises firms heavily reliant on seasonal workers.

Actions taken: The incentives to move from social assistance to work have improved since the mid-1990s because of the introduction of the National Child Benefit, which does not depend on work status. The EI premium rate has been set so as to balance premiums and benefits at the aggregate level. However, in 2004, the federal government increased access to EI benefits for seasonal workers.

Recommendations: Reduce the "welfare wall": Implement stricter job search and activation requirements, and coordinate abatement rates more tightly across programmes and jurisdictions. Shift the focus of the EI system towards its insurance objective: Introduce enterprise experience rating, lenghten the relatively short qualification and stand-down periods, and phase out differences in eligibility rules between regions.

Reduce barriers to foreign ownership

Canada has one of the most widespread foreign ownership restrictions in the OECD, mainly in telecommunications, broadcasting and domestic airlines. These are holding back competition and innovation.

Actions taken: Two parliamentary committees have taken different positions on cable/broadcasting restrictions.

Recommendations: Eliminate ownership restrictions. For example, use content rules to safeguard Canadian culture.

Further liberalise services

Removal of obstacles to inter-provincial trade in professional services and full implementation of the *Agreement on Internal Trade* has been slow. Competition remains almost non-existent in the provincially-controlled electricity sector. Securities regulation is unduly fragmented.

Actions taken: In its latest budget, Ontario announced that electricity prices would evolve in line with costs.

Recommendations: Dismantle remaining barriers to inter-provincial trade, including the regulation of professional services. Streamline securities regulation. Open up electricity markets to competition in all provinces.

Other key priorities

● Restrain growth in public health costs by introducing a mixed remuneration system for primary-care providers, and by allowing for output-based hospital funding and more contracting out.

● Continue to examine capital cost allowances to ensure that they are aligned with useful economic lives and remove provincial taxes on the purchase of capital goods as well as on firms' ownership of capital assets.

CANADA

Structural indicators

	1990	1995	2000	2003
Trend GDP per capita (% growth rate)	0.7	1.6	2.5	1.7
Trend employment rate	70.3	70.4	72.2	72.8
Trend participation rate	76.6	76.4	77.5	78.5
Structural unemployment rate (NAIRU)	8.3	7.9	6.8	7.3

Source: Estimates based on *OECD Economic Outlook,* No. 76.

A. Divergence in GDP per capita has halted[1]

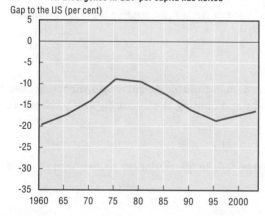

B. Annual growth in GDP per hour has risen

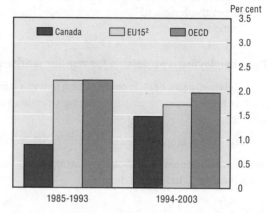

C. Health spending as a share of GDP is high[3]

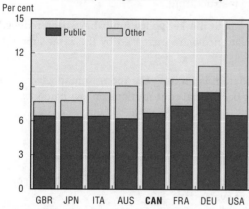

D. FDI restrictions are high, 2003[4]

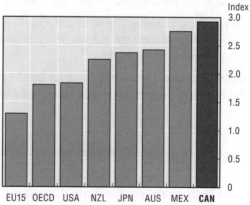

1. Percentage gap with respect to US GDP per capita (in constant 2000 PPPs).
2. Excluding Austria and Luxembourg.
3. Health expenditure as a percentage of GDP; 2002, except 2001 for Japan and Australia.
4. Index scale of 0-6 from least to most restrictive.

Source: Charts A and B: *National Accounts of OECD Countries,* 2004; *OECD Labour Force Statistics,* 2004; *OECD Economic Outlook,* No. 76; Chart C: *OECD Health database;* Chart D: OECD Regulation database.

CZECH REPUBLIC

Growth in GDP per capita has not been sufficiently high in recent years to allow for a significant catch-up in income. Strong productivity growth has been partly offset by falling employment rates.

Priorities supported by indicators

Reduce administrative burden on start-ups

Cumbersome bankruptcy proceedings reduce the efficiency of capital and the pace of structural change. Complex and sometimes lengthy procedures to enter the commercial registry dissuade business start-ups.

Actions taken: The government is in the process of putting together reform proposals for improving bankruptcy legislation and the commercial registry.

Recommendations: The intended reforms need to be implemented, and continued efforts are required to shorten the length of bankruptcy proceedings and lighten the administrative burden of business registration.

Ease employment protection for regular workers

Relatively strict EPL is contributing to weak labour demand and inefficient employment practices. This is hindering progress in reducing unemployment and limiting re-structuring and productivity growth.

Actions taken: Employment protection legislation is currently under review by the authorities.

Recommendations: Significant reform efforts are needed, in particular to reduce overall costs associated with individual dismissal.

Reduce the tax wedge for low-income workers

A high tax wedge on low-paid jobs restricts employment opportunities for low-productivity workers that have lost their job as a result of industrial restructuring.

Actions taken: Employers' contributions to the active labour market policy funds have been reduced by 2 percentage points, but contributions to social insurance were increased by the same amount, leaving the wedge unchanged.

Recommendations: While the need for fiscal consolidation is limiting the room to manoeuvre, the authorities should nevertheless put priority on cutting back social contributions on low-paid jobs.

Other key priorities

● Increase labour mobility through further liberalisation of the rental housing market.

● Reduce poverty traps for non-employed households generated by the combined effects of social welfare, housing and child allowances in the tax-benefit system.

ECONOMIC POLICY REFORMS – ISBN 92-64-00836-5 – © OECD 2005

CZECH REPUBLIC

Structural indicators

	1990	1995	2000	2003
Trend GDP per capita (% growth rate)	..	2.4	2.3	2.7
Trend employment rate	..	68.8	66.9	66.0
Trend participation rate	..	72.6	71.8	71.4
Structural unemployment rate (NAIRU)	..	5.3	6.9	7.6

Source: Estimates based on *OECD Economic Outlook*, No. 76.

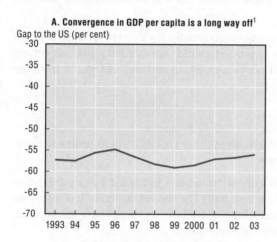

A. Convergence in GDP per capita is a long way off[1]

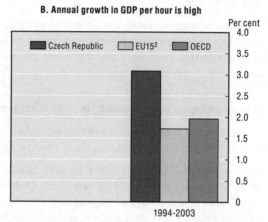

B. Annual growth in GDP per hour is high

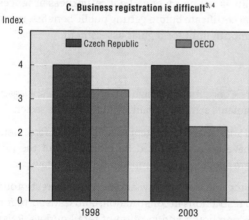

C. Business registration is difficult[3, 4]

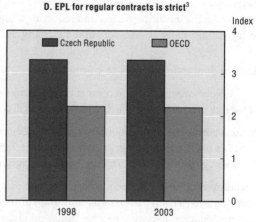

D. EPL for regular contracts is strict[3]

1. Percentage gap with respect to US GDP per capita (in constant 2000 PPPs).
2. Excluding Austria and Luxembourg.
3. Index scale of 0-6 from least to most restrictive.
4. Business registration refers to licences and permits.
Source: Charts A and B: *National Accounts of OECD Countries*, 2004; *OECD Labour Force Statistics*, 2004; *OECD Economic Outlook*, No. 76; Chart C: OECD Regulation database; Chart D: *OECD Employment Outlook*, 2004.

DENMARK

Faster growth in GDP per capita over the past decade has contributed to maintain relatively high income levels by international standards, even though the gap vis-à-vis the United States has further widened.

Priorities supported by indicators

Reduce tax wedge on labour income

Tax rates on earned income are high, with the top marginal rate payable as from around the average wage. This reduces the incentive to work and discourages entrepreneurship.

Actions taken: The threshold for the intermediate tax bracket has been raised and an in-work benefit has reduced the tax wedge for people on low incomes. Marginal tax rates have therefore been lowered by about 6 percentage points for middle-income earners. A tax freeze was implemented in 2002 and remains in place.

Recommendations: Modify the tax freeze so that revenue-neutral changes can be made at all levels of government (for example, raising taxes on immovable property, which are relatively low, and cutting taxes on earned income). Cutting the top marginal tax rate or lifting its threshold would have the largest impact on labour supply.

Reform sickness and disability benefit schemes

Around 12 per cent of the working-age population receives either a disability pension or a sickness benefit. Benefits are relatively high and easily accessible.

Actions taken: Eligibility criteria for the disability benefit have been tightened by requiring that working capacity be reduced by two-thirds (previously one-half). The benefit structure has also been simplified. The government has proposed that municipalities should pay a greater share of long-term sickness benefits, and that medical assessments be made earlier.

Recommendations: Make it easier for disability benefit recipients to rejoin the labour force on a part-time basis, and periodically review all cases where a disability is not permanent. Reduce sickness absences by introducing a waiting period and requiring a medical certificate before getting public benefits, using independent medical assessors and enforcing the 12-month limit for regular assessment.

Reduce domestic barriers to competition

Regulations unduly limit competition in many sectors. Concentration is high in some industries, a legacy of the lack of merger control in the past. Some local governments compete unfairly with the private sector.

Actions taken: The competition law has been modernised and cartel control stepped up, but the enforcement agencies need streamlining. Pro-competition reforms have been announced for electricity, but the two dominant generators plan to merge. Local governments are opening up to competition, but at a slow pace.

Recommendations: Cut the number of agencies applying competition law and remove interest-group representatives from their boards. Eliminate unneeded restrictions in construction, land transportation and professional services. Reduce limits on shop-opening hours and location of retail outlets. Raise public-sector outsourcing by enforcing current laws.

Other key priorities

● Reduce work disincentives in the early retirement scheme, *e.g.* by linking the entry age to life expectancy and raising the cash bonus for later retirement.

● Improve the under-performing school system. Denmark has one of the most expensive school systems in the world; however, students need to be more challenged (*e.g.* through testing), and teachers need to spend longer time in class, be better trained and specialise more.

DENMARK

Structural indicators

	1990	1995	2000	2003
Trend GDP per capita (% growth rate)	1.4	1.8	1.7	1.7
Trend employment rate	75.5	75.7	76.3	76.3
Trend participation rate	81.0	80.5	80.2	80.2
Structural unemployment rate (NAIRU)	6.8	6.1	4.8	4.8

Source: Estimates based on *OECD Economic Outlook,* No. 76.

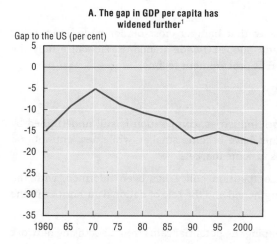

A. The gap in GDP per capita has widened further[1]

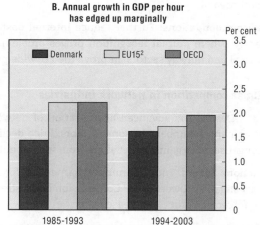

B. Annual growth in GDP per hour has edged up marginally

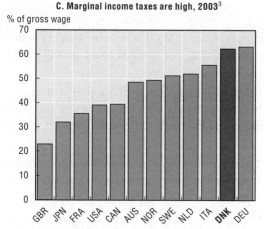

C. Marginal income taxes are high, 2003[3]

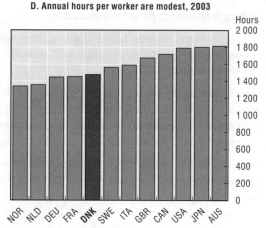

D. Annual hours per worker are modest, 2003

1. Percentage gap with respect to US GDP per capita (in constant 2000 PPPs).
2. Excluding Austria and Luxembourg.
3. Marginal income tax plus employee contributions less cash benefits for a one-earner family with no children, 167% of average worker's earnings.

Source: Charts A and B: *National Accounts of OECD Countries,* 2004; *OECD Labour Force Statistics,* 2004; *OECD Economic Outlook,* No. 76; Chart C: *OECD Taxing Wages,* 2003/2004; Chart D: *OECD Economic Outlook,* No. 76.

EUROPEAN UNION

A slowdown in labour productivity growth since the mid-1990s combined with weak growth in labour resource utilisation has resulted in a widening of the per capita income gap vis-à-vis the United States.

Priorities supported by indicators

Ease regulatory burden on business operations

The single-market strategy has only partly fulfilled its objective of fostering economic integration. Substantial barriers remain in service sectors, including impediments to cross-border establishment and the recognition of diplomas, and the lack of mutual recognition for business licenses.

Actions taken: An EU-wide system of protecting intellectual property rights has been adopted. A directive on services in the internal market to underpin the mutual recognition principle has been proposed.

Recommendations: Further reduce internal obstacles that hamper cross-border trade and market entry. Where mutual recognition proves problematic, adopt EU-wide standards. Liberalise fully the postal and railway sectors. Improve the EU-wide public procurement regime.

Raise competition in network industries

Despite the advanced liberalisation of network industries, competition is still undermined by dominant incumbent in some sectors. Price declines have become smaller, while new entrants no longer seem to gain market share from incumbents in some markets.

Actions taken: The Community framework for competition policy has been reformed, with the investigative powers of the Commission being strengthened and the role of national authorities in the enforcement process increased.

Recommendations: Focus competition policy on reaping the potential gains from liberalising network industries.

Reduce producer support to agriculture

Agricultural support under the Common Agriculture Policy (CAP) is distorting, keeping excess resources in low-productivity activities. The recent accession of 10 new member countries will put the CAP under strain.

Actions taken: Following the 2003 reform of the CAP, the composition of support will change substantially, but not the overall level. Support will be further de-coupled from production and made conditional on compliance with, *inter alia*, environmental and food safety standards. Even so, market price support will remain high.

Recommendations: Improve market access for non-EU countries. Move further away from production towards income support, and ensure that the recent agreement on a framework for continuing the Doha trade round – including notably the commitment to eliminate export subsidies – results in reforms.

Other key priorities

● Improve intra-European labour mobility by enhancing the portability of accrued pension rights and pension capital in occupational schemes as well as of other benefit entitlements.

● Fully implement the Financial Services Action Plan in order to foster economic integration. Ensure legal certainty for third-country securities issuers. Resist attempts to favour national champions.

EUROPEAN UNION

Structural indicators

	1990[1]	1995	2000	2003
Trend GDP per capita (% growth rate)	1.8	1.6	1.8	1.7
Trend employment rate	63.0	63.6	65.3	66.4
Trend participation rate	68.5	69.2	70.8	71.8
Structural unemployment rate (NAIRU)	8.2	8.3	7.9	7.7

Note: The 15 European Union countries prior to the 2004 enlargement, excluding Luxembourg.
1. To avoid break in the series due to the reunification in Germany, 1992 is used instead of 1990.
Source: Estimates based on *OECD Economic Outlook*, No. 76.

A. The gap in GDP per capita has widened[1]

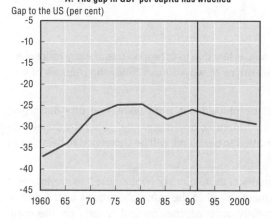

B. Annual growth in GDP per hour has fallen

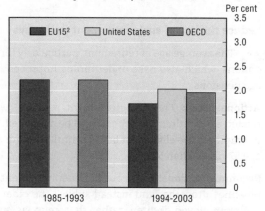

C. High dispersion of electricity prices for industries, 2003[3]

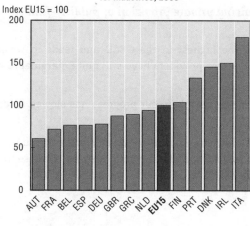

D. Agricultural support is still high
Producer support estimate

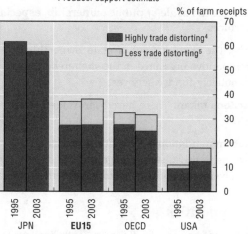

1. Percentage gap with respect to US GDP per capita (in constant 2000 PPPs). Break in series in 1991 due to reunification of Germany.
2. Excluding Austria and Luxembourg.
3. 2000 for Austria and Belgium, 2001 for Italy and the Netherlands, 2002 for Germany and Spain. EU15, excluding Luxembourg and Sweden.
4. Market price support and payments based on output and input use.
5. Payments based on area planted/animal numbers, historical entitlements and overall farm income.
Source: Charts A and B: *National Accounts of OECD Countries,* 2004; *OECD Labour Force Statistics,* 2004; *OECD Economic Outlook,* No. 76; Chart C: *OECD Energy Prices and Taxes,* 2004; Chart D: OECD, Producer and consumer support estimates database.

FINLAND

Growth performance has been impressive but largely driven by the ICT sector, while the performance in many others sectors has been poor. Structural unemployment remains high.

Priorities supported by indicators

Reduce the tax wedge on labour income

Average and marginal tax rates on labour income are among the highest in the OECD and pose a particular problem in combination with a compressed wage structure.

Actions taken: Tax rates on labour income have been steadily reduced over recent years, and the earned income tax allowance has been extended to benefit the low-paid in particular.

Recommendations: Continue to reduce high marginal tax rates on labour, not just for the low-paid but throughout the earnings distribution. If the fiscal room for action remains tight, then switch the tax burden from labour to property.

Reduce the use of early retirement pathways

The average age of retirement, particularly for men, is low due to extensive use of early retirement options, which also risks undermining improved incentives to work longer following reforms of old-age pensions.

Actions taken: The "unemployment pension" will be phased out from 2009, and one disability-related early retirement scheme will be abolished. The "unemployment pipeline", whereby the elderly unemployed are eligible for benefits until they are entitled to pensions, will be shortened to begin from age 57 rather than 55.

Recommendations: Phase out the unemployment pension more quickly, abolish the "unemployment pipeline" altogether and instead subject the older unemployed to the same obligations as the rest of the unemployed. Tighten, rather than relax as currently planned, the medical criteria for the main disability pension scheme.

Reduce the scale of public ownership, especially raising private provision of publicly-funded services

The current level of state ownership is among the highest in the OECD and leads to weak competitive pressures in the sheltered sectors. Private-sector providers have still quite marginal role in publicly-funded services.

Actions taken: There have been some privatisation measures taken, but progress has slowed since 2000.

Recommendations: Separate more clearly the state's ownership and regulatory roles. Pursue an extensive privatisation programme and ensure vertical separation in network industries. Increase the involvement of private-sector providers in publicly-funded services.

Other key priorities

● Promote greater flexibility in centralised wage determination (*e.g.* by allowing wages to reflect local labour market conditions) to prevent low-skilled service jobs from being further crowded out and to facilitate structural adjustment across sectors.

● Net replacement rates are among the highest in the OECD after long unemployment spells. Taper unemployment benefits with duration to encourage job search and reduce the unemployment trap.

FINLAND

Structural indicators

	1990	1995	2000	2003
Trend GDP per capita (% growth rate)	1.9	1.3	2.7	2.1
Trend employment rate	71.6	67.5	67.3	68.1
Trend participation rate	75.2	74.4	74.6	74.5
Structural unemployment rate (NAIRU)	4.8	9.4	9.8	8.6

Source: Estimates based on *OECD Economic Outlook*, No. 76.

A. Relative GDP per capita is still below the late 1980s level[1]

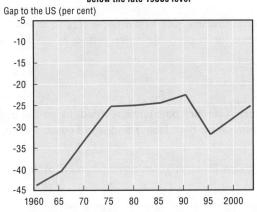

B. Annual growth in GDP per hour remains strong

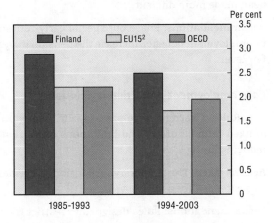

C. Average tax wedge is high[3]

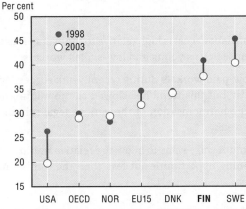

D. Implicit tax on continued work is high, 2003

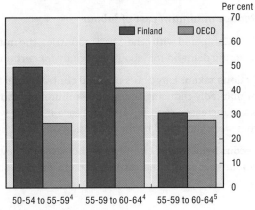

1. Percentage gap with respect to US GDP per capita (in constant 2000 PPPs).
2. Excluding Austria and Luxembourg.
3. Direct tax wedge including employer's social security contributions for a couple with two children. Average of 3 family situations with earnings at 100% of average worker's earnings.
4. Implicit tax embedded in early-retirement schemes on continued work from age 50-54 to age 55-59 and 55-59 to 60-64, respectively.
5. Implicit tax embedded in old-age pension schemes on continued work from age 55-59 to age 60-64.

Source: Charts A and B: *National Accounts of OECD Countries*, 2004; *OECD Labour Force Statistics*, 2004; *OECD Economic Outlook*, No. 76; Chart C: *OECD Taxing Wages*, 2003/2004; Chart D: Chapter 5 in this publication.

FRANCE

Despite improved employment rates, unemployment remains high. GDP per capita has not grown strongly enough to narrow the income gap vis-à-vis the United States.

Priorities supported by indicators

Reduce implicit tax on continued work at older ages

A low official retirement age, high implicit tax rates on working longer, state-funded early-retirement and extended unemployment-insurance (UI) programmes contribute to very low employment rates of older workers.

Actions taken: Retirement ages are being raised in line with life expectancy. Private-sector rules have been changed to increase the net income of those working beyond the official retirement age. Early-retirement programmes have been scaled back. Using the UI system as a form of early-retirement has been made more difficult.

Recommendations: Phase out special early-retirement schemes. Further tighten access to extended unemployment benefits. Increase the pension increments for longer contribution periods to actuarially fair levels.

Ease employment protection legislation

Rules governing large-scale layoffs, high statutory severance payments, restrictions on the use of fixed-term contracts and limitations on working time raise both labour and layoff costs, thereby reducing hiring.

Actions taken: The temporary suspension of legislation significantly tightening employment protection was extended for a further year.

Recommendations: Rules designed to restrict the use of fixed-term contracts should be relaxed and regulations concerning "social plans" (mass layoffs) amended. Limit the role of the judiciary system to intractable cases.

Reduce minimum cost of labour

Compared with other OECD countries, the minimum labour cost is high relative to the average cost, lowering demand for labour, especially for certain groups such as young and low-skilled workers.

Actions taken: Large cuts in social contributions for low-paid workers during recent years succeeded in markedly reducing the relative minimum labour cost, but this trend has slowed as the minimum wage increased (and is set to increase in 2005) with the harmonisation of the various legal minima that were generated by the legislation on the 35 hours week.

Recommendations: Limit future increases in the minimum wage so as to allow the relative minimum labour cost to decline further. Expand on-the-job training opportunities at less than the minimum wage.

Other key priorities

● Reduce barriers to entry in network industries that contribute to higher prices and limit choice. Introduce competition in rail transport and secure non-discriminatory third-party access in telecommunications and air transport.

● Ease the regulatory environment by simplifying the compulsory social security system, replacing the administrative approval of retail outlet locations with zoning requirements and scaling back pricing rules in place between producers and retailers.

FRANCE

Structural indicators

	1990	1995	2000	2003
Trend GDP per capita (% growth rate)	1.4	1.4	1.9	1.6
Trend employment rate	60.5	60.7	63.0	63.5
Trend participation rate	66.7	67.8	69.4	69.8
Structural unemployment rate (NAIRU)	9.3	10.4	9.2	9.1

Source: Estimates based on *OECD Economic Outlook*, No. 76.

A. The gap in GDP per capita has widened[1]

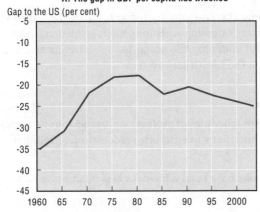

B. Annual growth in GDP per hour has remained robust

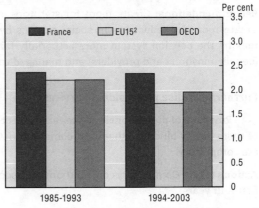

C. Employment rates are low for youth and older workers, 2003

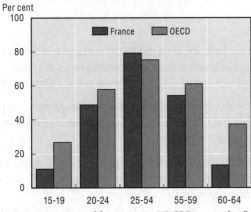

D. Minimum labour cost is high, 2002[3]

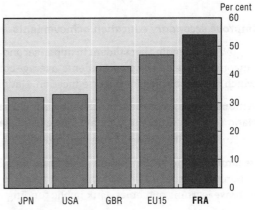

1. Percentage gap with respect to US GDP per capita (in constant 2000 PPPs).
2. Excluding Austria and Luxembourg.
3. Minimum labour cost as a percentage of labour cost of average worker.
Source: Charts A and B: *National Accounts of OECD Countries*, 2004; *OECD Labour Force Statistics*, 2004; *OECD Economic Outlook*, No. 76; Chart C: *OECD Labour Force Statistics*, 2004; Chart D: *OECD Employment Outlook*, 2004 and *OECD Taxing Wages*, 2004.

GERMANY

For more than ten years economic growth in Germany has been weak, resulting in a widening of the gap in GDP per capita vis-à-vis the United States and several EU countries.

Priorities supported by indicators

Reduce average tax wedge on labour income

Because of high social charges, Germany's tax wedge on labour income is in the upper range among OECD countries and the rise in ageing-related pension and social expenditures will put further upward pressures.

Actions taken: Personal income taxes have been lowered. Pension contribution rates have been temporarily stabilised by raising ecological taxes. Cost containment measures have been introduced in the public pension and health care systems with a view to reduce contribution rates.

Recommendations: Create room for statutory income tax rate cuts by reducing tax expenditures. Create room for reductions in social charges by better targeting unemployment-related transfers, making the pension system more actuarially fair and widening the scope for selective contracting (between insurers and providers) and managed care in the health care system.

Further liberalise professional services

Providers of professional services are subject to fee schedules of professional associations – some of them legally binding – that limit competition. Contributions to enterprise associations (chambers) are compulsory.

Actions taken: Compulsory contributions to associations have been waived for new businesses for the first four years.

Recommendations: Binding fee schedules for architects and engineers should be eliminated and deregulation in other professions should be considered. Compulsory contributions to associations should be phased out.

Improve secondary education achievements

While spending per student in upper-secondary education exceeds the OECD average, educational outcomes are relatively poor. Students' average competence levels differ significantly across the Länder, which are responsible for public education. Nation-wide educational standards are mostly lacking.

Actions taken: Investment in schooling infrastructure is being co-financed by the federal government. Nation-wide educational standards have been agreed by the Länder in some fields. Language training for students with immigrant background is being stepped up.

Recommendations: Set nation-wide standards for educational attainment and regularly monitor adherence to them. Give schools more freedom in determining their own programmes on how to improve learning outcomes. Link public funding of schools to educational outcomes.

Other key priorities

- Reduce disincentives to work at older ages. Abolish preferential benefit eligibility conditions for older workers and cut subsidies for working time reductions of this group.
- Increase competition in government procurement. Widen publication of contracts, simplify rules across the Länder and eliminate the role of business associations in setting these rules.

ECONOMIC POLICY REFORMS – ISBN 92-64-00836-5 – © OECD 2005

GERMANY

Structural indicators

	1992[1]	1995	2000	2003
Trend GDP per capita (% growth rate)	2.2	0.9	0.9	1.4
Trend employment rate	67.7	68.8	69.4	70.2
Trend participation rate	72.5	73.5	75.2	76.0
Structural unemployment rate (NAIRU)	6.5	6.4	7.6	7.7

1. To avoid break in the series due to the reunification in Germany, 1992 is used instead of 1990.
Source: Estimates based on *OECD Economic Outlook*, No. 76.

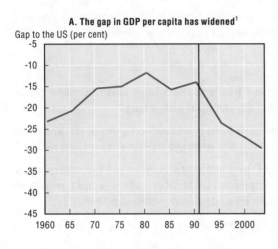

A. The gap in GDP per capita has widened[1]

Gap to the US (per cent)

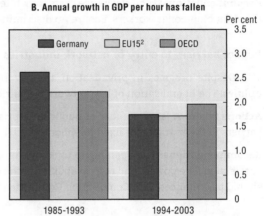

B. Annual growth in GDP per hour has fallen

Per cent

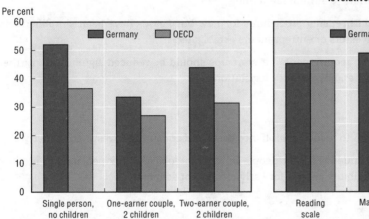

C. Average tax wedges are high, 2003[3]

Per cent

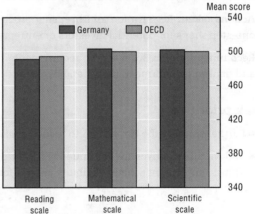

D. Educational achievement of 15 year-olds is relatively low, PISA 2003

Mean score

1. Percentage gap with respect to US GDP per capita (in constant 2000 PPPs). Break in the series in 1991.
2. Excluding Austria and Luxembourg.
3. Income tax plus employee and employer social security contributions less cash benefits as a percentage of labour costs, using average worker's earnings for the primary earner, 67% of this wage for secondary earner.
Source: Charts A and B: *National Accounts of OECD Countries*, 2004; *OECD Labour Force Statistics*, 2004; *OECD Economic Outlook*, No. 76; Chart C: *OECD Taxing Wages*, 2003/2004; Chart D: *OECD Learning for Tomorrow's World*, PISA 2003.

GREECE

Despite brisk growth in the past decade, a large gap in GDP per capita remains vis-à-vis the leading EU countries. Labour productivity has accelerated sharply, but the increase in employment rates has been small.

Priorities supported by indicators

Ease employment protection legislation

Employment protection legislation is among the strictest in the OECD, and this may have contributed to low labour turnover and to persistently high unemployment rates for women and youth.

Actions taken: The rule which allowed collective dismissals of only 2 per cent of the workforce per month for medium-sized firms has been abolished. Provisions for smaller firms have been tightened.

Recommendations: High severance costs for white-collar workers should be brought more in line with those for blue-collar workers. Ensure no discrimination against part-time employment.

Reduce barriers to entry in network industries

Despite progress in privatisation, the government has retained a large stake in major public utilities. The liberalisation of key network industries is advancing at a slow pace.

Actions taken: A large number of public enterprises have been privatised in recent years, and entry barriers in the markets for fixed telephony, electricity and domestic sea transport have been reduced.

Recommendations: The opening up to competition of the electricity and other key sectors should be accelerated. The powers and responsibilities of the Competition Committee and the sectoral regulators should be enhanced. The Competition Committee should be adequately staffed and funded.

Reduce administrative burdens on start-ups

By international comparison, self-employment rates are high but enterprise creation rates are low, suggesting substantial barriers to entrepreneurship.

Actions taken: Registration and licensing procedures for new businesses have been simplified and one-stop shops for potential investors or entrepreneurs established.

Recommendations: Bureaucratic requirements for start-ups should be reduced significantly further and flanked by reforms to labour and bankruptcy legislation.

Other key priorities

● Further simplify the tax system to reduce compliance costs and encourage investment activity.

● Reduce disincentives for continued work for people in arduous jobs and link pensions to lifetime earnings. Implement stricter eligibility criteria for early retirement schemes.

GREECE

Structural indicators

	1990	1995	2000	2003
Trend GDP per capita (% growth rate)	1.2	1.6	1.0	3.7
Trend employment rate	56.1	56.0	56.4	57.5
Trend participation rate	60.6	61.6	63.2	64.3
Structural unemployment rate (NAIRU)	7.4	9.2	10.8	10.5

Source: Estimates based on OECD Economic Outlook, No. 76.

A. Divergence in GDP per capita has halted[1]

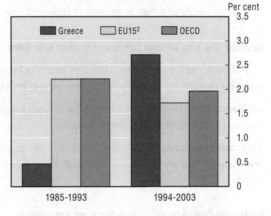

B. Annual growth in GDP per hour has increased markedly

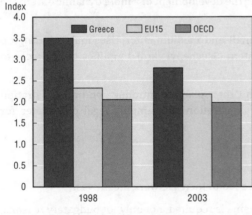

C. EPL is among the strictest in the OECD[3]

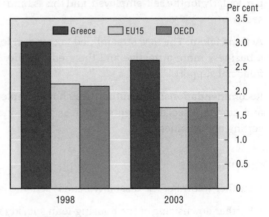

D. Administrative burden on start-ups is still high[3]

1. Percentage gap with respect to US GDP per capita (in constant 2000 PPPs).
2. Excluding Austria and Luxembourg.
3. Index scale of 0-6 from least to most restrictive.
Source: Charts A and B: National Accounts of OECD Countries, 2004; OECD Labour Force Statistics, 2004; OECD Economic Outlook, No. 76; Chart C: OECD Employment Outlook, 2004; Chart D: OECD Regulation database.

HUNGARY

GDP growth has been brisk in recent years, but registered labour force participation and employment rates remain low despite having risen rapidly relative to other countries.

Priorities supported by indicators

Reduce state control on the operations of network industries

After years of transition to a market-based economy, the key issues with respect to state control relate principally to regulations of the operations of network industries.

Actions taken: The authorities have begun deregulating prices in retail gas and electricity markets and have a schedule for complete liberalisation.

Recommendations: The price liberalisation schedule needs to be followed, and preferably brought forward, and the government's role in setting network access charges reduced. This would be helped by greater independence accorded to industry regulators.

Reduce the tax wedge for low-income workers

A high tax wedge for low-income workers is contributing to a relatively low recorded employment rate and reportedly high levels of grey-sector activity.

Actions taken: The abolition of the fixed health-care insurance contribution has helped to bring down the cost of employing low-wage workers.

Recommendations: While the need for fiscal consolidation constrains the options to cut taxes, lowering the tax wedge on low earnings should be given some priority, not least to reduce underground activity.

Reduce administrative burdens on start-ups

Both the number of administrative procedures and time taken to complete them is burdensome, particularly for the self-employed, and this is hindering the development of a more dynamic enterprise sector.

Actions taken: The new streamlined tax system for small-and-medium enterprises makes setting-up a business more attractive and the credit facility system (Szechenyi card) simplifies their access to financial support.

Recommendations: The authorities should implement their plans to introduce on-line registration and standardised documents, cut fees for business registration and simplify legal procedures for setting up a business.

Other key priorities

● Further reform of the disability benefit scheme is needed to increase work incentives.

● Further downsizing of the housing-loan subsidy scheme is required, not only for budgetary reasons, but also to reduce distortions in housing markets and increase labour mobility.

HUNGARY

Structural indicators

	1990	1995	2000	2003
Trend GDP per capita (% growth rate)	..	..	4.4	4.1
Trend employment rate	..	..	54.6	54.1
Trend participation rate	..	..	58.4	58.1
Structural unemployment rate (NAIRU)	..	..	..	..

Source: Estimates based on *OECD Economic Outlook*, No. 76.

A. Convergence in GDP per capita is a long way off[1]

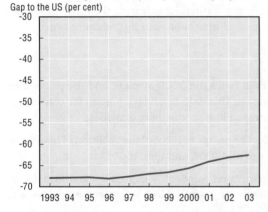

B. Annual growth in GDP per hour is above average

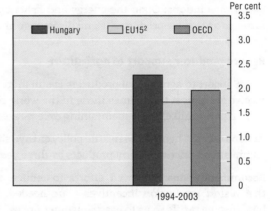

C. State control over business enterprises remains high[3]

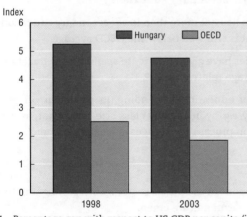

D. Administrative burden to set up a small business is high[3]

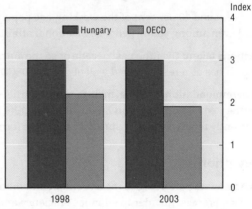

1. Percentage gap with respect to US GDP per capita (in constant 2000 PPPs).
2. Excluding Austria and Luxembourg.
3. Index scale of 0-6 from least to most restrictive.
Source: Charts A and B: *National Accounts of OECD Countries*, 2004; *OECD Labour Force Statistics*, 2004; *OECD Economic Outlook*, No. 76; Charts C and D: OECD Regulation database.

ICELAND

Economic performance has improved significantly since the mid-1990s, allowing Iceland to narrow its income gap vis-à-vis the United States. However, the labour productivity gap remains large.

Priorities supported by indicators

Lower barriers to entry for domestic and foreign firms

Despite market liberalisation since Iceland joined the European Economic Area (EEA) in 1994, relatively high barriers to the entry of domestic and foreign firms remain in some sectors, *e.g.* energy and fisheries.

Actions taken: The sale of the government's stake in Iceland Telecom has resumed after being halted in 2002 due to adverse market conditions. The authorities do not intend to privatise the major national electricity company.

Recommendations: Open the energy and fisheries sectors further, including to the entry of foreign firms, so as to raise productivity and discourage anti-competitive behaviour by dominant firms.

Reduce producer support to agriculture

Support to agricultural producers is still more than twice the OECD average, and the prices they receive are almost three times those in the world market. This entails a heavy burden for consumers and taxpayers alike, while maintaining excess resources in low-productivity activities.

Actions taken: There has been little policy change since the postponement of the abolition of remaining administered prices for dairy products by three years to mid-2004, and then to 2012.

Recommendations: Renewed efforts to reduce agricultural support – especially in those forms that distort production incentives – are needed. Eliminate heavily binding protective quotas and burdensome tariffs so as to ease consumer prices.

Improve access to, and graduation rates from, upper-secondary education

Around 40 per cent of the working-age population has not more than lower secondary education, and even among young people educational attainment is still well below the OECD average.

Actions taken: Over the past decade or so the authorities have given priority to spending on education, which has as a result moved well above the OECD average relative to GDP.

Recommendations: While maintaining high levels of educational spending, in particular on pre-tertiary education, focus on quality and cost efficiency, *e.g.* by increasing class size somewhat, as it is currently relatively low. Ensure that the wage formation process encourages skills development.

Other key priorities

● Accelerate performance measurement and management in the public sector by integrating it in the budget process, in order to enhance efficiency and curb expenditure creep.

● Reduce government backing of bonds issued by the Housing Finance Fund, which distorts investment choice between housing and other assets.

ECONOMIC POLICY REFORMS – ISBN 92-64-00836-5 – © OECD 2005

ICELAND

Structural indicators

	1990	1995	2000	2003
Trend GDP per capita (% growth rate)	0.8	0.9	2.9	2.0
Trend employment rate	85.1	83.1	84.3	84.3
Trend participation rate	86.7	86.7	86.7	86.7
Structural unemployment rate (NAIRU)	1.8	4.1	2.8	2.8

Source: Estimates based on *OECD Economic Outlook*, No. 76.

A. Convergence in GDP per capita has resumed[1]

B. Annual growth in GDP per hour has increased

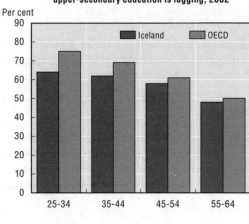

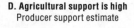

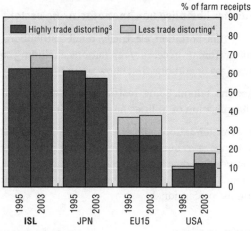

C. The proportion of the population with at least upper-secondary education is lagging, 2002

D. Agricultural support is high
Producer support estimate

1. Percentage gap with respect to US GDP per capita (in constant 2000 PPPs).
2. Excluding Austria and Luxembourg.
3. Market price support and payments based on output and input use.
4. Payments based on area planted/animal numbers, historical entitlements and overall farm income.
Source: Charts A and B: *National Accounts of OECD Countries*, 2004; *OECD Labour Force Statistics*, 2004; *OECD Economic Outlook*, No. 76; Chart C: *OECD Education at a Glance*, 2004; Chart D: OECD, Producer and consumer support estimates database.

IRELAND

With the fastest growth rate of GDP per capita in OECD countries over the past decade, Ireland has largely caught-up with leading countries in terms of productivity and, to a lesser extent, income levels.

Priorities supported by indicators

Strengthen work incentives for second earners

The rapid pace of economic growth over the past decade has been underpinned by a substantial increase in labour force participation. However, growth in female participation needs to be encouraged further to respond to continued strong growth in the demand for labour.

Actions taken: A change in the personal income tax system has reduced the effective marginal tax rates for second earners closer to the low rates applied for primary earners. The National Employment Action Plan foresees significant investment in childcare structures to reduce the relatively high childcare costs.

Recommendations: Strengthen work incentives further, especially for those seeking part-time work and lower-skilled second earners, through a non-wastable tax credit for childcare.

Ease the regulatory burden on business operations

Neglect of regulatory policy has resulted in a framework that burdens business and constrains the degree of competition. Improving the regulatory framework and establishing a better mix of regulatory policies, tools and institutions will enhance transparency and lower the regulatory burden on business operations.

Actions taken: The government has issued a *White Paper on Better Regulation*, aiming for a regulatory system that abides by the OECD guidelines on better regulation.

Recommendations: Implement swiftly the regulatory framework proposed in the *White Paper on Better Regulation*.

Further liberalise non-manufacturing sectors

Transportation, electricity, retail distribution, professions and, to some extent, telecommunications suffer from unnecessary regulations, including barriers to entry, price controls and other rules limiting business operations that show up in high prices.

Actions taken: Some restrictions to entry have been removed, for example for retail pharmacies. Liberalisation of utilities has started, in line with the EU agenda.

Recommendations: Pursue liberalisation of network industries, by ensuring that incumbents do not engage in business practices that prevent newcomers from entering the market. Eliminate anti-competitive devices in retail distribution, such as the "Groceries order" and the "Retail planning guidelines", and abolish other price controls. Pursue efforts to open professional services to foreign-trained professionals.

Other key priorities

● Phase out tax deductibility of mortgage interest payments. Avoid frequent changes in stamp duties, which lead to undue volatility in house prices.

● Improve the enforcement system for competition. Give the competition authorities more enforcement power and the possibility of imposing sanctions, such as fines.

IRELAND

Structural indicators

	1990	1995	2000	2003
Trend GDP per capita (% growth rate)	4.8	6.6	6.4	3.8
Trend employment rate	54.2	57.9	63.7	65.8
Trend participation rate	63.3	65.2	68.2	69.8
Structural unemployment rate (NAIRU)	14.4	11.1	6.6	5.7

Source: Estimates based on *OECD Economic Outlook,* No. 76.

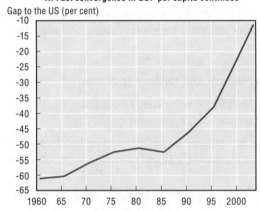

A. Fast convergence in GDP per capita continues[1]

Gap to the US (per cent)

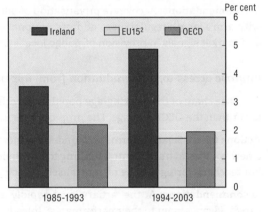

B. Annual growth in GDP per hour has risen further

Per cent

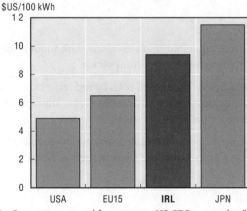

C. Electricity prices for industries are relatively high, 2003[3]

$US/100 kWh

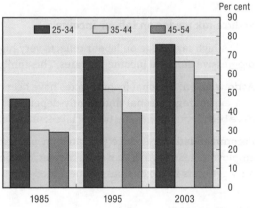

D. Female labour force participation is rising

Per cent

1. Percentage gap with respect to US GDP per capita (in constant 2000 PPPs).
2. Excluding Austria and Luxembourg.
3. 2002 for Japan and the EU15. EU15 excluding Luxembourg and Sweden.
Source: Charts A and B: *National Accounts of OECD Countries,* 2004; *OECD Labour Force Statistics,* 2004; *OECD Economic Outlook,* No. 76; Chart C: *OECD Energy Prices and Taxes,* 2004; Chart D: *OECD Labour Force Statistics,* 2004.

ITALY

Since the mid-1990s, labour productivity has slowed. The employment rate has risen but remains one of the lowest in OECD.

Priorities supported by indicators

Reduce public ownership

Despite divestitures, the state still holds controlling interest or "golden shares" in key industries, notably energy, transportation and telecommunications. Most utilities at local levels remain under public ownership.

Actions taken: The state tobacco company was recently privatised, 26.6 per cent of the electricity incumbent sold, and golden shares are under review. However, the tendering obligation for public local service providers has been relaxed.

Recommendations: Accelerate privatisation of public companies. Replace golden shares in companies with arm's length regulation to address national security concerns. Increase reliance on competition and market signals in provision of public local services.

Improve access to, and graduation from, upper-secondary and tertiary education

The share of the working-age population with at least upper-secondary education is significantly lower than the OECD average. The drop-out rate from tertiary education is especially high.

Actions taken: School reforms now underway increase compulsory schooling by 2 years and introduce a new vocational track. Central funding to universities is increasingly linked to academic performance, but teachers' hiring is to be re-centralised.

Recommendations: At the tertiary level, rapidly implement the vocational track and relate teachers' career advancement to their performance. Introduce a system of co-payments and loans with income-contingent re-payments. Decentralise further universities' financing and management, and allow professional managers to run such establishments.

Reduce tax wedge on labour income

A high tax wedge on labour reflects very high pension contribution rates along with moderately progressive personal income tax rates. This inhibits employment in the formal sector.

Actions taken: Personal income taxes have been reduced across the board, both by reducing tax rates and expanding personal and family-dependant tax allowances. Around 800 000 illegal immigrants have been brought into the tax/social security net, and other tax amnesties implemented.

Recommendations: Reduce tax rates, in particular applied to lower-middle earning levels to boost employment. Strengthen tax enforcement, discontinue tax amnesties, and expand further deductions for wage costs in the business value added tax (IRAP).

Other key priorities

● Corporate control reforms should focus on strengthening independent directors and minority shareholder rights. The bankruptcy law should be reformed by strengthening creditor rights and reducing borrower penalties in case of insolvency.

● The public sector should take a lead in decentralising wage bargaining arrangements, taking into account regional differences in both productivity and cost of living.

ITALY

Structural indicators

	1990	1995	2000	2003
Trend GDP per capita (% growth rate)	2.5	1.2	1.3	1.3
Trend employment rate	54.7	53.3	54.2	55.8
Trend participation rate	59.5	58.9	60.2	61.5
Structural unemployment rate (NAIRU)	8.1	9.6	9.9	9.3

Source: Estimates based on *OECD Economic Outlook*, No. 76.

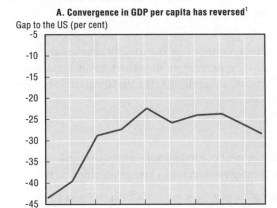

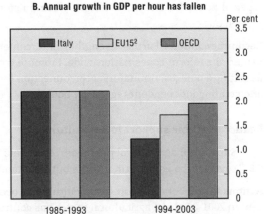

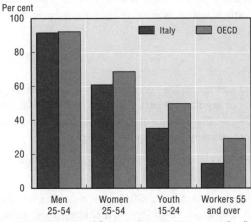

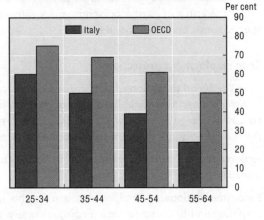

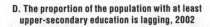

1. Percentage gap with respect to US GDP per capita (in constant 2000 PPPs).
2. Excluding Austria and Luxembourg.
Source: Charts A and B: *National Accounts of OECD Countries*, 2004; *OECD Labour Force Statistics*, 2004; *OECD Economic Outlook*, No. 76; Chart C: *OECD Labour Force Statistics*, 2004; Chart D: *OECD Education at a Glance*, 2004.

JAPAN

Labour productivity decelerated during Japan's decade of economic stagnation, thus widening the income gap with the leading OECD countries.

Priorities supported by indicators

Further liberalise services

Prices of services are relatively high, reflecting insufficiently strong enforcement of competition law, overly prescriptive regulations and inadequate regulatory frameworks in network industries, including electricity.

Actions taken: The resources of the Fair Trade Commission have been increased and its independence strengthened. Joint-stock companies have been allowed to enter the health and education sectors in "special zones for structural reform". Compulsory fee-setting by professional associations is being phased out.

Recommendations: Further strengthen enforcement of competition law and impose heavier sanctions. Extend the reform zones nation-wide. Promote competition in network industries by such measures as setting a non-discriminatory interconnection framework, unbundling vertically integrated activities and creating independent regulatory bodies.

Reduce producer support to agriculture

Support for agricultural producers represents 59 per cent of total farm receipts, nearly double the OECD average, boosting farm income but maintaining excess resources in low-productivity activities.

Actions taken: Total support to agriculture has been cut from 2.3 per cent of GDP in 1986-88 to 1.4 per cent in 2001-03 as the agricultural sector has contracted. Measures to deregulate rice distribution have been introduced.

Recommendations: Further reduce the level of support to agriculture, while shifting its composition from market price support to direct payments, which cause less distortion of trade and production. Allow the entry of joint-stock companies into agriculture, which was recently permitted in some special zones, on a nation-wide basis.

Ease employment protection

The broad definition of unfair dismissal by courts has made the requirement for dismissal less transparent and this could have discouraged the hiring of regular workers. Also, the difference in the strictness of regulation between regular and non-regular workers is one of the factors contributing to the rise in the share of non-regular workers, raising both efficiency and equity concerns.

Actions taken: The requirements for dismissals have been elaborated in labour law, thus enhancing transparency.

Recommendations: To reduce dualism in the labour market and facilitate restructuring of the corporate and financial sectors, a comprehensive approach should be adopted, including a reduction of employment protection for regular workers.

Other key priorities

● Reform the financial sector by resolving the non-performing loan problem, requiring banks to strengthen their capital base and scaling back the role of public financial institutions.

● Remove impediments to foreign direct investment in Japan, currently receiving the lowest inflow in the OECD area, by implementing the action plan aimed at doubling the stock of FDI over five years.

JAPAN

Structural indicators

	1990	1995	2000	2003
Trend GDP per capita (% growth rate)	2.8	1.4	1.3	1.4
Trend employment rate	72.3	73.9	74.7	75.1
Trend participation rate	74.4	76.2	77.6	78.1
Structural unemployment rate (NAIRU)	2.8	3.0	3.6	3.9

Source: Estimates based on *OECD Economic Outlook*, No. 76.

A. Convergence in GDP per capita reversed in the 1990s[1]

Gap to the US (per cent)

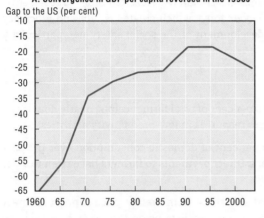

B. Annual growth in GDP per hour has fallen

Per cent

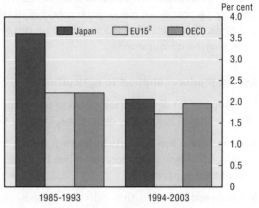

C. Electricity prices for households are high
Pre-tax price per 100 kWh, 2002

US dollars

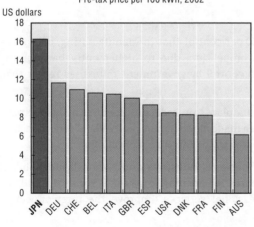

D. Agricultural support is high
Producer support estimate

% of farm receipts

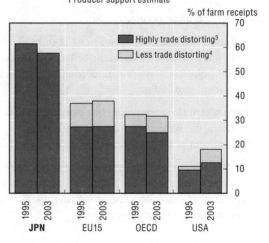

1. Percentage gap with respect to US GDP per capita (in constant 2000 PPPs).
2. Excluding Austria and Luxembourg.
3. Market price support and payments based on output and input use.
4. Payments based on area planted/animal numbers, historical entitlements and overall farm income.
Source: Charts A and B: *National Accounts of OECD Countries*, 2004; *OECD Labour Force Statistics*, 2004; *OECD Economic Outlook*, No. 76; Chart C: *OECD Energy Prices and Taxes*, 2004; Chart D: OECD, Producer and consumer support estimates database.

KOREA

With growth rates of labour productivity and GDP per capita remaining well above most other OECD countries, Korea has continued to narrow its substantial income gap relative to the average OECD level.

Priorities supported by indicators

Ease employment protection for regular workers

Although collective dismissals of regular workers for economic reasons have been allowed since 1998, this reform has failed to promote flexibility in practice, given the constraints imposed on management.

Actions taken: An expert committee has recommended some easing of the conditions on collective dismissals.

Recommendations: The conditions on collective dismissals should be relaxed in order to reverse the growing proportion of non-regular workers in the labour force, which creates equity and efficiency concerns. This should be accompanied by further development of the social safety net, particularly unemployment insurance.

Reduce producer support to agriculture

Support for agricultural producers represents 60 per cent of total farm receipts, nearly double the OECD average. This creates distortions, keeping excess resources in low-productivity activities.

Actions taken: Rice imports have risen from 1 to 4 per cent of domestic consumption over the past decade, while overall support has fallen by 13 per cent. Direct payments to farmers have risen to 9 per cent of total support.

Recommendations: Further shift the composition of assistance from market price support to direct payments, and reduce the overall level. Eliminate remaining restrictions on farm size, so as to raise productivity.

Further liberalise services

Labour productivity in services is only about 60 per cent of that in manufacturing, one of the largest gaps in the OECD area, reflecting weaker competition, due to higher entry barriers and tighter regulation. Network industries are subject to control by government ministries rather than independent regulators.

Actions taken: The government has launched restructuring plans to introduce competition in the electricity and natural gas sectors. Collusion in fee-setting has been made illegal in nine professional service sectors, while a reform of 152 trade associations has been launched by the Fair Trade Commission.

Recommendations: Accelerate the restructuring of network industries and establish independent regulators to promote competition. Simplify procedures for opening large retail stores. Extend the prohibition on collusion in fee-setting to all professional services. Improve the interconnection framework in telecommunications.

Other key priorities

● Remove ownership, procedural and regulatory barriers to foreign direct investment, which is currently relatively low. Extend the incentives offered in the three Free Economic Zones to the rest of the country.

● Improve the functioning of the financial sector by completing the privatisation of banks, resolving the instability in the non-bank sector, notably the credit card companies, the investment trust companies and the fixed-income sector, and by shifting to a more pre-emptive approach to financial supervision to deal with emerging risks in this sector.

ECONOMIC POLICY REFORMS – ISBN 92-64-00836-5 – © OECD 2005

KOREA

Structural indicators

	1990	1995	2000	2003
Trend GDP per capita (% growth rate)	6.7	5.3	3.7	3.6
Trend employment rate	60.4	62.7	63.4	64.5
Trend participation rate	62.3	64.4	66.2	67.1
Structural unemployment rate (NAIRU)	3.0	2.6	4.2	3.8

Source: Estimates based on *OECD Economic Outlook*, No. 76.

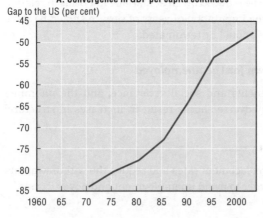

A. Convergence in GDP per capita continues[1]

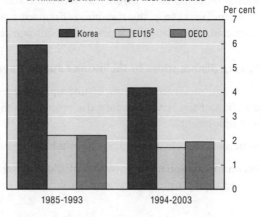

B. Annual growth in GDP per hour has slowed

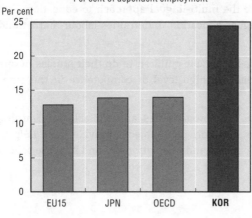

C. The share of temporary workers is very high, 2003

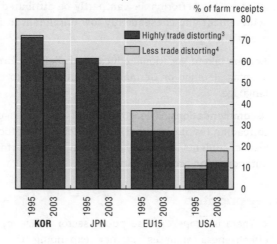

D. Support for agriculture remains high

1. Percentage gap with respect to US GDP per capita (in constant 2000 PPPs).
2. Excluding Austria and Luxembourg.
3. Market price support and payments based on output and input use.
4. Payments based on area planted/animal numbers, historical entitlements and overall farm income.
Source: Charts A and B: *National Accounts of OECD Countries*, 2004; *OECD Labour Force Statistics*, 2004; *OECD Economic Outlook*, No. 76; Chart C: *OECD Economic Survey, Korea* 2004 and *OECD Labour Force Statistics*, 2004; Chart D: OECD, Producer and consumer support estimates database.

LUXEMBOURG

Despite a deceleration in GDP per capita in recent years, Luxembourg maintains one of the highest income levels in OECD countries. Employment rates remain relatively low.

Priorities supported by indicators

Reduce implicit tax on continued work at older ages

Disability pension and pre- and early-retirement pensions provide attractive routes to early retirement, resulting in a low average age of withdrawal from the labour market.

Actions taken: Access to general disability pensions has been tightened, and a new redeployment procedure for the partially disabled has been established. However, early retirement and old-age pension replacement rates have been increased.

Recommendations: Early retirement pension should be reduced on an actuarially fair basis in relation to a pension taken at the standard retirement age, the imputation of years of service should be more restricted, and subsidies for pre-retirement pensions should be terminated.

Reduce disincentives in the income support system for the unemployed

High replacement rates of unemployment benefits and social assistance, and the unlimited duration of the latter, increase the probability that adverse shocks result in increases in structural unemployment.

Actions taken: No actions have been taken in recent years.

Recommendations: The government should lower replacement rates and reduce the withdrawal rate for social assistance as recipients' incomes rise in order to avoid unemployment and poverty traps.

Raise achievement in primary and secondary education

Achievement of Luxembourg students is low, and the gap between nationals and immigrants is large. This performance can partly be attributed to the multi-lingual approach to education. Low achievement and consequently low enrolment in higher education undermines labour-market and productivity performance.

Actions taken: Vocational education is being reformed to enable children to do their studies in one language (French or German) without having to achieve a high level of competence in the other language.

Recommendations: The government should ensure that programmes are available for learning to read and write in either German or French, focus more on core subjects, provide more help to weaker students in primary education, define performance standards nationally, and increase school autonomy and accountability.

Other key priorities

● There is scope to raise public-sector efficiency by making more use of cost-benefit and cost-effectiveness analyses, further expanding the role of e-government, increasing managerial independence and accountability, and *via* administrative simplification.

● The government should reduce barriers to competition in broadband services by imposing lower access charges to the local loop and by restricting the scope for the incumbent telecom's company to cross-subsidise other activities.

ECONOMIC POLICY REFORMS – ISBN 92-64-00836-5 – © OECD 2005

LUXEMBOURG

Structural indicators

	1990	1995	2000	2003
Trend GDP per capita (% growth rate)	4.3	3.2	3.6	2.4
Trend employment rate	60.0	60.3	60.8	61.7
Trend participation rate	60.9	61.4	62.4	63.6
Structural unemployment rate (NAIRU)	..	..	..	..

Source: Estimates based on *OECD Economic Outlook*, No. 76.

A. Relative GDP per capita continues to rise[1]

Gap to the US (per cent)

B. Annual growth in GDP per hour has fallen below average[2]

Per cent

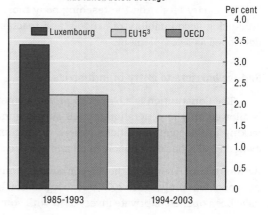

C. Participation rates of older workers are low, 2002

Per cent

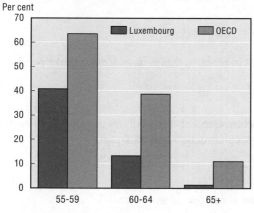

D. Educational achievement is low, 2000

Mean score

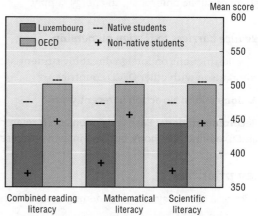

1. Percentage gap with respect to US GDP per capita (in constant 2000 PPPs). The development of GDP is biased upwards by the large share of cross-border workers (33 per cent of domestic employment).
2. GDP per hours worked in the economy (*i.e.* including that of cross-borders workers).
3. Excluding Austria and Luxembourg.

Source: Charts A and B: *National Accounts of OECD Countries,* 2004; *OECD Labour Force Statistics,* 2004; *OECD Economic Outlook,* No. 76; Chart C: *OECD Labour Force Statistics,* 2004; Chart D: *OECD Knowledge and Skills for Life,* PISA 2000.

MEXICO

Economic growth has been too slow to reduce the large gap in living standards with other OECD countries. Employment rates are high and rising, but productivity has stagnated in the past decade.

Priorities supported by indicators

Improve access to upper-secondary education

Mexico ranks last in the OECD in terms of educational attainment of the population (even for young adults) and for student performance. Reducing the gap would help boost growth by enhancing human capital, and by facilitating the adoption of new technologies.

Actions taken: Measures have been taken to increase participation in upper-secondary education of students from low-income families and to increase the quality of teaching.

Recommendations: Efforts should concentrate on making the existing school system, including at the secondary level, and the teaching body more effective by further modernising curricula and by enhancing accountability of schools and teachers. Effective on-the-job training should be further developed as a complement.

Reduce barriers to entry in industries

The Constitution is a barrier to private ownership in the entire electricity sector: private capital is allowed only in generation for self-supply and small-scale cogeneration. Effective competition is lacking in telecommunications, where the incumbent TELMEX retains a dominant position. State-owned PEMEX has a monopoly in oil and gas extraction.

Actions taken: A reform of the Telecommunications Law, reducing TELMEX control over communication networks, was proposed in 2002, but no legislation has resulted as yet. PEMEX secondary petrochemicals have been opened to private investment with some restrictions.

Recommendations: Approve the proposed Telecommunications Law and implement it effectively, thereby eliminating barriers to entry (domestic and foreign) by simplifying procedures. Reduce the share of public enterprises in energy supply.

Reduce barriers to foreign ownership

Restrictions on foreign direct investment are still in place. In this respect Mexico ranks poorly in comparison with other OECD countries.

Actions taken: No action in recent years.

Recommendations: Ease restrictions on foreign direct investment, especially in the electricity sector and fixed-line telephony, but also in some professions, construction and transport.

Other key priorities

● Reform the tax system, broadening the VAT base and simplifying the system.

● Improve the "rule of law" (*i.e.* the effectiveness of the judiciary and enforceability of contracts).

MEXICO

Structural indicators

	1990	1995	2000	2003
Trend GDP per capita (% growth rate)	..	..	1.7	1.6
Trend employment rate	..	..	57.7	57.8
Trend participation rate	..	..	59.7	59.7
Structural unemployment rate (NAIRU)	..	..	..	..

Source: Estimates based on *OECD Economic Outlook,* No. 76.

A. Convergence in GDP per capita is a long way off[1]

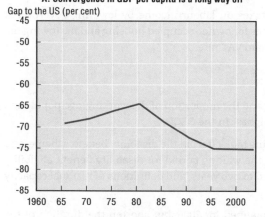

B. Annual growth in GDP per hour is stagnating

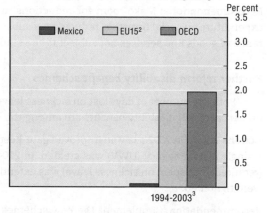

C. The proportion of the population with at least upper-secondary education is low, 2002

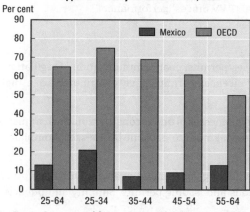

D. Explicit barriers to trade and investment are high[4]

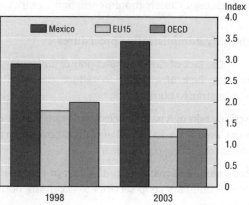

1. Percentage gap with respect to US GDP per capita (in constant 2000 PPPs).
2. Excluding Austria and Luxembourg.
3. Earlier period not shown because of lack of consistent data for Mexico.
4. Index scale of 0-6 from least to most restrictive.

Source: Charts A and B: *National Accounts of OECD Countries,* 2004; *OECD Labour Force Statistics,* 2004; *OECD Economic Outlook,* No. 76; Chart C: *OECD Education at a Glance,* 2004; Chart D: OECD Regulation database.

NETHERLANDS

Despite a decline in the unemployment rate to one of the lowest levels in the OECD area, labour resource under-utilisation in the Netherlands still accounts for most of the wide income gap vis-à-vis the United States.

Priorities supported by indicators

Reduce tax wedge on labour income

The high tax wedge on labour income and the "tax-like" (*i.e.* redistributive) elements in the almost universal second-pillar pension system weaken incentives to join the labour force (for low-income earners) and to increase hours worked (for high-income earners).

Actions taken: The special treatment of employers' social security contributions for low-paid workers (SPAK) was abolished in 2003. Pension fund contributions have been increased sharply to bring fund solvency back to a sustainable track.

Recommendations: Make room for reductions in taxes on labour income by lowering government expenditure on social transfers, reducing tax subsidies for owner-occupied housing and narrowing the range of goods and services not subject to the standard VAT rate.

Further reform disability benefit schemes

Both the number of days lost on sickness leave and the proportion of the working-age population on partial or full disability benefits are among the highest in the OECD.

Actions taken: In 2002 a law on improved gate-keeping took effect in the disability benefit scheme, and a single benefit agency (UWV) was created. In 2004 the waiting period for disability benefit eligibility (required to be spent on sickness leave) was extended to two years, and definitions of residual capacity were tightened.

Recommendations: Implement the new schemes planned for 2006, but shorten the duration of the first-stage disability benefit (which lasts up to 5 years depending on age and employment history) and prevent social partners from topping up benefits by denying sector extension to agreements containing such clauses. Closely monitor and benchmark regional UWV offices' performance.

Simplify administrative procedures

The lack of single contact points for issuing licenses/permits, poor communication of regulations and the lack of a policy to reduce the number of licenses/permits have contributed to a high administrative burden.

Actions taken: A national electronic one-stop shop for businesses is under construction. Each ministry must produce a list of all simplification opportunities, taking into account businesses' complaints about conflicting regulations.

Recommendations: Reduce the cost of compliance by linking government agencies with each other. Extend one-stop shop services to accepting notifications and issuing permits. Simplify and publicise regulations.

Other key priorities

● Remove barriers to product market competition by privatising the retail end of electricity and gas distribution networks, eliminating unwarranted anti-competitive practices in the professions and easing restrictions on large-format retail store operators.

● Ease residential zoning restrictions to stimulate supply of housing, and phase out tax subsidies to owner-occupiers so as to reduce the excess burden of taxation.

NETHERLANDS

Structural indicators

	1990	1995	2000	2003
Trend GDP per capita (% growth rate)	1.7	2.0	2.0	1.6
Trend employment rate	63.4	68.8	73.6	76.1
Trend participation rate	68.6	72.7	77.1	78.7
Structural unemployment rate (NAIRU)	7.5	5.3	4.5	3.3

Source: Estimates based on *OECD Economic Outlook*, No. 76.

A. Convergence in GDP per capita has stalled[1]

B. Annual growth in GDP per hour has fallen

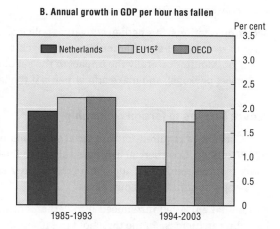

C. Working time lost due to sickness and disability is high, 1999

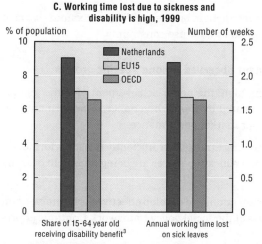

D. Tax disincentives result in low hours worked, 2002

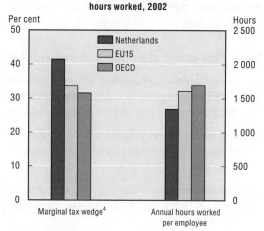

1. Percentage gap with respect to US GDP per capita (in constant 2000 PPPs).
2. Excluding Austria and Luxembourg.
3. Excluding Finland, Greece, Ireland and Luxembourg.
4. Marginal tax wedge, averaged over five representative household and earnings types.
Source: Charts A and B: *National Accounts of OECD Countries*, 2004; *OECD Labour Force Statistics*, 2004; *OECD Economic Outlook*, No. 76; Chart C: *OECD Transforming Disability into Ability*, 2003, *OECD Employment Outlook*, 2004 and US Bureau of Labor Statistics; Chart D: *OECD Taxing Wages*, 2003/2004 and *OECD Economic Outlook*, No. 76.

NEW ZEALAND

Growth in GDP per capita has risen markedly in New Zealand in the past decade, albeit not sufficiently for a catch-up with the top half of OECD countries. The large gap in labour productivity has widened.

Priorities supported by indicators

Strengthen incentives to move from welfare to work

Nine per cent of working-age New Zealanders have been on public income support for more than a year, and incentives to move from welfare to work are weak.

Actions taken: The "Jobs Jolt" provides more active case management for job seekers. The child tax credit will be replaced with an in-work payment, and abatement thresholds for in-work payments, family support and parental tax credits will rise from April 2006. Work testing of sole-parent benefits was abolished in 2003.

Recommendations: Strengthen activation policies, for example, by re-introducing work testing for sole parents with school-age children. Consider back-to-work bonuses for long-term beneficiaries moving into a job. Monitor carefully the impact of the set of measures unveiled in the last budget (the *Working for Families* package), and make adjustments if the labour supply response is not significant.

Reduce barriers to foreign ownership

Consent is required for foreign acquisitions of 25 per cent or more of firms worth more than NZ$ 50 million. Commercial fishing is subject to foreign ownership restrictions, and any single foreign entity requires ministerial approval to own more than 49.9 per cent of Telecom New Zealand. Consent rules apply to certain land purchases.

Actions taken: A bill introduced into Parliament in November 2004 proposes a number of changes, including an increase in the threshold to $100 million, but also a tightening of conditions for sensitive land.

Recommendations: Remove restrictions on foreign investment in business activities. Examine ways of protecting sensitive land through other instruments such as land-use constraints.

Reduce the extent of educational under-achievement observed among specific groups

Although average student achievement remains high, the under-achievement of some groups, particularly among ethnic minorities, persists as indicated by the high variance in performance on standardised tests. This undermines subsequent labour market performance.

Actions taken: The government is developing a "Schooling Strategy" to efficiently boost performance, including that of under-achievers. More early childhood education places are being phased in over the next four years.

Recommendations: Further expand early childhood education, and develop effective early intervention programmes that are well coordinated with other parts of the social policy framework. Continue efforts to raise teaching quality.

Other key priorities

● Reconsider recent measures that have raised labour costs, and ensure that employment relations legislation supports efficient labour market outcomes.

● Create a business environment more conducive to growth by improving the regulatory framework for addressing infrastructure bottlenecks, especially in transport and energy.

ECONOMIC POLICY REFORMS – ISBN 92-64-00836-5 – © OECD 2005

NEW ZEALAND

Structural indicators

	1990	1995	2000	2003
Trend GDP per capita (% growth rate)	0.5	1.6	2.0	2.0
Trend employment rate	71.7	70.0	71.9	73.2
Trend participation rate	76.9	75.4	76.8	77.6
Structural unemployment rate (NAIRU)	6.7	7.1	6.3	5.7

Source: Estimates based on *OECD Economic Outlook*, No. 76.

A. Divergence in GDP per capita has stopped[1]

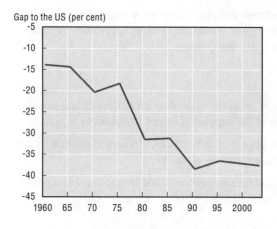

B. Annual growth in GDP per hour has remained below average

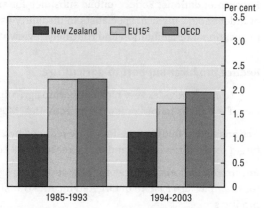

C. Variation in student performance has been high, 2000[3]
OECD = 100

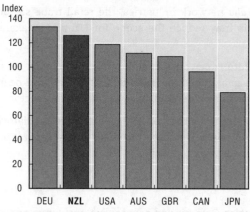

D. FDI restrictions are relatively high, 2003[4]

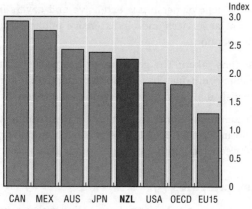

1. Percentage gap with respect to US GDP per capita (in constant 2000 PPPs).
2. Excluding Austria and Luxembourg.
3. Percentage of average variation of student performance in OECD countries.
4. Index scale of 0-6 from least to most restrictive.

Source: Charts A and B: *National Accounts of OECD Countries*, 2004; *OECD Labour Force Statistics*, 2004; *OECD Economic Outlook*, No. 76; Chart C: *OECD Knowledge and Skills for Life*, PISA 2000; Chart D: OECD Regulation database.

NORWAY

GDP per capita is one of the highest in the OECD, reflecting in part a strong labour productivity performance. Rising employment rates have been more than offset by a large decline in average hours worked.

Priorities supported by indicators

Reform disability and sickness benefits schemes

There has been a surge in lost working time due to sickness leaves, and the disability recipient rate is one of the highest in the OECD, reflecting the system's generosity and loose eligibility criteria.

Actions taken: Stricter regulations on the entitlement to long-term sick leave have recently been introduced. Reduced replacement rates and mandatory assessment for vocational rehabilitation are being implemented. Temporary disability pensions are replacing permanent ones for those with uncertain future work capacity.

Recommendations: Reduce public subsidies for sickness benefits. Make mandatory the involvement of independent medical specialists in disability assessment. Make job search compulsory for workers in vocational rehabilitation and routinely review its cost-effectiveness.

Reduce producer support to agriculture

Norway provides very high support to agriculture, resulting in production surpluses and excessive use of resources in low-productivity activities. Most of the support is linked to output or inputs.

Actions taken: Budget transfers were reduced by 2½ per cent during 2002, but this was offset by higher target prices for livestock and an increase in tax concessions for all farmers.

Recommendations: Reduce producer support to agriculture and decouple aid from output or input use, for example *via* a system of targeted income transfers. Reduce very high external tariffs on agricultural products.

Reduce the scope of public ownership

Public ownership is extensive and covers *inter alia* network industries, the retail trade sector, financial services and oil. Extensive public ownership may reduce the scope for FDI and weakens competition.

Actions taken: The government has published a White Paper on reducing public ownership. Most public companies have been incorporated, and state guarantees for loans to such firms have been abolished. However, the government has been increasing its ownership stake in the banking sector.

Recommendations: Implement a privatisation programme in the context of extensive regulatory reform. Further liberalise sectors such as railways and postal services. Introduce formal separation between competitive and non-competitive activities in network industries.

Other key priorities

● Implement a pension reform in line with recent Pension Commission proposals. Consider using the Petroleum Fund to pre-fund part of pension liabilities, so as to underpin fiscal sustainability.

● Reduce the regional emphasis in policies related to communication and transport, social security, labour markets, welfare, and natural resources. Pursue regional goals by more transparent cash transfers, and use any freed up resources to cut taxes.

NORWAY

Structural indicators

	1990	1995	2000	2003
Trend GDP per capita (% growth rate)	1.2	2.1	2.3	1.9
Trend employment rate	75.2	75.5	76.6	76.6
Trend participation rate	78.3	79.0	79.6	79.9
Structural unemployment rate (NAIRU)	3.9	4.4	3.8	4.1

Source: Estimates based on *OECD Economic Outlook,* No. 76.

A. GDP per capita is above the US level[1]

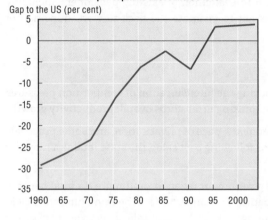

B. Annual growth in GDP per hour remains high

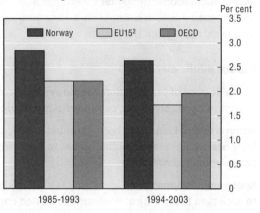

C. Public ownership remains high[3]

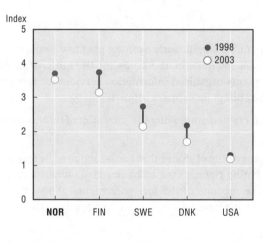

D. Agricultural support is high
Producer support estimate

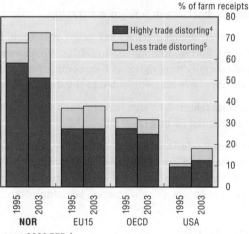

1. Percentage gap with respect to US GDP per capita (in constant 2000 PPPs).
2. Excluding Austria and Luxembourg.
3. Index 0-6 scale from lowest to highest share of public enterprises.
4. Market price support and payments based on output and input use.
5. Payments based on area planted/animal numbers, historical entitlements and overall farm income.
Source: Charts A and B: *National Accounts of OECD Countries,* 2004; *OECD Labour Force Statistics,* 2004; *OECD Economic Outlook,* No. 76; Chart C: OECD Regulation database; Chart D: OECD, Producer and consumer support estimates database.

POLAND

Despite substantial growth since the start of the transition, participation rates have fallen, unemployment is very high and GDP per capita income is well below OECD average.

Priorities supported by indicators

Reform entitlement conditions in disability benefit schemes

The disability system provides net incomes twice as large as those from minimum-wage work, thereby creating a serious dependency trap and substantially weakening work incentives.

Actions taken: Inflow rates have been reduced and plans made to reduce the number and categories of disability and associated pensions, including a one-time re-evaluation of all disability pensioners below the age of 55.

Recommendations: Implement a stricter and regular re-evaluation of existing pensioners, including permanent pensioners. Establish a time-limited benefit to facilitate the back-to-work transition of people excluded from the system.

Reduce public ownership

The pace of privatisation has slowed down, delaying the intensification of competition pressures in some sectors. Moreover, continued support of loss-making firms curbs overall productivity growth.

Actions taken: Plans have been announced to accelerate the pace of privatisation, and some proposals have been made to sell residual stakes in firms where, following past sales, the state retains a majority or controlling interest.

Recommendations: Place less emphasis on raising government revenues and more on total benefits to society in the selling of government-owned companies. Seek investors for the remaining state-held companies. Reconsider the strategy of merging state-owned firms before sale so as to avoid creating monopoly power.

Reduce barriers to foreign ownership

Even though barriers to foreign ownership have fallen significantly over the past few years, they remain among the highest in OECD. Widespread public ownership, the scope for the authorities to use special voting rights as a screening device and poorly organised information services for foreign investors have all contributed to the decline in foreign direct investment inflows.

Actions taken: A foreign investment agency has been created, improving the provision of information for potential investors.

Recommendations: Raise the statutory limit on the proportion of shares that can be acquired by foreign investors and limit the use of government special voting rights that can be exercised when foreign investors seek to acquire domestic firms. Improve the capacity of the foreign investment agency, so that it becomes a one-stop shop advising potential foreign investors on investment opportunities.

Other key priorities

● Improve transport and housing infrastructure so as to increase labour mobility to areas with higher levels of employment and better-paid jobs.

● Improve employment prospects for youth and low-skilled workers by ensuring that the minimum wage does not rise significantly relative to average wages and by using in-work benefits to raise labour income. The reduced-minimum-wage programme should be extended to include the long-term unemployed and individuals no longer receiving disability pensions.

POLAND

Structural indicators

	1990	1995	2000	2003
Trend GDP per capita (% growth rate)	..	4.1	5.0	3.3
Trend employment rate	..	57.9	55.4	54.2
Trend participation rate	..	67.3	65.2	64.0
Structural unemployment rate (NAIRU)	..	13.9	15.0	15.3

Source: Estimates based on *OECD Economic Outlook,* No. 76.

A. Convergence in GDP per capita is slow[1]

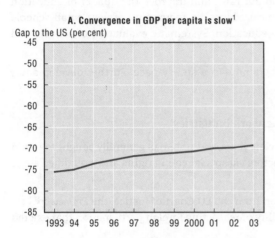

B. Productivity growth is high[2]

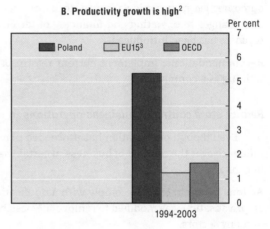

C. Disability and pre-retirement benefit recipients as a share of population is high, 2002

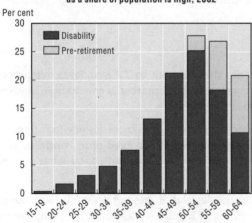

D. The pace of privatisation has slowed down[4]

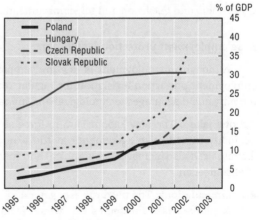

1. Percentage gap with respect to US GDP per capita (in constant 2000 PPPs).
2. Annual growth in GDP per employed person.
3. Excluding Austria and Luxembourg.
4. Cummulative privitisation revenues as a share of GDP.

Source: Charts A and B: *National Accounts of OECD Countries,* 2004; *OECD Labour Force Statistics,* 2004; *OECD Economic Outlook,* No. 76; Charts C and D: *OECD Economic Survey, Poland* 2004.

PORTUGAL

Convergence in living standards with the more advanced OECD average seems to have halted in recent years. With employment rates above EU average, the income gap essentially reflects low productivity.

Priorities supported by indicators

Improve upper-secondary education attainments

Portugal's human capital base still lags the rest of the OECD, with low educational attainment of the population (even for young adults) and poor student performance. Reducing the gap would help boost growth by improving the quality of labour input and by facilitating the adoption of new technologies.

Actions taken: Current reforms aim to reduce drop-out rates and improve the quality of education outcomes *via* new curricula, a new focus on technical education, regrouping of very small schools and changes to operating and financing of tertiary education. Systematic evaluation of schools and teachers has been introduced.

Recommendations: Implement current reform programme at a steady pace. Further develop adult training as a complement.

Reduce state control of business operations in network industries

Even though privatisation has proceeded in recent years, the state has generally sought to retain influence over the conduct of business in certain sectors *via* special voting rights and a qualified stake in capital.

Actions taken: In order to comply with a notification from the EU Court of Justice, the *Framework Law* on privatisation was modified to remove the possibility of restricting foreign participation that existed in many sectors.

Recommendations: Replace special voting rights with arm's length regulation where genuine national security concerns are involved. Promote effective competition in sectors such as energy, transportation, water, radio and television and telecommunications.

Ease employment protection legislation

Although unemployment is low and employment rates are high by EU standards, restrictive employment protection legislation for regular workers creates labour market segmentation, hinders mobility and discourages technological and managerial innovation.

Actions taken: The new Labour Law, in force since December 2003, gives more leeway to introduce flexibility in collective agreements at the firm level regarding rules for fixed-term contracts and dismissals. It also increases geographical and functional mobility of workers and allows better control of absenteeism.

Recommendations: The need to ease general job protection legislation has not been fully addressed. EPL should be eased further, as this would facilitate hiring of regular workers and be conducive to higher productivity growth.

Other key priorities

● Step up implementation of the public administration reform to enhance effectiveness, as this will accelerate the pace of reform in many other areas.

● Simplify the tax system and broaden the income tax base to reduce compliance costs for businesses and the scale of informal activities.

PORTUGAL

Structural indicators

	1990	1995	2000	2003
Trend GDP per capita (% growth rate)	3.5	2.2	2.6	1.2
Trend employment rate	68.3	70.1	72.1	73.1
Trend participation rate	71.5	73.4	75.2	76.2
Structural unemployment rate (NAIRU)	4.5	4.5	4.1	4.1

Source: Estimates based on *OECD Economic Outlook,* No. 76.

A. Convergence in GDP per capita has stalled[1]

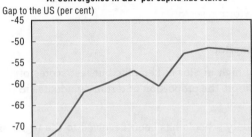
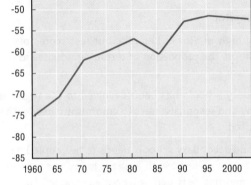

B. Annual growth in GDP per hour has fallen

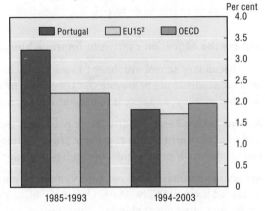

C. The proportion of the population with at least upper-secondary education is low, 2002

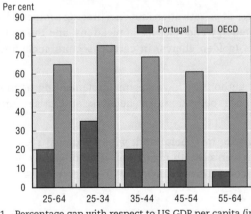

D. EPL is among the strictest in the OECD[3]

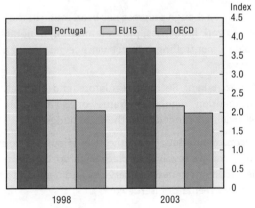

1. Percentage gap with respect to US GDP per capita (in constant 2000 PPPs).
2. Excluding Austria and Luxembourg.
3. Index scale of 0-6 from least to most restrictive.
Source: Charts A and B: *National Accounts of OECD Countries,* 2004; *OECD Labour Force Statistics,* 2004; *OECD Economic Outlook,* No. 76; Chart C: *OECD Education at a Glance,* 2004; Chart D: *OECD Employment Outlook,* 2004.

SLOVAK REPUBLIC

Strong growth in GDP per capita has contributed to a narrowing of the large income gap vis-à-vis OECD countries and has helped boosting employment. However, unemployment remains high.

Priorities supported by indicators

Reduce the tax wedge for low-income workers

A high tax wedge (due to high social insurance contributions) is reducing formal-sector employment and contributing to high rates of unemployment in regions with a high concentration of low-skilled workers.

Actions taken: Tax and social security reforms have significantly reduced marginal income tax rates faced by low-income earners, facilitating the transition from unemployment to work.

Recommendations: Social security contribution rates should be reduced, in particular for lower-wage earners so as to stimulate low-skill job creation in the formal sector.

Reform the education system to improve human capital

Secondary school enrolment rates are relatively high in Slovak Republic but test scores of 15-year old students are below the OECD average. In addition, the proportion of tertiary graduates in the population is low, and access to programmes is restricted.

Actions taken: Responsibility for primary and secondary schools has been devolved to the regional and municipal authorities to provide greater autonomy and responsiveness to community needs. The establishment of private universities has been authorised.

Recommendations: Increased autonomy in primary and secondary schools needs to be coupled with increased accountability. At the tertiary level, tuition fees combined with student loans and income-contingent re-payment should be introduced, and competition between universities encouraged.

Reduce state control of business operations in network industries

Even though progress has been made in the process of privatisation and encouraging competition in network industries, prices remain high, notably in energy and telecommunications, and the state holds a controlling interest *via* special voting rights (golden shares) in certain sectors, including railways.

Action taken: Sectoral regulators and competition authorities have begun implementing a pro-competition regulatory framework. The public service obligations of network enterprises are increasingly funded from the state budget.

Recommendation: Limit the use of special voting rights in general and, where national security concerns are involved, replace such voting rights with arm's length regulation. Monitor closely price development in network services and respond to anti-competitive behaviour with full enforcement of the new regulatory framework.

Other key priorities

● Strengthen the governance of the judicial and law enforcement systems to ensure a more efficient, transparent, and rules-based business environment.

● Progressively increase the statutory retirement age for public pension eligibility towards 65 years for both men and women in order to make the pay-as-you-go pension system sustainable.

ECONOMIC POLICY REFORMS – ISBN 92-64-00836-5 – © OECD 2005

SLOVAK REPUBLIC

Structural indicators

	1990	1995	2000	2003
Trend GDP per capita (% growth rate)	..	..	3.2	4.0
Trend employment rate	..	..	59.5	58.7
Trend participation rate	..	..	69.1	69.3
Structural unemployment rate (NAIRU)	..	..	..	..

Source: Estimates based on *OECD Economic Outlook,* No. 76.

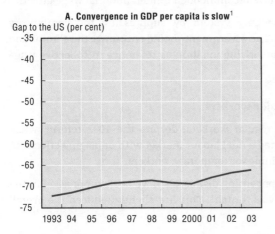

A. Convergence in GDP per capita is slow[1]
Gap to the US (per cent)

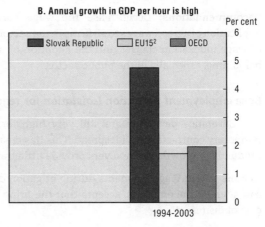

B. Annual growth in GDP per hour is high
Per cent

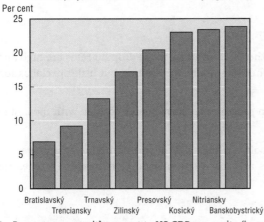

C. Unemployment outside Bratislava is very high, 2003
Per cent

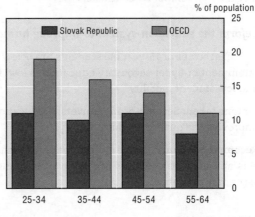

D. Tertiary education is lagging, 2002[3]
% of population

1. Percentage gap with respect to US GDP per capita (in constant 2000 PPPs).
2. Excluding Austria and Luxembourg.
3. Tertiary type A programmes, providing qualifications for advanced research or higher skill professions.
Source: Charts A and B: *National Accounts of OECD Countries,* 2004; *OECD Labour Force Statistics,* 2004; *OECD Economic Outlook,* No. 76; Chart C: *Statistical office of the Slovak Republic;* Chart D: *OECD Education at a Glance,* 2004.

SPAIN

The Spanish economy has been resilient to the last international slowdown. Strong employment growth has led to a substantial decline in the high structural unemployment rate but labour productivity has stagnated.

Priorities supported by indicators

Limit the extent of administrative extension of collective agreements

Wages are bargained mainly at the provincial and sectoral level, with adverse effects on international competitiveness and for employment opportunities for certain groups and/or regions. Catch-up clauses for inflation are widespread, increasing the risk of an inflationary spiral when negative shocks hit the economy.

Actions taken: Recent national wage agreements have recommended limited nominal wage growth.

Recommendations: Decentralise the wage bargaining system by suppressing the compulsory application of agreed wages to all firms in the sector. The government should encourage the elimination of wage indexation clauses and the adoption of underlying inflation as reference in collective wage bargaining, especially in the public sector.

Ease employment protection legislation for regular workers

Severance payments are still very high for regular workers, despite the 1997 reform, while temporary contracts are widespread. This has created a dual labour market with damaging effects on productivity growth as employers provide little training for temporary workers.

Actions taken: Wage payments during litigation concerning dismissals have been suppressed in the cases where the employer accepts that the firing was "unfair". This has slightly reduced the overall cost of dismissal.

Recommendations: Reduce the gap in protection between regular and temporary workers by further lowering severance payments for workers on regular contracts and strengthening controls on the illegal use of temporary contracts.

Reform the education system to improve human capital

Test scores of 15-year old students are below the OECD average, while dropout rates are high and attainment of upper-secondary education is low. There are many universities, but little specialisation and low student mobility.

Actions taken: Secondary and university education programmes have been reformed with the aim of improving the quality of education.

Recommendations: Provide more autonomy to schools and university departments. Increase university fees and use extra receipts to improve the grants and loans system and to increase resources for secondary education.

Other key priorities

● Land regulations should be reformed, while tax advantages for home ownership should be phased out to restore fiscal neutrality *vis-à-vis* the rental market.

● The public pension system should be made actuarially fair so as to ease the strong pressure on public finances expected as from 2015-20, which would require a sharp increase in taxes and labour costs in the absence of reforms.

SPAIN

Structural indicators

	1990	1995	2000	2003
Trend GDP per capita (% growth rate)[1]	3.1	2.8	2.3	1.3
Trend employment rate	49.6	52.1	57.2	60.6
Trend participation rate	57.2	59.6	64.7	68.2
Structural unemployment rate (NAIRU)	13.3	12.7	11.5	11.0

1. The regularisation process of immigrants in 2002 and 2003, which raised official population figures, partly accounts for the deceleration of trend per capita GDP in 2003.
Source: Estimates based on *OECD Economic Outlook*, No. 76.

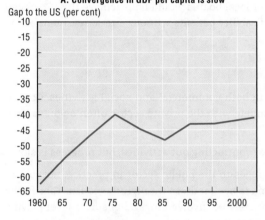

A. Convergence in GDP per capita is slow[1]

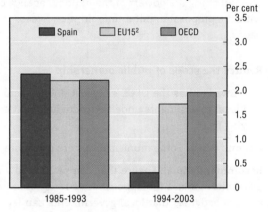

B. Growth in GDP per hour has fallen to a very low level

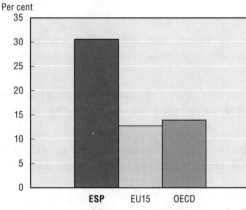

C. The share of temporary workers is very high, 2003[3]

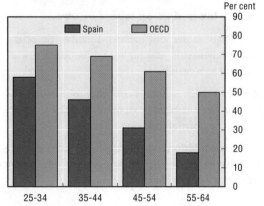

D. The proportion of the population with at least upper-secondary education is lagging, 2002

1. Percentage gap with respect to US GDP per capita (in constant 2000 PPPs).
2. Excluding Austria and Luxembourg.
3. Share of temporary workers in total employment.
Source: Charts A and B: *National Accounts of OECD Countries*, 2004; *OECD Labour Force Statistics*, 2004; *OECD Economic Outlook*, No. 76; Chart C: *OECD Labour Force Statistics*, 2004; Chart D: *OECD Education at a Glance*, 2004.

SWEDEN

Productivity growth over the past decade has picked up, helping Sweden to slightly narrow its income gap vis-à-vis the United States.

Priorities supported by indicators

Reform sickness and disability benefit schemes

On an average day, one out of eight workers is absent on sick leave. Whereas employment rates have risen since the mid-1990s, the number of people actually at work as a share of population has not and growth in total hours worked has been subdued.

Actions taken: Employers now pay a bigger share of sickness benefits, administration has been tightened, sickness certificates give a better assessment of ability to work, and the benefit rate has been cut slightly.

Recommendations: Ensure the reforms are carried out as intended in all local social insurance offices. Strengthening the powers of the national agency over local boards would help achieve this. Go ahead with the proposal to put a time limit on access to disability benefits without a re-assessment of the needs.

Reduce the scope of public ownership

Sweden has the OECD's biggest public sector, in both commercial and social activities. Central and local governments undertake activities that compete with the private sector, often on an uneven playing field.

Actions taken: Some municipalities are privatising or contracting out activities, but progress is slow.

Recommendations: Ensure that competition law applies to the public sector in practice, not just in principle. Increase the opportunities for private firms to seek redress through the courts. Clarify the sorts of activities that local governments can legitimately be involved in, and ensure a level playing field. Streamline and strengthen the public procurement supervisory agencies, and give them power to enforce sanctions.

Reduce tax wedges on labour income

High taxes on earned income discourage labour supply and reduce the returns from entrepreneurship and higher education. Growth, innovation and human capital development are all harmed as a result.

Actions taken: Tax rates continue to rise, especially at the local level. A planned reduction in the state income tax has been postponed, and the threshold for the top marginal rate was boosted by less than under the normal indexing rules.

Recommendations: Cut overall marginal income tax rates by raising the threshold for the state tax. Broaden tax bases by restoring and then increasing the property tax and by removing exemptions from the value-added tax.

Other key priorities

● Boost working hours. Government plans to introduce a legal right to a year of sabbatical leave and pilot schemes for lower working hours should both be reconsidered.

● Liberalise the housing market by phasing out rent controls and easing planning restrictions. Serious distortions have almost broken the link between supply and demand, leading to shortages in high-growth areas, reducing labour mobility.

SWEDEN

Structural indicators

	1990	1995	2000	2003
Trend GDP per capita (% growth rate)	1.7	1.4	2.7	2.1
Trend employment rate	80.1	75.4	72.6	72.6
Trend participation rate	81.9	79.2	76.3	76.2
Structural unemployment rate (NAIRU)	2.2	4.8	4.8	4.7

Source: Estimates based on *OECD Economic Outlook*, No. 76.

A. Divergence in GDP per capita has stopped[1]

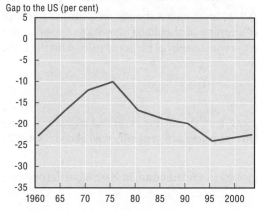

B. Annual growth in GDP per hour has picked up

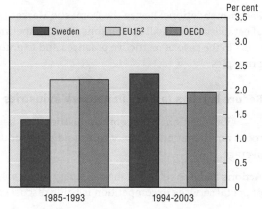

C. Sickness absence rates are high by EU standards, 1999

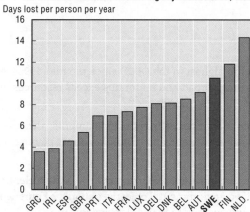

D. Share of public consumption in GDP is high, 2002

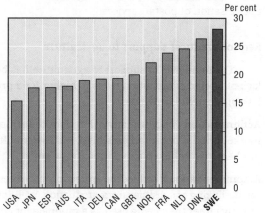

1. Percentage gap with respect to US GDP per capita (in constant 2000 PPPs).
2. Excluding Austria and Luxembourg.
Source: Charts A and B: *National Accounts of OECD Countries*, 2004; *OECD Labour Force Statistics*, 2004; *OECD Economic Outlook*, No. 76; Chart C: *Third European Survey of Working Conditions*, 2000; Chart D: *OECD Economic Outlook*, No. 76.

SWITZERLAND

GDP growth has been among the weakest in the OECD over the past two decades, reflecting mainly very low productivity growth. Nonetheless, income per capita remains high.

Priorities supported by indicators

Further liberalise professional services

The domestic market for professional services is characterised by excessive segmentation. Various cantonal regulations, such as special permits to work, constitute entry barriers and reduce competition.

Actions taken: A framework law for the domestic market has attempted to reduce this segmentation by imposing general guidelines for cantonal regulation affecting professional activities. Recognition of credentials across cantons has improved, but authorisation requirements are still widespread.

Recommendations: Revise the Domestic Market Act (DMA) to include a specific reference to freedom of establishment in all the cantons. The Competition Commission should be allowed to appeal to the court in the case of restrictive practices and to enforce the consistency of cantonal rules with the DMA principles.

Reduce barriers to entry in network industries

Liberalisation of network industries has been only partial and varies across sectors, leaving room for further productivity gains and price reductions, as prices are generally well above the OECD average.

Actions taken: A reform of the electricity sector was rejected in a referendum in 2002. A partial opening of postal services to competition is being discussed.

Recommendations: In telecommunications, the unbundling of the local loop is a priority. In the electricity and gas sectors, liberalise the markets in a manner compatible with the EU reform, and create strong and independent regulators to ensure equitable access to the market. Accelerate the liberalisation of postal services.

Reduce producer support to agriculture

The total level of support to agriculture has been the highest in the OECD since the mid-1990s. A lack of foreign competition leads to higher food prices than abroad and maintains excess resources in low-productivity activities.

Actions taken: Policy initiatives have shifted support to more market-friendly instruments, although market price support remains high. Aid to agriculture, which depends now more on direct payments, has been partly linked to environmental goals.

Recommendations: Reduce the protection and excessive assistance enjoyed by agriculture, and accelerate the de-linking of subsidies from production. Well-identified environmental objectives should be pursued directly rather than being used as a rationale for continuing with very high aid to agriculture.

Other key priorities

● The sharp rise in the tax burden since the 1990s needs to be halted, which calls for altering public outlay trends on a lasting basis. This requires structural reforms of social programmes, in particular the invalidity pension scheme to curb the rising number of disability pensions.

● The growth of medical costs should be contained by increasing competition in health care. In the ambulatory sector, abolishing the obligation of insurers to contract would stimulate competition between providers and enhance the control of supply. Obstacles to effective foreign competition in pharmaceuticals should be removed.

SWITZERLAND

Structural indicators

	1990	1995	2000	2003
Trend GDP per capita (% growth rate)	1.4	0.2	1.0	0.6
Trend employment rate	84.0	84.7	84.9	85.3
Trend participation rate	85.5	86.9	86.9	87.2
Structural unemployment rate (NAIRU)	1.7	2.5	2.2	2.2

Source: Estimates based on *OECD Economic Outlook,* No. 76.

A. Relative GDP per capita is on a declining trend[1]

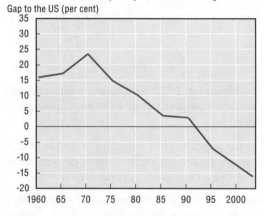

B. Annual growth in GDP per hour is below average

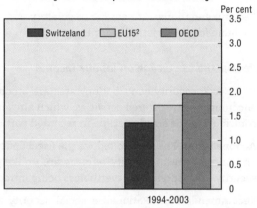

C. Prices of utility services are high[3]

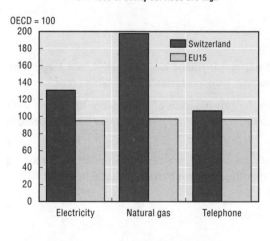

D. Agricultural support is high
Producer support estimate

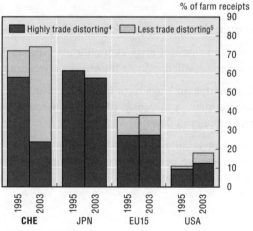

1. Percentage gap with respect to US GDP per capita (in constant 2000 PPPs).
2. Excluding Austria and Luxembourg.
3. 2003 or latest available data for electricity and natural gas; May 2004 for the OECD composite basket of business telephone charges.
4. Market price support and payments based on output and input use.
5. Payments based on area planted/animal numbers, historical entitlements and overall farm income.
Source: Charts A and B: *National Accounts of OECD Countries,* 2004; *OECD Labour Force Statistics,* 2004; *OECD Economic Outlook,* No. 76; Chart C: *OECD Energy Prices and Taxes,* 2004 and OECD Communications Outlook database; Chart D: OECD, Producer and consumer support estimates database.

TURKEY

Growth in trend GDP per capita has risen in recent years, but job creation remains too weak to reverse the sharp deterioration in labour market conditions in the 1990s.

Priorities supported by indicators

Reduce administrative burdens on start-ups

Until recently, the process of establishing a company had been very complex and time-consuming, with no fewer than 19 different procedures to complete. Substantial regulatory obligations contribute to pushing many small-scale companies into the informal sector.

Actions taken: The commercial law was amended in 2003, and the number of required administrative steps to create a company was cut to two. In contrast, efforts to improve enforcement of legal obligations in order to reduce the size of the grey economy have had limited effect.

Recommendations: Streamline regulatory requirements for small-scale enterprises in order to facilitate formal registration for them.

Reduce the tax wedge on labour income

Social security contribution rates are among the highest in OECD and create a vicious circle encouraging unregistered activities, which already account for more than half of all employment and contribute to the steady decline in recorded participation rates.

Actions taken: The need to reduce the fiscal deficit has not permitted any reduction in the tax wedge, and ongoing social security reforms are unlikely to create additional room. Labour tax and social security exemptions are nevertheless being introduced for new employees in poor regions.

Recommendations: Rationalise social security spending, cut social contribution rates, and offset revenue losses through indirect tax increases. Put in place a "company registration strategy" that would include a reduction, during a transition period, of the marginal tax and contribution rates faced by firms joining the formal sector.

Reduce the scope of public ownership

The share of state economic enterprises in total employment has decreased, but large state enterprises still dominate the energy, telecommunication, transportation and banking sectors.

Actions taken: Laws have been passed to facilitate the privatisation of these large firms, but with limited success. Recently, the judiciary cancelled some of the few large-scale sales because of legal and procedural flaws.

Recommendations: Clarify the policy and regulatory frameworks for network industries, including with regard to public service obligations and their funding. Remove barriers to foreign ownership of privatised companies.

Other key priorities

● Enhance the quality of public expenditures by implementing results-oriented budgeting in the core public services of justice, education and health.

● Improve educational opportunities for women by enforcing minimum schooling rules, and revise the curriculum of secondary schools to better align education with job-market requirements.

ECONOMIC POLICY REFORMS – ISBN 92-64-00836-5 – © OECD 2005

TURKEY

Structural indicators

	1990	1995	2000	2003
Trend GDP per capita (% growth rate)	2.2	1.8	0.8	2.7
Trend employment rate	59.2	55.7	53.5	51.7
Trend participation rate	64.1	60.7	57.9	56.1
Structural unemployment rate (NAIRU)	..	..	..	..

Source: Estimates based on *OECD Economic Outlook*, No. 76.

A. No convergence in GDP per capita for decades[1]

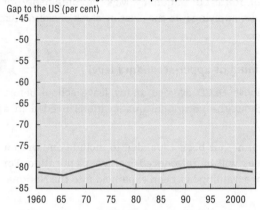

B. Annual growth in GDP per hour has fallen sharply

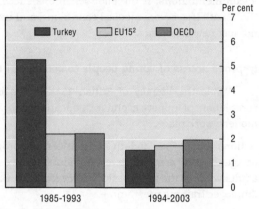

C. Unregistered employment is widespread, 2003
Per cent of total employment

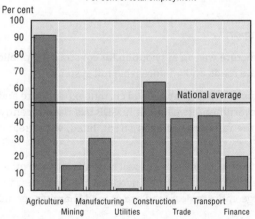

D. Labour force participation is low and falling

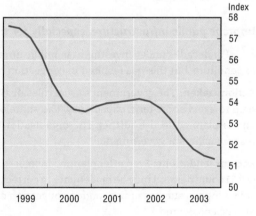

1. Percentage gap with respect to US GDP per capita (in constant 2000 PPPs).
2. Excluding Austria and Luxembourg.
Source: Charts A and B: *National Accounts of OECD Countries*, 2004; *OECD Labour Force Statistics*, 2004; *OECD Economic Outlook*, No. 76; Chart C: *OECD Economic Survey, Turkey* 2004; Chart D: *OECD Labour Force Statistics*, 2004.

UNITED KINGDOM

Economic growth has been resilient in the last downturn and structural unemployment has fallen to low levels. But the productivity gap with the leading OECD economies remains large.

Priorities supported by indicators

Reform disability benefit schemes

The proportion of the population claiming disability-related benefits is high relative to other countries, probably reflecting tightening eligibility criteria in the rest of the income support system.

Actions taken: A new approach for disabled people is being piloted with mandatory work-focused interviews for new claimants and a "Return to Work" credit paid for the first year for those taking up work.

Recommendations: If the pilot scheme is successful, roll it out nationally. Make it compulsory for those with less severe medical conditions, and consider applying it to the existing stock of claimants, not just new claimants.

Improve access of young people to vocational training at upper-secondary level

While the literacy of British 15 year-olds is above OECD average, many leave school before completion of upper-secondary education and without the vocational qualifications needed in a modern work place.

Actions taken: The Modern Apprenticeships programme has been expanded to include one in four at age 22 this year, and two-year foundation degrees will be introduced in higher education. For adults without the most basic literacy skills, workplace training has been expanded into the National Employer Training programme.

Recommendations: Extend eligibility of young people to these schemes. Expand adult training, but keep public costs under control by cost-sharing arrangements and by focussing content on what is relevant to work.

Improve public infrastructure, especially for transport

For decades under-investment in public infrastructure was an easy option for constraining public expenditure, but this has resulted in congestion on the roads and an unreliable rail system.

Actions taken: The government's fiscal rules distinguish between capital and current expenditure and help to avoid short-term expediency. The share of government investment in GDP has risen recently, and is planned to rise further. The organisation of the railways has been streamlined, with greater responsibility for government.

Recommendations: Even after planned increases, government investment will be low relative to other OECD countries and may be inadequate to correct years of neglect. Further increases may be necessary. Following the success of the London congestion charge, more widespread use of road charging should also be considered.

Other key priorities

● Enhance incentives to pursue performance targets in publicly-funded services. Reduce waiting times by expanding activity-based funding for hospitals, and by introducing incentive pay for hospital doctors (i.e. paying them through a combination of salaries and fees).

● Re-examine planning restrictions, which inhibit competition in key services and limit the supply of new housing. Give greater weight to economic considerations, and involve fewer layers of decision-making in the process.

UNITED KINGDOM

Structural indicators

	1990	1995	2000	2003
Trend GDP per capita (% growth rate)	2.2	2.2	2.4	2.3
Trend employment rate	69.4	70.4	71.8	72.1
Trend participation rate	75.4	75.9	76.1	76.2
Structural unemployment rate (NAIRU)	8.0	7.2	5.6	5.4

Source: Estimates based on *OECD Economic Outlook,* No. 76.

A.Convergence in GDP per capita has been slow and a large gap remains[1]

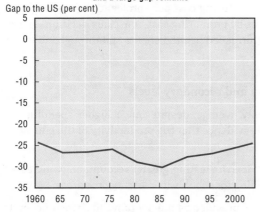

B. Annual growth in GDP per hour has edged up

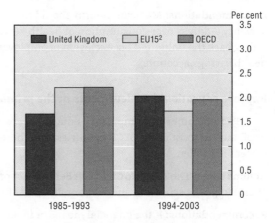

C. Government investment is relatively low

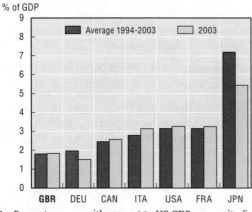

D. Educational attainment of adults aged 25-34 is low, 2002

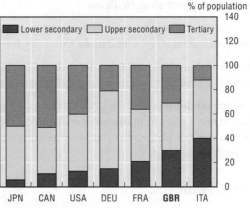

1. Percentage gap with respect to US GDP per capita (in constant 2000 PPPs).
2. Excluding Austria and Luxembourg.
Source: Charts A and B: *National Accounts of OECD countries,* 2004; *OECD Labour Force Statistics,* 2004; *OECD Economic Outlook,* No. 76; Chart C: *OECD Economic Outlook,* No. 76; Chart D: *OECD Education at a Glance,* 2004.

UNITED STATES

Labour productivity has accelerated significantly since the mid-1990s from an already high level, while employment rates have remained high.

Priorities supported by indicators

Restrain health care costs

With a renewed rise in cost pressures, health spending is likely to have absorbed 15½ per cent of GDP in 2004. This boosts non-wage labour costs and seems not to be fully reflected in current health outcomes.

Actions taken: The 2003 Medicare reform legislation included initiatives to introduce competition and increase efficiency in health care delivery, but these measures are not expected to offset the costs of introducing an outpatient prescription drug benefit.

Recommendations: Medicare reform should focus on reducing cost per enrolee to ensure long-term solvency. Address over-consumption of health services by promoting cost-conscious decisions (*e.g.* by rolling back the unlimited tax exclusion of employer-furnished health benefits and through individual health savings accounts).

Improve educational achievements at the primary and secondary levels

The outcomes of compulsory education are only average, despite much higher spending per pupil than in most other OECD countries, and there is evidence that the productivity of the education system has fallen.

Actions taken: The 2002 "No Child Left Behind" Act provided for testing, greater accountability, increased choice in public schooling and additional federal funding for schools in lower-income areas.

Recommendations: If the financial means or incentives provided by the Act prove to be insufficient to improve educational outcomes, further funding should be envisaged and other measures examined.

Reduce support to agriculture

While support to agricultural producers remains well below the OECD average, it is above the levels of the mid-1990s, and trade-distorting forms of support are still significant.

Actions taken: The 2002 Farm Act reversed the previously intended move toward liberalisation by both increasing support to farmers and doing so in a manner that is distorting production decisions.

Recommendations: Roll back the extra support given to farmers in the past few years, and reverse the recent move away from market-based outcomes. Ensure that the recent agreement on a framework for continuing the Doha trade round – including notably the commitment to eliminate export subsidies – results in reforms.

Other key priorities

● Broaden the tax bases where exemptions create inefficiencies and move from personal income taxation toward a consumption-based tax system to encourage saving.

● Stand firm on promoting transparency and accountability in corporate governance and accounting. Eliminate the special status of government-sponsored housing finance companies.

UNITED STATES

Structural indicators

	1990	1995	2000	2003
Trend GDP per capita (% growth rate)	1.7	2.0	2.1	1.8
Trend employment rate	71.6	73.7	74.2	71.5
Trend participation rate	76.1	77.9	78.1	75.1
Structural unemployment rate (NAIRU)	5.9	5.3	4.9	4.8

Source: Estimates based on *OECD Economic Outlook*, No. 76.

A. Annual growth in GDP per capita has picked up

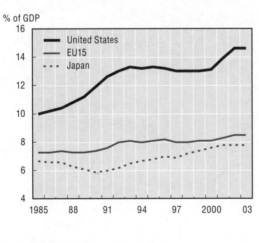

B. Annual growth in GDP per hour has improved

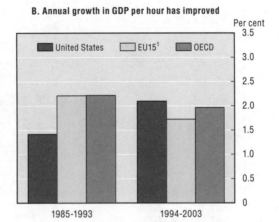

C. Health spending is absorbing a rising share of GDP

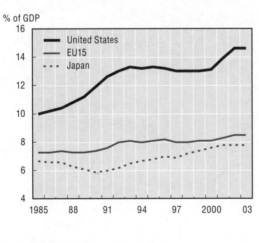

D. Agricultural support has risen
Producer support estimate

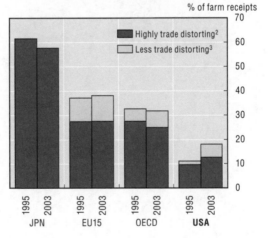

1. Excluding Austria and Luxembourg.
2. Market price support and payments based on output and input use.
3. Payments based on area planted/animal numbers, historical entitlements and overall farm income.
Source: Charts A and B: *National Accounts of OECD Countries*, 2004; *OECD Labour Force Statistics*, 2004; *OECD Economic Outlook*, No. 76; Chart C: OECD, Health database; Chart D: OECD, Producer and consumer support estimates database.

PART II

Thematic Studies

ISBN 92-64-00836-5
Economic Policy Reforms
© OECD 2005

Chapter 4

Product Market Regulation in OECD Countries: 1998 to 2003[1]

This chapter describes trends in product market regulation in OECD countries over the period 1998 to 2003. The analysis is based on summary indicators of product market regulation that measure the degree to which policies promote or inhibit competition. The results suggest that regulatory impediments to competition have declined in all OECD countries in recent years. Regulation has also become more homogenous across the OECD as countries with relatively restrictive policies have, in some areas, moved towards the regulatory environment of the more liberalised countries. Within some countries product market policies have become more consistent across different regulatory provisions, although relatively restrictive countries still tend to have a more heterogeneous approach to competition. In general, domestic barriers to competition tend to be higher in countries that have higher barriers to foreign trade and investment, and high levels of state control and barriers to competition tend to be associated with cumbersome administrative procedures and policies that reduce the adaptability of labour markets. Notwithstanding recent progress in product market reform, a "hard core" of regulations that impede competition still persists in virtually all countries.

Introduction

Regulation is perhaps the most pervasive form of state intervention in economic activity. It is also essential for the good working of market economies. Over recent decades, however, policymakers have become increasingly concerned about the potential for regulation to be too intrusive and stifle market mechanisms, possibly affecting resource allocation and productive efficiency. In light of this, most OECD governments have been reviewing and updating their regulatory environment. This process of reform has been closely intertwined with enhancing competition in product markets. Regulations that increase the role of competitive forces have been found to have important beneficial effects on GDP per capita – a common measure of welfare – through a number of channels. For instance, regulatory environments that favour competition can have a positive impact on economy-wide productivity, employment, and investment in some sectors.[2]

This chapter aims to describe changes in product market regulation in OECD countries from 1998 to the end of 2003. The analysis is based on the OECD indicators of product market regulation (PMR), which were developed in 1998 to describe broad differences in product market policies in OECD countries. The indicators are constructed from the perspective of regulations that have the potential to reduce the intensity of competition in areas of the product market where technology and market conditions make competition viable. The principal source of information used to construct the indicators is a questionnaire sent to OECD member countries.[3]

The structure of the indicator system is shown in Figure 4.1. The system is in the form of a pyramid with 16 low-level indicators at the base and one overall indicator of product market regulation at the top. The low-level indicators capture specific features of the regulatory regime and span the most important aspects of general regulatory practice as well as some aspects of industry-specific regulatory policies (in particular, in retail distribution, air and rail passenger transport, rail and road freight and telecommunications). At each step up the pyramid the regulatory domain summarised by the indicators becomes broader. Higher-level indicators are calculated as weighted averages of their constituent lower-level indicators. At the top of the structure the overall indicator of product market regulation summarises the main features of the regulatory framework in the product market of each country. At intermediate levels the indicators summarise information about broad regulatory areas and families of regulatory interventions (see Box 4.1).[4]

It is important to note that the PMR indicators are based primarily on explicit policy settings and only account for formal government regulation. "Informal" regulatory practices, such as administrative guidance or self-disciplinary measures of professional associations, are captured only to a very limited extent in the PMR indicators system. Similarly, the way in which regulations are applied by enforcement authorities, which can have a considerable impact on competition in a given market, is also reflected in a relatively minor way in the PMR indicator system.

Figure 4.1. **The PMR indicator system**

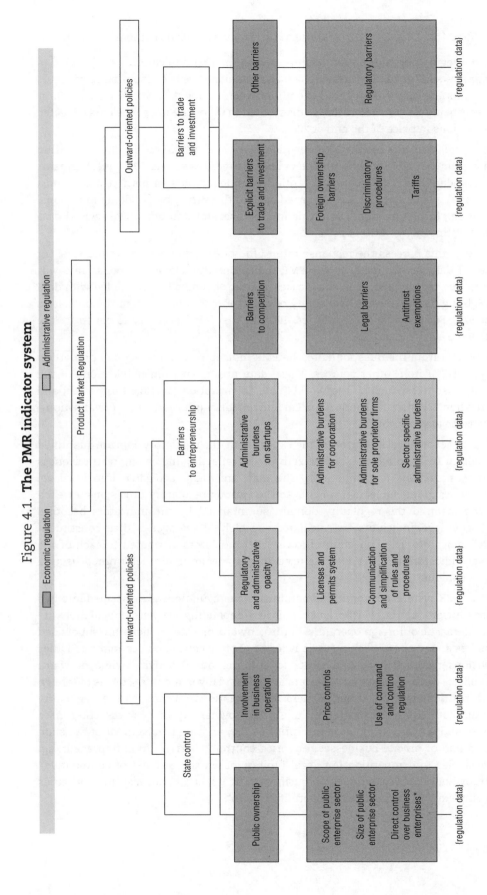

* Two indicators form the 1998 version of the PMR indicators ("Special voting rights" and "Control of public enterprise by legislative bodies") have been combined into this indicator.

Box 4.1. **The OECD regulation database and PMR indicators**

Most of the regulatory information summarised in the PMR indicators was collected in a questionnaire sent to OECD countries. The 2003 version of this questionnaire collected 805 data points for each country on general and sectoral regulatory policies as well as some aspects of industry structure. It was distributed in October 2003, so the data collected reflect regulations in place of the end of 2003.

After collection, responses to the 2003 questionnaire were systematically checked within and across countries as well as with the country responses to the 1998 questionnaire. This process identified a number of potentially erroneous data in both years. In most cases, potential inconsistencies were referred back to the survey respondents in national administrations for verification. Often this involved several iterations. The revised data were then scrutinised by OECD experts.

At the end of this process the response rate to the questionnaire was around 92%. For the subset of data used directly in the PMR indicators, the average response rate was also around this very high level. In some cases, gaps in this data set were filled with data from 1998, bringing the average availability of questionnaire data used in the indicators to almost 97%. For a number of countries, 100% of the data necessary to construct the indicators were available in 2003.

As well as data from the questionnaire, the PMR indicators also use a small proportion of data (about 7%) from other sources. These data are taken from publications of the OECD or other sources, such as the World Trade Organisation (average tariff rates) and the Privatisation Barometer – Fondazione Eni Enrico Mattei (proceeds from privatisation – *www.privatizationbarometer.net*).

To calculate the low-level indicators in the PMR system, the regulatory data are quantified and normalised so as to have a scale of zero to six, reflecting increasing restrictiveness of regulatory provisions to competition. The data are then aggregated into low-level indicators by assigning subjective weights to the various regulatory provisions. At each step up the pyramid the regulatory domain summarised by the indicators becomes broader. Higher-level indicators are calculated as weighted averages of their constituent lower-level indicators. The collection of lower-level indicators attributed to each of the higher-level indicators and the weights used in the averaging are determined using a statistical technique.

Within the PMR system, economic and administrative regulations are classified into two main areas – inward- and outward-oriented policies – depending on whether regulations are directed at domestic or foreign operators. In turn, inward-oriented policies are subdivided into measures aimed at establishing various forms of state control on economic activities and provisions resulting in impediments to entrepreneurial activity, while outward-oriented policies distinguish explicit barriers to trade and investment (*e.g.* tariffs or foreign ownership restrictions) from other barriers to international exchanges (*e.g.* regulatory hindrances). State control measures include public ownership of business enterprises (*e.g.* the size and scope of the public enterprise sector) and the involvement of the state in the operation of private businesses (*e.g.* price controls). Barriers to entrepreneurship include obstacles to competition (*e.g.* legal limitations on the number of competitors), administrative burdens (*e.g.* burdens on business start ups) and administrative opacities (*e.g.* the complexity of the licenses and permits system).

Progress in regulatory reform, 1998-2003

This section uses the updated PMR indicators to illustrate progress made by OECD countries in regulatory reform. It begins with a brief review of the indicator values for OECD countries in 1998, and then outlines the broad trends in regulatory policy that have occurred between 1998 and 2003. It finishes with a review of regulatory patterns in OECD countries in 2003.

1998 revisited

Figure 4.2 graphs the PMR indicators for OECD countries in 1998, as well as the three constituent indicators of state control, barriers to entrepreneurship, and barriers to foreign trade and investment.[5] A number of broad observations of important differences in product market regulation across countries are apparent from the figure. The United Kingdom, Australia, the United States, Canada, New Zealand, Denmark, and Ireland are estimated to have had the least restrictive overall regulatory environments in 1998. Within this group, the United Kingdom was estimated to be relatively liberal in all three of the broad policy domains further down the PMR pyramid. Australia, the United States, Canada, and especially New Zealand, however, are estimated to have had a more restrictive approach to foreign trade and investment relative to the inward-oriented policies of state control and barriers to entrepreneurship. Conversely, Ireland and Denmark were estimated to be highly open to trade and investment in 1998, but were deemed more restrictive in terms of state control.

At the other end of the spectrum, Poland, Turkey, the Czech Republic, Greece, and Italy are estimated to have had regulatory environments that were the least conducive to product market competition in the OECD in 1998. A relatively high degree of state control was a feature of product market regulation in all these countries and barriers to entrepreneurship were also high in Turkey, Poland, and Italy. Poland, the Czech Republic, and to a lesser extent, Turkey also stand out as having had particularly restrictive barriers to foreign trade and investment in comparison to the other OECD countries.

To assess the statistical significance of the estimated differences in product market regulation, Figure 4.3 graphs 90% confidence intervals for the 1998 PMR indicators calculated using a "random weights" technique (Box 4.2). Across a number of countries the PMR indicators were not statistically different when uncertainty about the weights used to construct them is taken into consideration. However, at this level of confidence, two broad country groupings with clearly distinct regulatory regimes can be identified in 1998: a "relatively liberal" group of countries – including the common-law countries and Denmark – and a "relatively restrictive" group of countries – including Poland, Turkey, Czech Republic, Greece, Italy, France, Mexico, Korea, Hungary and Spain. The rest of the OECD countries – the "middle of the road" group – were not statistically distinguishable from these two groups at the 90% level of confidence.

Figure 4.2. **The situation in 1998**[1]

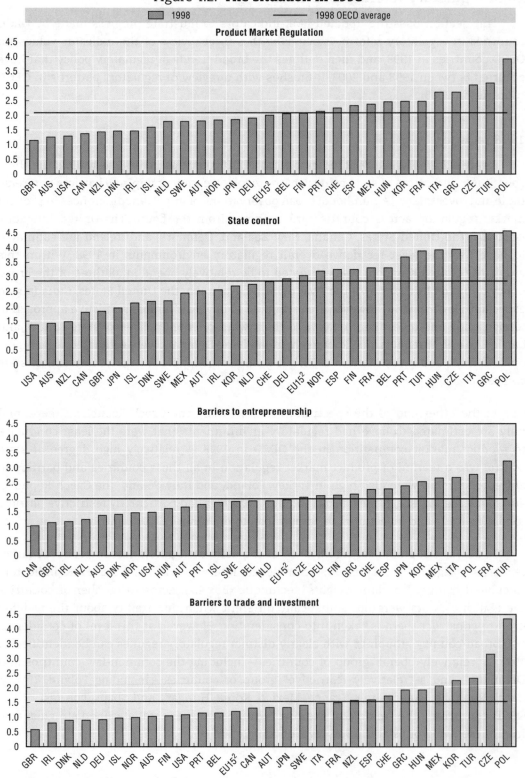

1. The scale of the indicators is 0-6 from least to most restrictive of competition.
2. EU15 (simple average).

ECONOMIC POLICY REFORMS – ISBN 92-64-00836-5 – © OECD 2005

Figure 4.3. **Confidence intervals for the PMR indicators, 1998**[1, 2]

At 90% levels

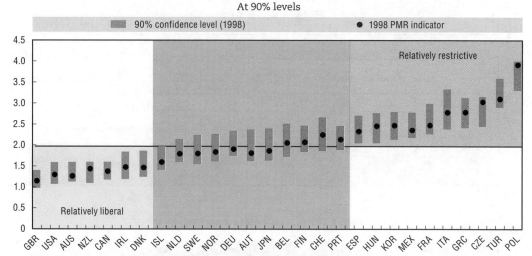

1. The scale of the indicator is 0-6 from least to most restrictive of competition.
2. The confidence intervals are calculated using stochastic weights on the low-level indicators to generate a distribution of overall PMR indicators for each country. The 90% confidence intervals are calculated from that distribution. Indicator values for the "relatively liberal" and "relatively restrictive" countries are significantly different at the 90% level of confidence.

Box 4.2. **The random weights technique**

Starting with the 16 low-level indicators, this technique uses 10 000 sets of randomly-generated weights to calculate 10 000 overall indicators for each country.[1] The random weights are drawn from a uniform distribution between zero and one and then normalised so as to sum to one. This is equivalent to assuming complete uncertainty about the most appropriate value of each of the individual weights used to construct the PMR indicators. Accordingly, the resulting distribution of indicators for each country reflects the possible range of values given no *a priori* information on the most appropriate value for each of the weights. Confidence intervals and the probability of a given country achieving a given rank are calculated from these distributions.

The confidence intervals are centred on the mean value of each country's 10 000 indicator values. Given that the weights are drawn from a uniform distribution between zero and one, the mean indicator values are asymptotically equivalent to indicators calculated using equal weights on each of the 16 low-level indicators. These differ from the PMR indicators, given that the weights in the PMR system are not equal. In all cases, however, the PMR indicator values fall within the confidence intervals.

1. The sensitivity of the indicators to changes in the subjective weights used to construct the low-level indicators has not been tested.

A *degree of policy convergence over the past five years*

On (unweighted) average across OECD countries, product market regulation has become more conducive to competition since 1998 (Figure 4.4a). Visible progress has been made in reducing barriers to competition in all three of the broad areas of regulation captured in the PMR indicators. Slightly more progress, however, has been made in reducing state control and barriers to trade and investment than in reducing barriers to entrepreneurship (Figure 4.4b).

Figure 4.4. **Progress in regulatory reform, 1998 to 2003**

Panel A. OECD-wide average of PMR Indicator levels[1]

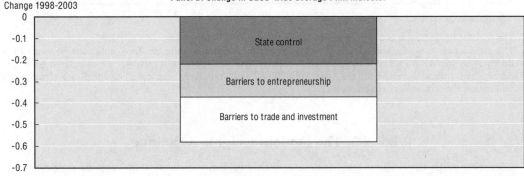

Panel B. Change in OECD-wide average PMR indicator

1. OECD-wide average is a simple average of the overall PMR indicators for 29 OECD countries. The scale of the indicator is 0-6 from least to most restrictive of competition.

As is apparent from Figure 4.5, the reduction in state control in the OECD has, in large part, been due to the easing or elimination of coercive forms of regulation (command-and-control measures, price controls) and less state interference in the choices of public or private business enterprises (direct control over business enterprises). In contrast, on average, there has not been a great deal of privatisation undertaken (as reflected in the indicators of the scope and size of the public enterprise sector).[6] Hence, by and large, reform in this policy domain is successfully moving away from "command-and-control" to "incentive-based" regulations, but the extent of the state's commercial interests has not decreased substantially since 1998. As well as being beneficial in its own right, the move away from command-and-control regulation could also be an important prequel to further privatisations. A greater reliance on incentive-based regulation lessens the need for the state to be directly involved in product markets and increases the attractiveness of state-owned assets to the private sector.

In the policy domain of barriers to entrepreneurship, progress across the OECD has been particularly limited with respect to removing remaining legal barriers to new entry in product markets that are sheltered from competition, such as several non-manufacturing industries. The simplification of administrative procedures and reduction of burdens on business start-ups has also been limited, except for a marked improvement in licence and permit systems due to more widespread use of one-stop shops and, to a lesser extent, "silence is consent" rules.

ECONOMIC POLICY REFORMS – ISBN 92-64-00836-5 – © OECD 2005

Figure 4.5. **Sources of change in the OECD-average PMR indicator, 1998 to 2003**[1]

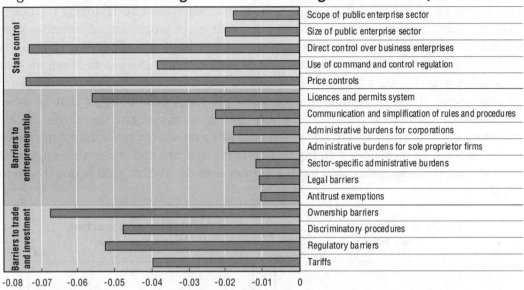

1. Shows the contribution of each of the 16 low level PMR indicators to the change of the OECD-average overall PMR indicator.

In contrast, significant easing was recorded in all types of barriers to foreign trade and investment, further increasing the outward orientation and the trade integration of OECD economies. Average most-favoured-nation tariff rates have declined in most countries and restrictions on foreign direct investment have also softened somewhat over the past five years.[7] In most countries, ceilings on foreign ownership and limitations on management and business choices are the main remaining impediments (Golub, 2003).

As a result of regulatory reform since 1998, there is now less variation in overall product market policies across countries (Figure 4.6). To a significant extent, this reduction

Figure 4.6. **Smaller cross-country variance in regulatory approaches**[1]

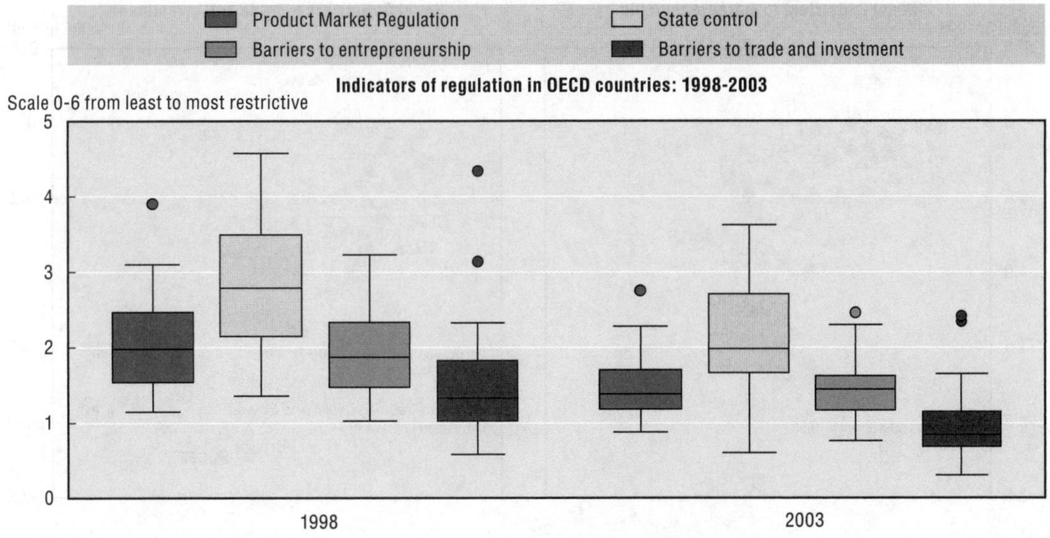

| ■ Product Market Regulation | □ State control |
| ■ Barriers to entrepreneurship | ■ Barriers to trade and investment |

Indicators of regulation in OECD countries: 1998-2003

Scale 0-6 from least to most restrictive

1. Box plots of the overall PMR indicator and its three components. The horizontal line in the middle of the box is the median value of the indicator OECD wide. The edges of the box are the 2nd and 3rd quartile of the cross-country distribution. The two whiskers are the extreme values and the dots represent outliers.

in cross-country dispersion is due to convergence towards the regulatory practices of the most liberal OECD economies. In other words, countries that had relatively restrictive product market policies in 1998 have generally made more progress than countries with policies that were already more conducive to product market competition, implying a positive relationship between the initial level of regulation and the extent of reform over the past five years (Figure 4.7*a*). For the group of EU member countries in 2003 convergence towards lower barriers to product market competition has been stronger than in other OECD member countries, perhaps reflecting efforts to implement the single market programme.[8] If confirmed, this trend would constitute a reversal of previous findings based on the analysis of regulatory reforms in non-manufacturing industries that suggested relatively weaker convergence within EU countries over the 1975 to 1998 period (Nicoletti and Scarpetta, 2003).

Figure 4.7. **Examining convergence in regulatory approaches**[1]

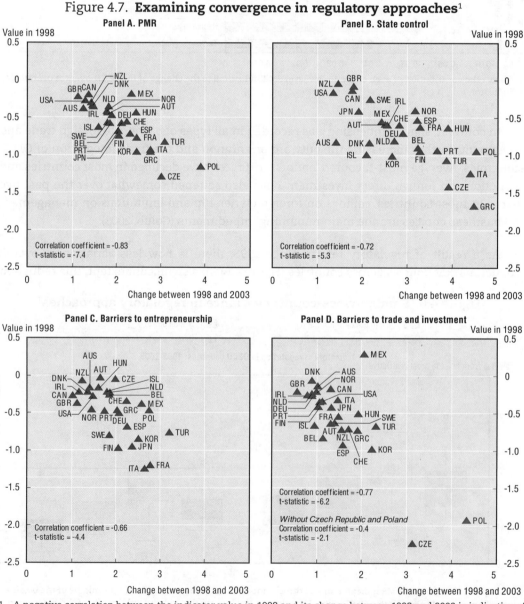

1. A negative correlation between the indicator value in 1998 and its change between 1998 and 2003 is indicative of convergence in regulation given that the scale of the indicators is 0 to 6 from least to most restrictive.

ECONOMIC POLICY REFORMS – ISBN 92-64-00836-5 – © OECD 2005

Convergence in the overall PMR indicator is due in large part to convergence in policies governing the extent of state involvement in product markets. Countries that had a relatively high degree of state control in 1998 have since made visible progress in this area (Figure 4.7b). The dispersion of barriers to entrepreneurship has also fallen since 1998 (Figure 4.6) and there is evidence of convergence (Figure 4.7c). In 2003, barriers to trade and investment are the most homogenous of the three broad policy domains (Figure 4.6). This reflects the fact that many of these regulations are determined by multilateral agreements and/or supranational institutions that often impose high standards of openness to trade and investment on their constituent countries. These institutions also tend to spread reform in this area across countries irrespective of their starting level; hence, the evidence of convergence in this sub-indicator is less compelling (Figure 4.7d).

Product market regulation to 2003

The overall PMR indicators and three constituent indicators for each country in 1998 and 2003 are shown in Figure 4.8. According to the PMR indicators, the regulatory environment has become more conducive to product market competition in all countries for which 1998 data are available. Given the volume of regulatory information contained in the system, only the most apparent policy developments are discussed here on a country-by-country basis. For expositional purposes, countries are split into three groups – as identified above – depending on their estimated degree of product market regulation in 1998.

The "relatively restrictive" countries

Consistent with the pattern of convergence identified earlier, countries that were estimated to have had relatively restrictive product market regulations in 1998 – Poland, Turkey, Czech Republic, Greece, Italy, France, Mexico, Korea, Hungary, and Spain – have, in most cases, also recorded a relatively large easing of overall product market regulation. For most of these countries the reform of product market regulations since 1998 has led to substantial improvements in all three of the broad policy domains captured by the sub-indicators. In particular:

- *State control*, which was generally relatively pervasive in 1998, has been reduced substantially. In all cases this reflects the removal of price controls – especially in the air transport and telecommunications sectors – and, except for France and Spain, reductions in the extent of direct government control over firms. For example, legal restrictions on the sale of state-owned equity have been removed in the Czech Republic, Poland, and Italy; "golden shares" have been redeemed in Korea and Greece; and the legislature no longer controls directly the strategic choices of public firms in the Czech Republic and Greece.

- Progress in reducing *barriers to entrepreneurship* has been more disparate in this group of countries. Italy, France, Korea, Turkey, and Spain, which were estimated as having some of the most restrictive barriers to entrepreneurship in 1998, have since made substantial progress. In Italy, France, and Spain, this was driven predominantly by substantial reductions in the administrative burdens on start-up firms. Italy and Turkey also removed legal barriers to entry in some sectors, while Korea improved some aspects of public governance. Poland has made progress in this policy domain by reducing legal barriers to entry in some sectors while Greece and Mexico have improved the system of

Figure 4.8. **Regulation in 1998 and 2003**[1]

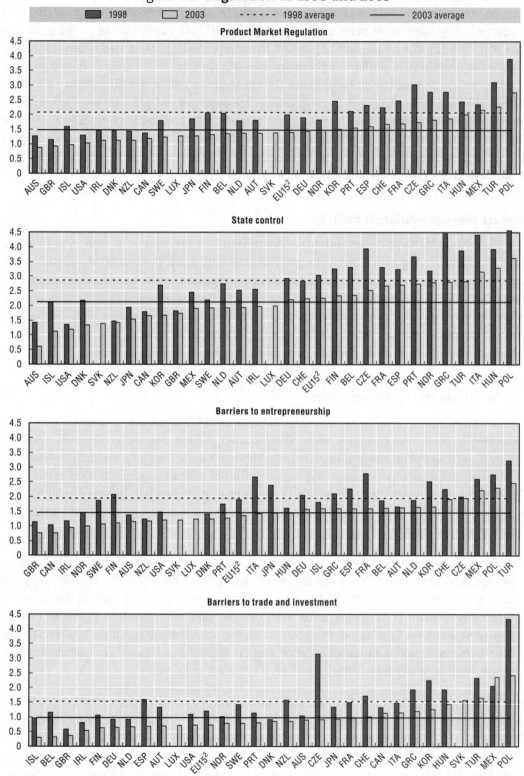

1. Sorted by 2003 values. The scale of the indicators is 0-6 from least to most restrictive of competition.
2. EU15 (simple average).

ECONOMIC POLICY REFORMS – ISBN 92-64-00836-5 – © OECD 2005

licences and permits. In the Czech Republic and Hungary, progress in this policy domain has been more limited.

- In the policy domain of *barriers to international trade and investment*, all the countries in this group have become more open as a result of higher ceilings on foreign investment in the airline and telecommunication sectors and, except for Mexico, lower average tariffs. In the Czech Republic and Poland, a range of other measures – such as explicit recognition of the national treatment principle, the use of Mutual Recognition Agreements, and access for foreigners to regulatory appeal procedures – have also contributed to large improvements in this area. This may reflect reforms implemented in the run up to accession to the European Union.

For all countries in this group, except Mexico and Hungary, the improvement in the PMR indicator between 1998 and 2003 is statistically significant at the 90% level of confidence (Figure 4.9).[9] Although progress has, in most cases, been substantial, reforms have not always been sufficiently deep to close the gap relative to other OECD countries, which have also implemented reforms over the same period. To varying degrees, countries in this group are still estimated to have some of the most restrictive product market regulations in the OECD. A continuing high level of state control is generally the most significant difference between these countries and the rest of the OECD. In particular, the scope and size of the public enterprise sector is still estimated to be relatively large and policy objectives tend to be achieved by coercive forms of regulation.

Figure 4.9. **Confidence intervals for the PMR indicators, 1998 and 2003[1, 2]**

At 90% levels

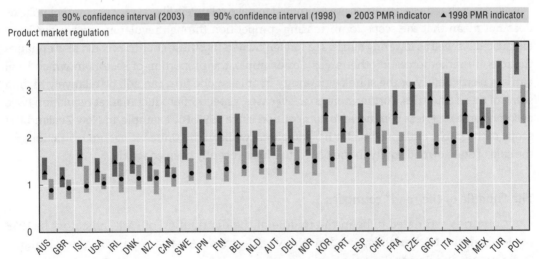

1. The scale of the indicators is 0-6 from least to most restrictive of competition.
2. The confidence intervals are calculated using stochastic weights on the low-level indicators to generate a distribution of overall PMR indicators for each country. The 90% confidence intervals are calculated from that distribution.

The "relatively liberal" countries

In line with the convergence theme, countries that were estimated to be relatively liberal in 1998 – the United Kingdom, the United States, Australia, New Zealand, Canada, Ireland, and Denmark – have tended to record relatively small relaxations of product market regulation. With a few exceptions, the pattern of product market reform in these countries has tended to consist of small incremental improvements across the range of PMR indicators. Most notably:

- In the policy domain of *state control*, Australia and Denmark have made progress by lessening recourse to "command-and-control" regulation. In Australia, regulations on retail trade have been decentralised and universal service requirements for airlines removed, while in Denmark policy alternatives to coercive regulations are being given greater consideration. Ireland has also improved in this policy domain due to marginal reforms in most of the areas covered by low-level indicators.

- All countries in this group have recorded some lowering of *barriers to entrepreneurship*, predominantly as a result of small reductions in administrative burdens on business start-ups and minor improvements in the communication and simplification of rules and procedures.

- *Barriers to trade and investment* have also fallen by minor amounts in all these countries. New Zealand recorded a more significant reduction in this policy domain due to lessening policy discrimination against foreign firms.

For all of these countries, the improvement in product market reform is not significant at the 90% level of confidence (Figure 4.9). However, these countries are still estimated to have some of the most liberal product market regimes in the OECD. This generally reflects lower barriers to entrepreneurship and less state control relative to other OECD countries. In contrast, many of these countries do not score well in the (relatively homogenous) sub-indicator of barriers to trade and investment, primarily because of relatively restrictive barriers to foreign ownership.

The fact that these countries are estimated to have relatively liberal product market policies does not mean that the scope for increasing competition through regulatory reform has been exhausted. As well as lowering barriers to foreign ownership, these countries could also enhance the role of market forces in other areas. For example, the proportion of sectors in which legal barriers restrict entry or the state owns equity in at least one firm can still be relatively high in some of these countries. Furthermore, in a few cases, aspects of product market regulation have become somewhat less conducive to competition since 1998. For example, in New Zealand the scope of the public enterprise sector has increased, while in the United Kingdom restrictions on the sale of state owned equity in the post office have recently been enacted.

The "middle of the road" countries

Countries estimated to be in the middle of the distribution of PMR indicators in 1998 are Iceland, the Netherlands, Sweden, Norway, Germany, Austria, Japan, Belgium, Finland, Switzerland, and Portugal.

- All of these countries have made progress in reducing the extent of *state control*. This has typically been achieved by removing price controls and relying less on "command-and-control" regulation to achieve policy objectives. The extent of direct government control over business has also been reduced in some of these countries, but not to the same extent as in the group of countries that were estimated to be "relatively restrictive" in 1998.

- Reductions in *barriers to entrepreneurship* have been more disparate across these countries. Sweden, Finland, and Japan have all made substantial progress by improving the system of licences and permits and government communication. Norway, Germany and Portugal have also made solid progress in this policy domain as a result of lower administrative burdens. The other countries in this group have virtually maintained the *status quo* in this policy domain since 1998.

● Reductions in *barriers to trade and investment* in this group of countries have been spread across the range of low-level indicators.

In Finland, Japan and Portugal the easing of product market regulation is significant at the 90% level of confidence (Figure 4.9). Notwithstanding this progress, state control is still relatively pervasive in Finland and Portugal, while barriers to foreign trade and investment remain in Japan. In the other countries in this group, the easing of product market regulations is not significant at the 90% level of confidence, although it comes close to significance in Sweden and Iceland.

Despite progress in some regulatory areas, the relative positions of Norway, the Netherlands, and, to a lesser extent, Switzerland and Austria have slipped somewhat, predominantly as a result of restrictive barriers to entrepreneurship in the Netherlands, Austria and Switzerland and persisting state control in Norway. On the other hand, Iceland, Finland, Japan and Belgium have improved their relative positions, and, to varying degrees, converged towards the most liberal countries.[10] The remaining countries – Sweden, Germany, and Portugal – have broadly maintained the relative positions they held in 1998.

As in 1998, the PMR indicators are in many cases not statistically different across countries in 2003 when uncertainty in the choice of weights used to calculate the overall PMR indicator is taken into account (Figure 4.10). However, once again, two broad groups

Figure 4.10. **Country groupings based on confidence intervals**[1,2]
for the PMR indicators, 2003
At 90% levels

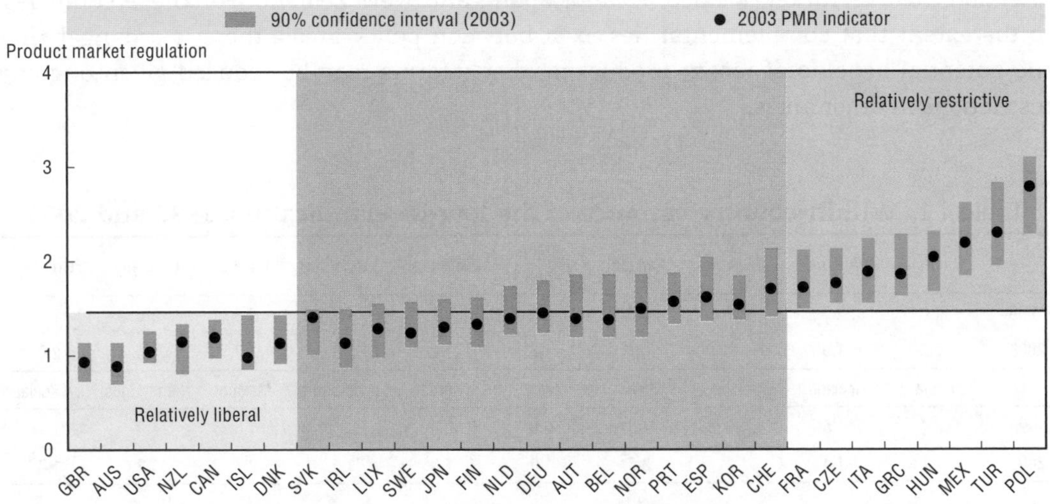

1. The scale of the indicators is 0-6 from least to most restrictive of competition.
2. The confidence intervals are calculated using stochastic weights on the low-level indicators to generate a distribution of overall PMR indicators for each country. The 90% confidence intervals are calculated from that distribution. Indicator values for the "relatively liberal" and "relatively restrictive" countries are significantly different at the 90% level of confidence.

of countries can be identified at conventional degrees of confidence. The "relatively liberal" countries have barely changed since 1998 and now include Iceland, in addition to the common-law countries and Denmark. The "relatively restrictive" countries in 2003 include Poland, Turkey, Mexico, Hungary, Greece, Italy, Czech Republic and France. Thus, Korea and Spain have moved to the group of "middle of the road" countries.

Consistency across policy domains

This section investigates the extent to which the policy approaches adopted by OECD countries in different regulatory areas are linked. It describes the observed empirical relationships between different aspects of product market regulation captured within the PMR indicators system as well as between product market and selected labour market policies.

Consistency across product market policies

One straight-forward method of assessing the extent of consistency in the policy areas covered by the 16 low-level indicators in the PMR system is simply to look at their variance within countries. A high variance would signal situations in which countries have relatively marked differences in the extent to which policies in different areas are conducive to competition; lower variances would point to policies that are either uniformly restrictive, or liberal, or somewhere in between, across the different areas of product market regulation.[11]

According to this metric, the dispersion of regulatory practice has declined between 1998 and 2003 for most countries, implying increased consistency of product market regulations (Table 4.1). Countries that have increased consistency most strongly include Italy, Japan, Sweden, and Korea. Given the overall improvement in product market regulation, this may indicate that recent reform efforts in these countries have been directed at regulatory domains that were problem areas in the past. Countries that have moved in the other direction include Turkey, Mexico, Poland, Spain, and New Zealand. For these countries, to the extent that complementarities exist between policy areas, there is a danger that the potential benefits of recent product market reforms may be reduced given ongoing restrictions in other areas.

Table 4.1. **Within-country variance of the low-level indicators, 1998 and 2003**

	Australia	Austria	Belgium	Canada	Czech Republic	Denmark	Finland	France	Germany	Greece
1998	1.0	2.5	2.7	0.8	2.3	1.7	1.7	2.3	1.6	2.3
2003	0.9	1.9	1.9	0.7	1.6	1.2	1.3	1.7	1.4	2.0
	Hungary	Iceland	Ireland	Italy	Japan	Korea	Luxembourg	Mexico	Netherlands	New Zealand
1998	2.4	1.5	1.9	4.0	2.6	2.0		1.6	1.3	1.1
2003	1.7	1.4	1.7	2.0	1.0	1.0	1.5	2.7	1.2	1.3
	Norway	Poland	Portugal	Slovak Republic	Spain	Sweden	Switzerland	Turkey	United Kingdom	United States
1998	1.9	2.1	1.5		1.9	2.1	2.9	2.1	0.8	1.2
2003	1.9	3.0	1.3	1.1	2.1	1.1	2.4	3.5	0.7	0.5

ECONOMIC POLICY REFORMS – ISBN 92-64-00836-5 – © OECD 2005

It is also interesting to note that the variability of regulatory approaches tends to increase as the regulatory environment (measured by the overall PMR indicator) becomes more restrictive across countries (Figure 4.11). Put differently, countries with relatively liberal product market policies also tend to have a more uniform approach across regulatory domains, and *vice versa*.[12] In countries with restrictive product market policies, the relatively diverse mix of policies could be open to two conflicting interpretations: it could be indicative of either inconsistent policy setting, or, more optimistically, an ongoing reform process.

Figure 4.11. **The relationship between the level of overall regulation and policy consistency in OECD countries**

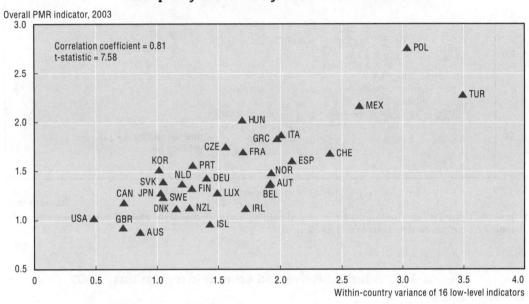

Across broader regulatory domains the consistency of product market regulations can be assessed by investigating relationships between pairs of PMR indicators at higher levels of the hierarchy. Three possible relationships are considered here: outward and inward-oriented policies;[13] economic and administrative regulations;[14] and, at a more detailed level, the scope of public enterprises and legal barriers to competition.

As mentioned above, supranational institutions and agreements tend to engender liberalisation in outward-oriented policies across all participant countries irrespective of their domestic policy settings. Notwithstanding this, there is a significant correlation between barriers to foreign trade and investment in OECD countries and domestic barriers to competition (Figure 4.12). In other words, relatively open economies also tend to have relatively liberal domestic policy settings. This may reflect a "political economy effect" whereby openness to trade and international investment generates pressures for domestic policy reform.

In 1998, countries that had restrictive economic regulations also tended to impose burdensome administrative procedures on business enterprises. Although subsequent reform has, in general, been somewhat asymmetric in favour of reducing economic regulations (especially state control), the positive correlation between these two regulatory areas has persisted into 2003 (Figure 4.13). There are at least two potential reasons to

Figure 4.12. **Outward and inward-oriented policies,**[1] **2003**

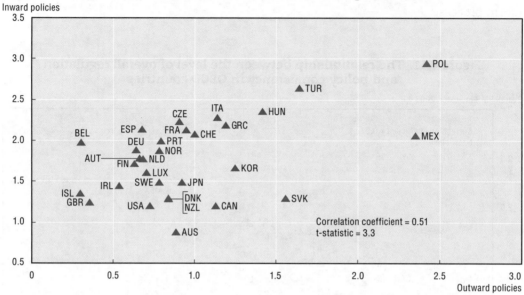

1. Inward-oriented policies include state control and barriers to entrepreneurship whereas outward-oriented policy indicators include barriers to trade and investment.

Figure 4.13. **Administrative and economic regulations,**[1] **2003**

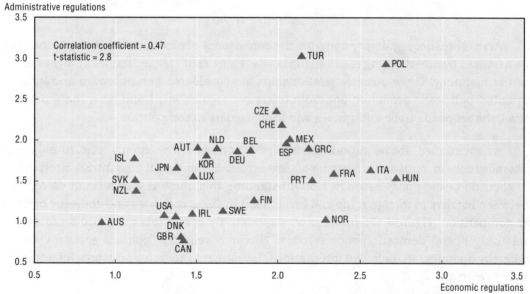

1. Administrative regulation includes reporting, information and application procedures, and the burdens on business start-ups, implied by both economy-wide and sector-level requirements. Economic regulation includes all other domestic regulatory provisions affecting private governance and product market competition (such as state control and legal barriers to entry in competitive markets). The scale of the indicators is 0-6 from least to most restrictive of competition.

Figure 4.14. **Public enterprises and legal barriers to competition, 1998 and 2003**

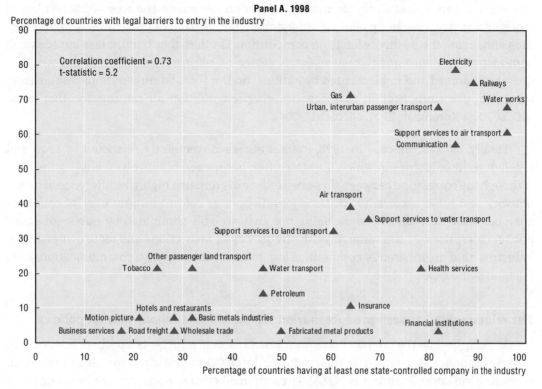

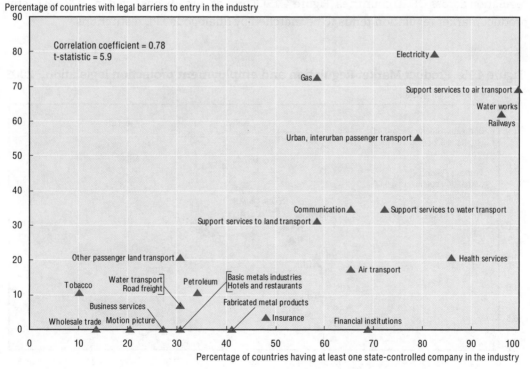

expect a degree of consistency between economic and administrative regulations. On the one hand, reforms that liberalise market access and enhance the role of market-based mechanisms may also bring about a reduction in administrative procedures and burdens, thus enhancing the positive effects on competition. On the other hand, a less burdensome administrative environment may make it easier to reform economic regulations that must be endorsed and implemented by national and/or local administrations. In this case, administrative simplification may constitute a pre-condition for reforms in other areas (OECD, 2003; Koromzay, 2004; Nicoletti, 2004).

Finally, as was the case in 1998, market access is frequently restricted by laws and regulations in industries in which the state often has ownership involvement (Figure 4.14). Although the correlation between these two indicators remains high, the difference between network and other sectors has become less distinct as reform in a number of countries has liberalised access to network industries that are still dominated by public (or semi-public) enterprises. At the same time, the frequency of restrictions and state ownership in industries that are inherently competitive (*e.g.* tobacco, air transport, communications) has fallen in some cases.

The relationship between product market regulation and labour market policies

Looking beyond the product market, empirical evidence suggests a positive relationship between product and labour market reforms in OECD countries with the former often preceding the latter (Brandt *et al.*, 2005). The empirical evidence also continues to suggest a positive relationship between employment protection legislation (EPL) and product market regulation across OECD countries (Figure 4.15). Thus, as already observed in 1998, restrictive product market regulation tends to be matched by analogous EPL restrictions.

Figure 4.15. **Product Market Regulation and employment protection legislation,**[1] **2003**

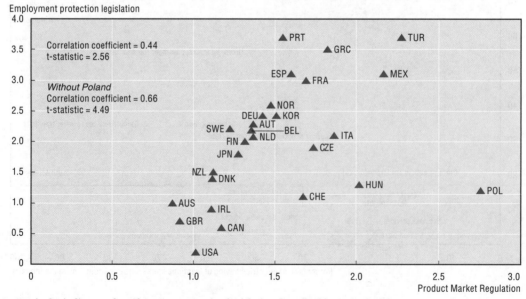

1. EPL is the indicator of employment protection legislation described in OECD (2004).

There are several potential reasons why some aspects of labour and product market policies might be positively correlated. For instance, because product market liberalisation reduces the rents accruing to firms, it may also reduce the incentive for labour to maintain or increase bargaining power aimed at capturing part of these rents (Blanchard and Giavazzi, 2003), or protecting "insiders" by means of restrictive EPL (Saint Paul, 1996). Firms in competitive markets may also find it less easy to bear the cost of restrictive EPL, while workers may have less incentive to protect their jobs if alternative employment opportunities are enhanced by the positive effect of easier product market regulation on overall employment (Koeniger and Vindigni, 2003).[15] As shown elsewhere (OECD, 2004), EPL has not changed a great deal over the past five years, especially for workers with permanent contracts. Thus, since the late 1990s, many OECD countries have made more progress in reforming product market regulation than EPL. If these policies are indeed political complements, this could suggest that better conditions for future labour market reforms may have been established.

Conclusions

Regulatory impediments to product market competition have declined in the OECD area in recent years. The extent of government involvement in product markets and barriers to international flows of capital and trade has fallen considerably. The fall in barriers to entrepreneurship has been somewhat less significant. However, notwithstanding recent progress, across virtually all OECD countries a "hard core" of regulations that impede competition still persists in some areas, such as barriers to entry in non-manufacturing industries.

In some respects, product market regulation has also become more homogenous across the OECD in the past five years as countries with relatively restrictive product market policies have moved towards the regulatory environment of the more liberalised countries. This convergence pattern has been most apparent in policies governing the extent of the state's involvement in product markets. There is also evidence of convergence in policy-induced barriers to entrepreneurship, whereas policies governing barriers to international trade and investment have tended to be relatively homogenous. However, despite a degree of convergence in product market regulation, differences between broad groups of countries that have "relatively liberal" and "relatively restrictive" regulatory environments are still significant.

The overall approach to product market regulation has also become more consistent across regulatory domains *within* many OECD countries, suggesting that recent reform efforts may have been focused on areas where regulation was previously particularly restraining. Also, countries with restrictive overall product market regulations tend to have a more heterogeneous approach to competition across different policy areas, which may imply additional efficiency losses.

Finally, as was the case in 1998, cross-country correlations between different aspects of product market regulation are also apparent in the 2003 indicators. Domestic impediments to competition tend to be lower in countries that have lower barriers to foreign trade suggesting a link between a country's degree of openness and domestic policy settings. In addition, restrictive economic regulations still tend to be associated with burdensome administrative environments, and legal barriers frequently block new entry into sectors in which publicly-controlled companies operate. Product market regulation also appears to be linked to employment protection legislation, raising the question of whether policies in the two regulatory areas are "political complements".

Notes

1. This chapter is based on recent more detailed OECD research (Conway *et al.*, 2005).

2. See, among others, Aghion *et al.* (2001), Nicoletti and Scarpetta (2003), Haefke and Ebell (2004), Nicoletti and Scarpetta (2004), Alesina *et al.* (2003), and Gust and Marquez (2002).

3. The values of all of the PMR indicators in 1998 and 2003, the underlying regulatory data used to construct them, and the questionnaire, called the OECD Regulatory Indicators Questionnaire are available via the OECD.stat Browser Web site at *http://stats.oecd.org/wbos/*.

4. A more detailed description of the way in which the PMR indicators are constructed can be found in Conway *et al.* (2004). The construction of the PMR indicators was originally described in Nicoletti *et al.* (1999).

5. Note that relative to the indicators shown in OECD (1999) the 1998 indicator values have been reviewed and revised as part of the current update.

6. This is in comparison to the early and mid-1990s when privatisation was more prevalent. See, for example, Megginson and Netter (2001).

7. The most-favoured-nation (MFN) tariff rates used in the PMR system are *ad valorem* and do not account for specific tariffs. The latter are frequently used on agricultural and food products with effects that are both less transparent and often more restrictive than *ad valorem* duties. MFN tariff rates also do not capture preferential tariffs, the trade importance of which has been growing over recent years with the expansion of regional trade agreements. The recent evolution of MFN tariff protection reflects reductions agreed in the Uruguay Round, with some differentiation according to sector, which a simple average may not accurately reflect. The tarification of non-tariff barriers in the agricultural sector is also an important determinant of recent changes in MFN tariffs.

8. The correlation coefficient between the 1998 levels of the overall PMR indicator and changes over the 1998-2003 period is -0.95 ($t = 10.54$) in the EU15 and -0.78 ($t = 4.16$) in non-EU15 countries.

9. That is, the confidence intervals around the 1998 and 2003 PMR indicators do not overlap, implying that the improvement between 1998 and 2003 is robust to the choice of weights used to calculate the indicator.

10. Note, however, that this result for Iceland is highly sensitive to the weights used in calculating the indicator (Figure 4.10).

11. The width of the confidence intervals calculated using the random weights technique is also a measure of variance in the 16 low-level indicators. Countries that have relatively similar scores for all of the low-level indicator values will score a relatively similar overall PMR indicator value irrespective of the weights used in the aggregation process. This will translate into a relatively narrow 90% confidence level. However, for countries with a larger variance across the low-level indicators the overall PMR indicator will vary considerably depending on the weights used in its construction and the confidence interval will be relatively wide. Hence, the width of the confidence interval also provides a graphical measure of policy consistency within each country at this level.

12. To some extent this is to be expected given that the variance of the low-level indicators in a perfectly liberal and perfectly restrictive country would be zero in both cases.

13. Inward-oriented policies include state control and barriers to entrepreneurship whereas outward-oriented policy indicators include barriers to trade and investment (see Figure 4.1).

14. Administrative regulation includes reporting, information and application procedures, and the burdens on business start-ups, implied by both economy-wide and sector-level requirements. Economic regulation includes all other domestic regulatory provisions affecting private governance and product market competition (such as state control and legal barriers to entry in competitive markets) (see Figure 4.1).

15. There is an increasing amount of research pointing to positive effects of product market competition on employment, both in theory (Blanchard and Giavazzi, 2003; Pissarides, 2001; Haefke and Ebell, 2004) and with reference to the experience of OECD countries (Boeri *et al.*, 2000; Nicoletti *et al.*, 2001; Kugler and Pica, 2003; Nicoletti and Scarpetta, 2004).

Bibliography

AGHION, P., C. HARRIS, P. HOWITT and J. VICKERS (2001), "Competition, Imitation and Growth with Step-by-Step Innovation", *Review of Economic Studies*, Vol. 68.

ALESINA, A., S. ARDAGNA, F. SCHIANTARELLI and G. NICOLETTI (2003), "Regulation and Investment", *NBER Working Papers*, No. 9560.

BLANCHARD, O. and F. GIAVAZZI (2003), "Macroeconomic Effects of Regulations and Deregulation in Goods and Labour Markets", *Quarterly Journal of Economics*, Vol. 118.

BOERI, T., NICOLETTI, G. and S. SCARPETTA (2000), "Regulation and Labour Market Performance", *CEPR Discussion Paper Series*, No. 2420.

BRANDT, N., J.M. BURNIAUX, and R. DUVAL (2005), "Assessing the OECD Jobs Strategy: Past Developments and Reforms", *OECD Economics Department Working Papers* (forthcoming).

CONWAY, P., V. JANOD and G. NICOLETTI (2005), "Product Market Regulation in OECD countries: 1998 to 2003", *OECD Economics Department Working Papers* (forthcoming).

GOLUB, S.S. (2003), "Measures of Restrictions on Inward Foreign Direct Investment for OECD Countries", *OECD Economics Studies Papers*, No. 36.

GUST, C. and J. MARQUEZ (2002), "International Comparisons of Productivity Growth: the Role of Information Technology and Regulatory Practices", *International Finance Discussion Papers*, No. 727.

HAEFKE, C. and M. EBELL (2004), "Product Market Deregulation and Labour Market Outcomes" *IZA Discussion Paper Series*, No. 957.

KOENIGER, W. and A. VINDIGNI (2003), "Employment Protection and Product Market Regulation", *IZA Discussion Paper Series*, No. 880.

KOROMZAY, V. (2004), "Some Reflections on Political Economy of Reform", comments presented to the International Conference on Economic Reforms for Europe: Growth Opportunities in an Enlarged European Union, Bratislava, Slovakia, 18 March.

KUGLER, A. and G. PICA (2003), "Effects of Employment Protection and Product Market Regulations on the Italian Labor Market", *Institute for the Study of Labor, Discussion Paper 948*. Bonn, Germany.

MEGGINSON, W. and NETTER, J (2001), "From State to Market: A Survey of Empirical Studies on Privatisations", *Journal of Economic Literature*, Vol. 39.

NICOLETTI, G., S. SCARPETTA and O. BOYLAUD (1999), "Summary Indicators of Product Market Regulation with an Extension to Employment Protection Legislation", *OECD Economics Department Working Papers*, No. 226.

NICOLETTI, G., R.C.G. HAFFNER, S. NICKELL, S. SCARPETTA and G. ZOEGA (2001), "European Integration, Liberalization and Labor Market Performance", in Bertola G., T. Boeri and G. Nicoletti (eds.), *Welfare and Employment in United Europe*, MIT Press, Cambridge, Mass.

NICOLETTI, G. and S. SCARPETTA (2003), "Regulation, Productivity and Growth: OECD Evidence", *Economic Policy*, No. 36.

NICOLETTI, G. and S. SCARPETTA (2004), "Do Regulatory Reforms in Product and Labor Markets Promote Employment? Evidence from OECD Countries". Paper presented at the ECB/CEPR Conference on "What Helps or Hinders Labour Market Adjustments in Europe", Frankfurt, 28-29 June.

NICOLETTI, G. (2004), "The Political Economy of Product Market Reform", paper presented at the Fondazione Rodolfo DeBenedetti conference on "Structural Reforms without Prejudices", Lecce, Italy, 19 June.

OECD (1999), *OECD Economic Outlook*, No. 66, Paris.

OECD (2003), *From Red Tape to Smart Tape, Administrative Simplification in OECD Countries*, Paris.

OECD (2004), *OECD Employment Outlook*, Paris.

PISSARIDES, C. (2001), "Employment Protection", *Labour Economics*, Vol. 8.

SAINT PAUL, G. (1996), *Dual Labour Markets*, The MIT Press, Cambridge, Mass.

ISBN 92-64-00836-5
Economic Policy Reforms
© OECD 2005

Chapter 5

The Retirement Effects of Old-age Pension and Early Retirement Schemes in OECD Countries[1]

OECD research summarised in this Chapter demonstrates that public pension systems and other social transfer programmes (such as unemployment, disability or special early retirement benefit systems) embody significant early retirement incentives. New empirical evidence shows that these schemes have played a major role in depressing employment at older ages, most prominently in a number of continental European countries where the work disincentives are particularly large. Therefore, a removal of early retirement incentives could raise effective retirement ages appreciably. For instance, labour force participation rates of older workers could be increased by over 15 percentage points in most continental European countries.

Introduction

Average effective retirement ages have declined in many OECD countries over the past three decades, and cross-country differences have become wide (Figure 5.1). Reversing this past decline would raise the labour force participation and employment of older workers. This in turn would ease the adjustment to ageing populations, curb age-related public spending and generate higher tax revenues to finance it.

Figure 5.1. **Retirement ages vary widely in the OECD**

Estimated effective retirement age of older male workers in 2000

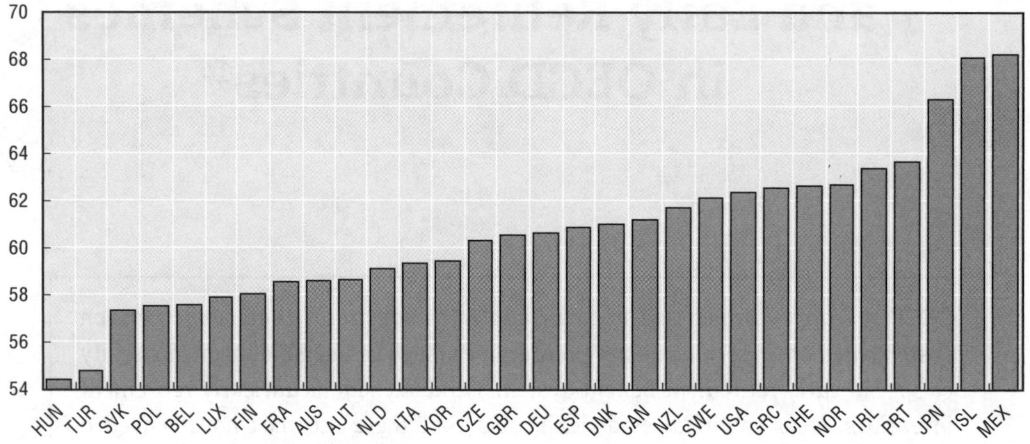

The main findings of the OECD research summarised in this chapter are:

● Public pension systems and other social transfer programmes (such as unemployment, disability or special early retirement benefits) embody significant early retirement incentives.

● These schemes have played a major role in depressing employment at older ages, most prominently in a number of continental European countries.

● A removal of such incentives could raise effective retirement ages appreciably. For instance, labour force participation rates of older workers could be increased by over 15 percentage points in most continental European countries.

Retirement incentives embedded in pension and other transfer systems

Three different characteristics of old-age pension systems affect the retirement decision of older workers: i) the age of entitlement to benefits; ii) the benefit level; and iii) the expected gain – in terms of higher future benefits – from continuing to work instead of retiring, weighed against the cost of doing so in terms of foregone pensions and contributions paid. In the following, these different – but interdependent – parameters of pension systems are presented for 22 to 30 OECD countries.

Standard and early ages of entitlement to old-age pension benefits

Many workers retire as soon as they reach the age of entitlement to a pension (see *e.g.* Gruber and Wise, 2002). This "bunching" of retirement occurs partly because social practice induces retirement at "customary" ages (see Lumdaine *et al.*, 1996). Another reason is that retirement before the minimum age of eligibility, even if desired, is inhibited by existing borrowing constraints. Some people may also retire as soon as benefits are available because they do not take proper account of financial incentives to continued work embedded in pension systems. Finally, in some cases, individuals may not be permitted to continue working after the standard retirement age.

The standard age of eligibility to pension benefits differs substantially across OECD countries (Table 5.1). It is currently set at 65 years in most of them, but ranges for males from a low of 60 in a few countries (France, Korea, Slovak Republic and Turkey) to a high of 67 in Norway and Iceland (and is gradually being raised to that age in the United States). There is wider cross-country variance in standard retirement ages for females; they have typically been lower than for males, and countries are at different stages of a process of gradual convergence towards male levels. There are even greater cross-country differences in eligibility ages for early pensions, but their interpretation is not straightforward because they do not necessarily allow access to full pension.

In the majority of OECD countries, standard and – to a lesser extent – early retirement ages have remained constant since the late 1960s. In those countries where changes have occurred, a general pattern emerges of reductions in the 1970s and 1980s, followed by stability. One striking exception in the 1990s was New Zealand, which raised its standard retirement age from 60 to 65. This was accompanied by a sharp increase in the labour force participation (over 15 percentage points) and – even more so – employment of the 55-64 age group.

Replacement rates

Older workers may choose to stay in employment after reaching the age of entitlement to a pension if their benefits are not seen to be high enough (Disney, 1996). Accordingly, an increase in pension benefits will push them to take advantage of pension entitlements. The most straightforward indicator of pension levels is the replacement rate, measured as the ratio of annual benefits to earnings just prior to retirement. For the purpose of this paper, *expected* replacement rates over a future five-year period are computed at ages 60 and 65. These figures are averages across stylised persons with different characteristics, and they refer to arrangements when recent reforms have been fully phased in.[2] The expected replacement rates at ages 60 and 65 differ noticeably across OECD countries (Figure 5.2). At age 60, they range from 0 in those countries where the earliest age of eligibility is at least 65 (including Austria,[3] Iceland, Ireland, Norway,[4] New Zealand, United Kingdom) to over 70% in several countries where people can claim generous old-age pension benefits in their early 60s (such as Korea, Luxembourg, Netherlands,[5] Portugal). At age 65, replacement rates range from less than 40% in Ireland and Norway to as high as 100% in Hungary and Luxembourg.

Table 5.1. **Standard and early ages of entitlement to old-age pension benefits**

	Males								Females			
	Early				Standard age				Standard age			
	1969	1979	1989	2003	1969	1979	1989	2003	1969	1979	1989	2003
Australia	..	..	..	55	65	65	65	65	60	60	60	62.5
Austria	..	..	..	..	65	65	65	65	60	60	60	60
Belgium	60	60	60	60	65	65	65	65	60	60	60	63
Canada	..	..	60	60	66	65	65	65	66	65	65	65
Czech Republic	..	..	..	58.5	..	..	..	61.5	..	..	..	59.5
Denmark	..	..	..	..	67	67	67	65	67	67	67	65
Finland	..	..	60	62	65	65	65	65	65	65	65	65
France	60	60	..	..	65	65	60	60	65	65	60	60
Germany	..	63	63	63	65	65	65	65	65	65	65	65
Greece	..	..	60	60	60	60	65	65	55	55	60	65
Hungary	..	..	..	..	..	..	60	62	..	..	55	62
Iceland	..	..	..	65	67	67	67	67	..	..	..	67
Ireland	..	65	65	65	70	66	66	66	70	66	66	66
Italy	55	55	55	57	60	60	60	65	55	55	55	65
Japan	60	60	60	60	65	65	65	65	65	65	65	65
Korea	..	..	..	55	..	..	60	60	..	..	60	60
Luxembourg	62	62	60	60	65	65	65	65	62	60	65	65
Mexico	..	..	..	..	..	65	65	65	..	65	65	65
Netherlands	..	62	60	60	65	65	65	65	65	65	65	65
Norway	..	..	..	..	70	67	67	67	70	67	67	67
New Zealand	60	..	..	..	65	60	60	65	65	60	60	65
Poland	..	..	..	..	..	..	..	65	..	..	..	60
Portugal	..	..	..	55	65	65	65	65	65	62	62	65
Slovak Republic	..	..	..	..	..	..	..	60	..	..	..	57
Spain	..	60	60	60	65	65	65	65	55	65	65	65
Sweden	63	60	60	61	67	65	65	65	67	65	65	65
Switzerland	..	..	..	63	65	65	65	65	62	62	62	63
Turkey	60	..	..	..	65	55	55	60	55	50	50	55
United Kingdom	..	..	..	..	65	65	65	65	60	60	60	60
United States	62	62	62	62	65	65	65	65	65	65	65	65

Notes:

Early ages of entitlement to old-age pension benefits are not indicated in the table when they are similar to standard ones or when early access to pensions is not possible.

Australia: Minimum retirement age (i.e. at which superannuation savings can be drawn) will increase to 60 over the period 2015-2025. Standard age for women to be increased from age 62.5 to age 65 between 2003 and 2013.

Austria: Early age of eligibility does not incorporate special early retirement for long insurance years, which will be progressively phased out (following the 2003 reform) but could still be accessed from age 61.5 in 2003 (60 in 1969, 1979 and 1989). Standard age for women to be increased from age 60 to age 65 between 2024 and 2033.

Belgium: Standard age for women scheduled to rise to age 65 by 2009.

Czech Republic: Standard and minimum retirement ages are scheduled to rise gradually to reach age 62 for men and age 61 for women (with no children) in 2007.

Greece: Standard age is 62 for men and 57 for women who first started to work before 1992.

Iceland: Early retirement age in 2003 is still 67 for the basic pension. However most occupational pension schemes, which are progressively maturing, set the minimum retirement age at 65.

ECONOMIC POLICY REFORMS – ISBN 92-64-00836-5 – © OECD 2005

Table 5.1. **Standard and early ages of entitlement to old-age pension benefits** (*cont.*)

Italy: Minimum retirement age is the minimum age of eligibility to a seniority pension, also equal to the minimum retirement age in the new pension system. Standard age is 60 (instead of 65) for women who first started to work before 1996.

Korea: Standard age scheduled to rise from age 60 to age 65 between 2011 and 2033.

Luxembourg: Early age of eligibility does not incorporate the special early retirement scheme ("pré-retraite"), which can be accessed from age 57 with 40 years of contribution.

Norway: Early age of eligibility does not incorporate the special early retirement (AFP) scheme, which can be accessed from age 62 in 2003.

Poland: Standard age is 55 for women with 30 years of insurance.

Slovak Republic: Standard age for women varies between 53 and 57 according to number of children raised.

Switzerland: Standard age for women will be 64 in 2005.

Turkey: Standard age is 55 for men and 50 for women who first started to work before 1990.

United Kingdom: Standard age for women will rise from age 60 to age 65 over 2010-2020 period.

United States: Standard age for both men and women scheduled to rise to age 67 over 2000-2022 period.

Source: US Department of Health and Human Services, Social Security Programs Throughout the World, various issues.

Figure 5.2. **OECD countries provide noticeably different replacement incomes**

Expected replacement rates over next 5 years in current old-age pension systems[1]

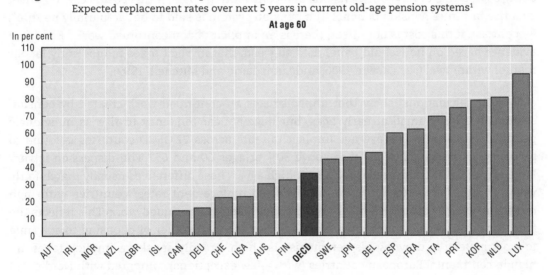

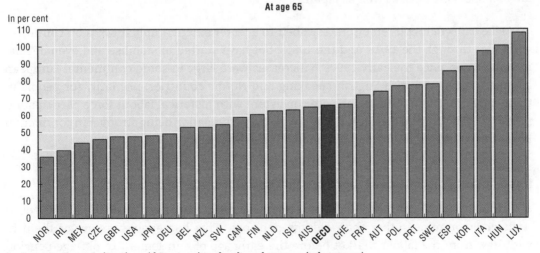

1. Average across 6 situations (three earnings levels and two marital statuses).
For the Netherlands, the calculations at age 60 is based on a "typical" VUT scheme.

Expected replacement rates rose in the vast majority of OECD countries between the end of the 1960s and the end of the 1980s. The rise at age 60 was mostly due to declines in entitlement ages to early pensions (increased eligibility), while at age 65 it was mainly caused by increased pension levels relative to earned income. By contrast, since the beginning of the 1990s expected replacement rates have stabilised (at age 65) or fallen (at age 60). However, these broad trends mask considerable differences across countries. While expected replacement rates remained fairly stable in some countries over the past three decades, they rose very significantly in others (Netherlands, Spain, Finland, Sweden (at age 60), Finland, Spain, Sweden and, to a lesser extent, Ireland and Norway (at age 65), in particular at early ages.[6]

Implicit taxes on continued work in old-age pension systems

When a worker reaches the age of eligibility to a pension, his retirement decision will depend not only on the current replacement rate but also on the expected gain – in terms of higher future benefits – if he or she stays in the labour force, weighed against the cost of doing so in terms of foregone pensions and contributions paid. If this cost is exactly offset by a rise in future pension benefits, the pension system is said to be "actuarially neutral". By contrast, if this cost is not offset, there is an implicit tax on continued work.[7] Empirical evidence based on household panel data suggests that implicit taxes induce early labour market withdrawal (see Lazear, 1986, and Lumsdaine and Mitchell, 1999).

OECD calculations[8] show that implicit taxes on continued work created by pension systems are fairly small at early ages, but have a clear tendency to rise as individuals get older (Figure 5.3). The average implicit tax rate across 22 OECD countries is found to be below 5% at age 55, while it is above 30% at ages 60 and 65.[9] The dispersion is very large across OECD countries, especially at high ages. These differences usually match fairly well – though not perfectly – those in expected replacement rates: countries with high replacement rates often also have large implicit taxes on continued work. This reflects the fact that when replacement rates are high, the cost to a worker of choosing to continue to work instead of drawing his benefits is also high. Broadly speaking, implicit taxes are high in continental European countries (with a few exceptions) compared with Nordic and English-speaking ones as well as Japan.

Like expected replacement rates, albeit to a lesser extent, implicit taxes on continued work rose through the 1970s and the 1980s, but have started to stabilise and even decline in some cases since the early 1990s.[10] Increases were large in some continental European countries compared with English-speaking and Nordic countries, primarily for people in their early 60s. These observations are consistent with historical labour force participation patterns, i.e. with trend declines in older workers' participation being stronger in continental European countries and having flattened out since the early 1990s.

Implicit taxes on continued work in other social transfer programmes

In many OECD countries, older workers have relatively easy access to various social transfer programmes other than old-age pensions. This has enabled many of them to withdraw from the labour market before the early age of entitlement to old-age pension benefits. Schemes that allow such early withdrawal include special early retirement

Figure 5.3. **Financial incentives to continue working decrease as individuals age**

Implicit tax rates on continued work over next 5 years in current old-age pension systems[1]

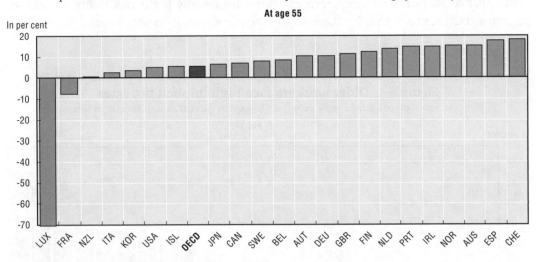

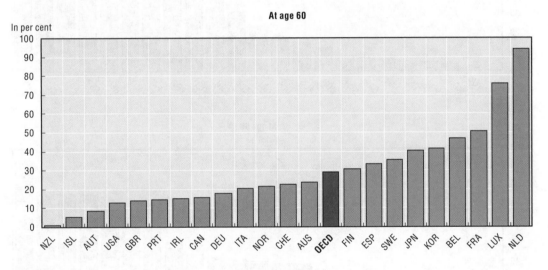

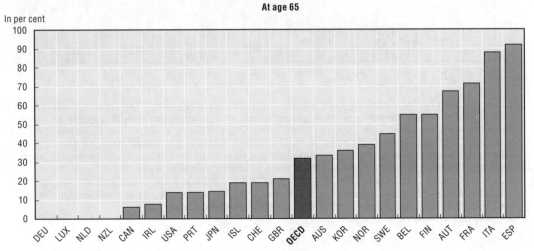

1. Single worker with average earnings.

provisions as well as unemployment-related and disability benefits (see Blöndal and Scarpetta, 1998; and Casey *et al.*, 2003). They often entail high implicit taxes on continued work, for two main reasons: replacement rates are usually high; and rights to ordinary pensions continue to accrue for those in the schemes even if, in some cases, at a reduced rate.

Figure 5.4. **Older workers face high implicit tax rates**

Implicit tax rates[1] on continued work over next 5 years in current social transfer programmes[2]

At age 55

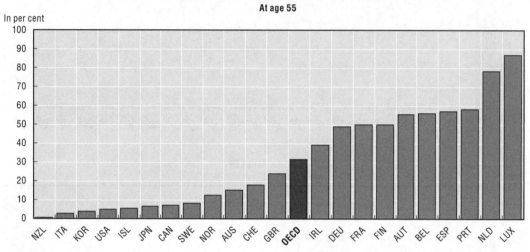

At age 60

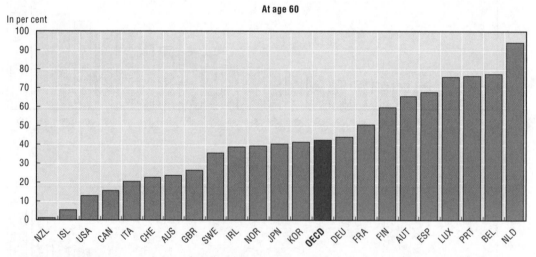

1. The implicit tax rate on continued work refers to an "early retirement route". The latter is modelled as the unemployment benefits/assistance pathway into retirement with the exception of Ireland, where the modelling refers to the pre-retirement allowance, and Luxembourg, where disability benefits were considered given their widespread incidence among pensioners. In those countries where it is considered that no early retirement scheme can be widely used to withdraw from the labour market before the minimum pensionable age (Australia, Canada, Iceland, Italy, Japan, Korea, New Zealand, Norway, Sweden, Switzerland and United States) the retirement scheme considered in the chart is simply the "regular" old-age pension system. Similarly, at those ages when people are entitled to an old-age pension (*e.g.* in France at 60), the retirement scheme considered in the chart is the "regular" old-age pension system rather than an early retirement scheme.
2. Single worker with average earnings.

No attempt is made here to be comprehensive in the coverage of these programmes.[11] Rather, in order to provide a rough assessment of early retirement incentives arising from them, implicit tax rates on continued work are computed for a "typical early retirement route".[12] These calculations take into account that a person will eventually move onto old-age pensions. In other words, they combine implicit taxes arising from old-age pension schemes and other transfer programmes into a single implicit tax rate which sums up retirement incentives embedded in the social system. The results underscore the strong incentives to retire in many countries. In particular, at age 55, when old-age pension schemes on their own do not provide strong retirement incentives (Figure 5.3), the overall implicit tax rate averages almost 30% across OECD countries (Figure 5.4). At the same time, the dispersion of implicit tax rates in the "early retirement route" is very large. Like for old-age pensions, overall implicit tax rates rose throughout most of the 1970s and the 1980s. This was especially the case at age 55, as early retirement schemes were created and/or became more generous. However, this expansion has come to a halt since the early 1990s, and has even been reversed in some countries (*e.g.* Sweden or Finland more recently).

Retirement incentives strongly affect labour market participation of older workers

The implicit tax on continued work is a key summary indicator of retirement incentives embedded in pension systems and early retirement schemes. This is not only because it represents the balance between economic costs and benefits of continued work but also because it captures some of the effects of eligibility ages and the level of benefits. Thus, in general, the higher the replacement rate, the higher the implicit tax on continued work. Similarly, the higher the minimum pensionable age, the lower is the implicit tax on continued work before this age. As a result, there is a good reason for focusing primarily on implicit taxes on continued work when assessing participation effects of retirement incentives embedded in pension and other retirement-income schemes.

To illustrate the effects of retirement incentives, Figure 5.5 plots, for successive five-year age spans, the fall in male labour force participation – a measure of labour market withdrawal – against the corresponding implicit tax on continuing working for five more years.[13] The significant and strong correlation between retirement incentives and labour force participation of older workers suggests that financial incentives have a sizeable impact on retirement behaviour. Both labour market withdrawal and implicit taxes are generally higher in continental European countries than in Japan, Korea, English-speaking and Nordic countries.

Figure 5.5. **High implicit taxes encourage labour market withdrawal**

Fall in male labour force participation between two consecutive age groups
and implicit tax rates on continued work, 1999[1]

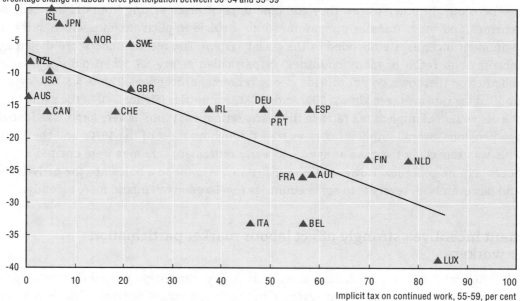

Panel A

Percentage change in labour force participation between 50-54 and 55-59[2]

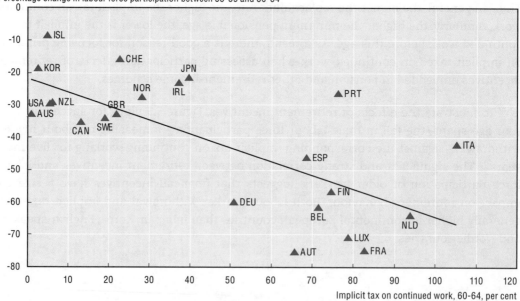

Panel B

Percentage change in labour force participation between 55-59 and 60-64[3]

1. Implicit tax rates are calculated for a single worker with average earnings in 1999. In some cases, the results differ from those presented in Figure 5.4, which refer to currently legislated systems. These differences reflect either policy changes that took place after 1999 (*e.g.* Finland, France) or the future implementation of measures that were already legislated but had not yet come into effect in 1999 (*e.g.* the future maturation of the Superannuation Guarantee Scheme in Australia, the transition from the "old" to the "new" pension system in Italy).
2. (Pr55-59-Pr50-54)/Pr50-54%.
3. (Pr60-64-Pr55-59)/Pr55-59%.

ECONOMIC POLICY REFORMS – ISBN 92-64-00836-5 – © OECD 2005

Taken at face value, the simple cross-country relationship suggests that a 10 percentage points decline in the implicit tax rate reduces the fall in participation rates between two consecutive (five-year) age groups of older workers by three to four percentage points.[14] More comprehensive empirical analysis, based on panel data regressions,[15] points to an effect of about a third of this size.[16] The difference to some extent reflects that over and above the effect of implicit taxes, the study identifies a specific, independent effect from eligibility ages on the labour force participation of the 60-64 and 65+ age groups.

These estimates can be used to assess the potential impact of various policy reforms on the labour force participation of older workers. Taking as an example a comprehensive overhaul of pension and transfer schemes that removed early retirement schemes and made old-age pension systems "actuarially neutral", there would be sizeable positive effects on the labour force participation of older workers, even if the "low" estimate of the more comprehensive empirical analysis is used.[17] However, there are reasons to believe that the elaborate empirical analysis underlying these calculations under-estimates the true effects of changes in retirement incentives.[18] If instead the simple cross-country correlations shown in Figure 5.5 are used, these effects could be almost three times larger. In particular, the participation rate of the 55-64 age group could rise significantly in a number of continental European countries (Figure 5.6). [19]

Figure 5.6. **Removing implicit taxes could encourage participation**

Projected labour force participation rates of the 55-64 age group in 2025 under different scenarios

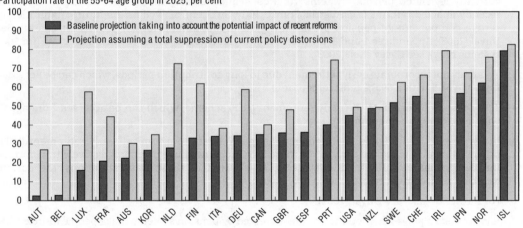

Participation rate of the 55-64 age group in 2025, per cent

Baseline projection taking into account the potential impact of recent reforms

Projection assuming a total suppression of current policy distorsions

Conclusion

Current old-age pension systems and other social transfer programmes induce older workers to withdraw early from the labour market. Suppressing these incentives – particularly in a number of continental European countries where they are strong – would delay retirement and help alleviate the burden of ageing.

The most straightforward step towards reducing incentives for early withdrawal from the labour force is to close early pathways into retirement, for three main reasons: i) it would leave older workers in their late 50s and early 60s facing only the – significantly lower – retirement incentives embedded in old-age pension systems; ii) reforming old-age pension systems could well have fairly small participation effects unless the access to early retirement schemes for people without special needs is removed; and iii) early pathways into retirement reflect the vestiges of a mistaken, and ultimately unsuccessful, attempt to deal with rising unemployment in the 1970s and 1980s by reducing the size of the labour force. It should also be borne in mind that reforming only some pathways into early retirement is likely to be ineffective because workers may leave the labour market via other schemes.

Nevertheless, suppressing early retirement schemes would not eliminate early retirement incentives, because these also arise from old-age pension schemes, especially in some (mostly continental European) countries and at high ages. Elimination of these incentives would require the value of pension benefits to be adjusted in case of anticipated and deferred retirement. While such adjustments currently apply in a number of OECD countries, they are insufficient to generate actuarial neutrality.[20]

Notes

1. This chapter is based on recent, more detailed OECD research (Duval, 2003).

2. Replacement rates are calculated before tax and are computed for, and averaged across, six different stylised workers (corresponding to three earnings levels and two marital situations), under the main assumption that these persons enter the labour market at age 20 and have an uninterrupted full-time career in the private sector until retirement. Only mandatory or quasi-mandatory components of pension systems are incorporated. In addition, the figures refer to currently legislated pension systems. As a consequence, they incorporate all future effects of recently enacted reforms (e.g. Austria, France, Italy, Sweden), as well as the future maturation of certain components of pension provision (e.g. Australia, Korea, Norway to a lesser extent). See Duval (2003), Appendices 1 and 3, for details. For a presentation of net replacement rates (for 2003 systems only), see Casey et al. (2003).

3. This does not incorporate early retirement due to long contribution periods, which can be accessed from age 61.5 with a 69.5% replacement rate.

4. This does not incorporate the early retirement (AFP) scheme, which can be accessed from age 62 with a 34.5% replacement rate.

5. In the case of Netherlands, the modelling at age 60 refers to a "typical" early retirement (VUT) scheme. However since the early 1990s these PAYG schemes have been progressively transformed into less generous, fully-funded, systems. As a result of these transformations, the current expected replacement rate at age 60 may be overstated.

6. For further details, see Duval (2003).

7. It is not clear a priori whether implicit taxes created by pension systems make people retire earlier or later (Mitchell and Fields, 1984). Changes in implicit tax rates on continued work are similar to changes in wages, i.e. they produce opposite income and substitution effects. An increase in the implicit tax – due for instance to a cut in the pension accrual rate – lowers the financial gain from postponing retirement, thereby reducing the opportunity cost of retiring earlier (negative substitution effect). At the same time, it provides lower income for each future year of work, thereby inducing later retirement (positive income effect).

8. These implicit tax rates are based on the same assumptions used to compute expected gross replacement rates, but they are computed only for one stylised worker (single worker with average earnings). An additional hypothesis is the following. When making his decision to withdraw from the labour market or to continue to work, the individual is assumed to expect constant economy-wide real earnings if choosing to work. While this has no impact on implicit tax rates in flat-rate schemes, it tends to over-estimate them in earnings-related ones, all the more so as the reference period for earnings used in the benefit formula is long (e.g. the "new" pension system in Italy). See Duval (2003), Appendix 2, for details.

9. Implicit tax rates at age 65 are actually higher than at age 60 in the majority of OECD countries. Nevertheless they are very low in those countries (*e.g.* Canada, Germany, Luxembourg, Netherlands and New Zealand) where it is possible to combine work with the receipt of a full or reduced pension (see Duval, 2003, Appendix 2), which lowers the OECD average.

10. For further details, see Duval (2003).

11. For more comprehensive coverage for 15 OECD countries, see recent OECD work by Casey *et al.* (2003).

12. For further information, see footnote 1 in Figure 5.4.

13. As already noted, the "early retirement route" simply corresponds to retirement via the normal old-age pension system when no alternative, more generous, pathway into retirement is accessible.

14. An effect of such magnitude is roughly consistent with existing microeconometric studies of the retirement decision: see for instance Gruber and Wise (1999, 2002).

15. See Duval (2003) for details.

16. These latter results are broadly in line with previous macroeconometric estimates by Johnson (2000) or Blöndal and Scarpetta (1998).

17. See Burniaux *et al.* (2003), Annex 7 for details.

18. See Duval (2003) for details.

19. Figure 5.6 presents projected labour force participation rates of older workers in 2025 under both baseline (*i.e.* assuming no change in legislation compared with the present situation) and reform scenarios. The main reason for considering participation rates in 2025 rather than current levels is to incorporate in the baseline scenario the projected, gradual impact of recently enacted reforms and the maturation of some components of pension systems.

20. In particular, many PAYG schemes do not provide actuarial bonuses for deferred retirement beyond the standard age, and where they exist, they usually do not rise enough with age to compensate for increasing mortality risks.

Bibliography

AARON, H. (1982), "Economic Effects of Social Security", *Studies of Government Finance*, The Brookings Institution, Washington DC.

BLÖNDAL, S. and S. SCARPETTA (1998), "The Retirement Decision in OECD Countries", *OECD Economics Department Working Papers*, No. 98.

BURNIAUX, J.-M., R. DUVAL and F. JAUMOTTE (2003), "Coping with Ageing: a Dynamic Approach to Quantify the Impact of Alternative Policy Options on Future Labour Supply", *OECD Economics Department Working Papers*, No. 371.

CASEY, B., H. OXLEY, E. WHITEHOUSE, P. ANTOLIN, R. DUVAL and W. LEIBFRITZ (2003), "Policies for an Ageing Society: Recent Measures and Areas for Further Reform", *OECD Economics Department Working Papers*, No. 369.

DISNEY, R. (1996), *Can We Afford to Grow Older: A Perspective on the Economics of Aging*, Cambridge, Massachussets, MIT Press.

DUVAL, R. (2003), "The Retirement Effects of Old-Age Pension and Early Retirement Schemes in OECD Countries", *OECD Economics Department Working Papers*, No. 370.

GRUBER, D. and D. WISE (2002), "Social Security Programs and Retirement around the World: Micro Estimation", *NBER Working Paper*, No. 9407, December.

GRUBER, D. and D. WISE (eds.) (1999), *Social Security Programs and retirement Around the World*, University of Chicago Press, Chicago.

JOHNSON, R. (2000), "The Effect of Old-Age Insurance on Male Retirement: Evidence from Historical Cross-Country Data", *Federal Reserve Bank of Kansas City Working Paper*, No. 00-09.

LAZEAR, E. (1986), "Retirement from the Labor Force", in ASHENFELTER O. and R. LAYARD (eds), *Handbook of Labor Economics*, Vol. 1, North Holland, Amsterdam.

LUMSDAINE, R. and O. MITCHELL (1999), "New Developments in the Economic Analysis of Retirement", in ASHENFELTER, O. and D. CARD (eds.), *Handbook of Labor Economics*, Vol. 3, North Holland, Amsterdam.

LUMSDAINE, R., J. STOCK and D. WISE (1996), "Why are Retirement Rates so High at Age 65?" in WISE, D. (eds.), *Advances in the Economics of Aging*, The University of Chicago Press, Chicago.

MITCHELL, O. and G. FIELDS (1984), "The Economics of Retirement Behaviour", *Journal of Labour Economics*, Vol. 2.

OECD (2003), *OECD Employment Outlook*.

OECD (2002), "Increasing Employment: the Role of Later Retirement", Chapter V, *OECD Economic Outlook*, No. 72, December, Paris.

ISBN 92-64-00836-5
Economic Policy Reforms
© OECD 2005

Chapter 6

Female Labour Force Participation: Past Trends and Main Determinants in OECD Countries[1]

Policy and market failures can depress female participation in the labour force and current participation rates are below levels desired by women. Female participation can be boosted by a more neutral tax treatment of second earners (relative to single individuals), stronger tax incentives to share market work between spouses, childcare subsidies, and paid maternity and parental leaves. Married women indeed remain more highly taxed than men and single women, and the level of family support (through childcare subsidies and paid parental leaves) differs widely across countries. Part-time employment can also help reconcile work and family demands. However, preferences for part-time labour vary across countries.

Introduction and summary

Female labour-force participation is much lower than men's in many countries. These differences are to some extent rooted in culture and social norms but they also reflect economic incentives. The female participation behaviour has attracted increasing interest because of concerns that population ageing will put downward pressure on labour supply, with negative implications for material living standards and public finances. An increase in female participation could help mitigate this (see Burniaux *et al.* 2003). This chapter focuses on the effects of market failures and policy distortions in depressing female participation and the likely results of policy reforms. The main findings of the chapter can be summarised as follows:

- A more neutral tax treatment of second earners in a household compared with single earners leads to an increase in female participation.

- Childcare subsidies and paid parental leaves boost female participation, but child benefits reduce it.

- More part-time work opportunities, *e.g.* through policies that remove barriers on part-time work, increase female participation.

- Simulations of comprehensive policy reforms in these areas suggest that they could close most of the gap between participation rates of prime-age women and men.

Trends in female participation

Over the past few decades, the labour force participation of women has increased strongly in most OECD countries. This process started earlier in some countries (*e.g.* the Nordic countries and the United States). More recently the increases have been greatest in countries where female participation was particularly low. This development has narrowed cross-country differences somewhat, but they still remain large (Figure 6.1). The participation rates of prime-age women (aged 25-54) range from about 60% (or below) in Korea, Mexico, Turkey and Southern European countries (with the exception of Portugal) to well above 80% in the Nordic countries and some Central European countries.

Preferences for female labour force participation are high in most countries. Indeed, surveys suggest that actual participation rates are below desired levels.[2] A survey carried out in EU countries in 1998 examined the preferences of couples with small children and found that only one in ten couples preferred the traditional male-only breadwinner model, while it actually applied to four in ten couples. The European Labour Force Survey, which covers all women irrespective of their marital status and number of children, indicates that the percentage of inactive women who would like to work is, on average, 12% in the 19 covered countries. This may be an underestimate since in responding to such questions, people may not take into account that policies could be changed. Finally, another international survey, which is more dated (carried out in 1994) but has a wider country coverage, suggests that

Figure 6.1. **The labour force participation of women has strongly increased**

Labour force participation rates of prime-age women (aged 25-54)

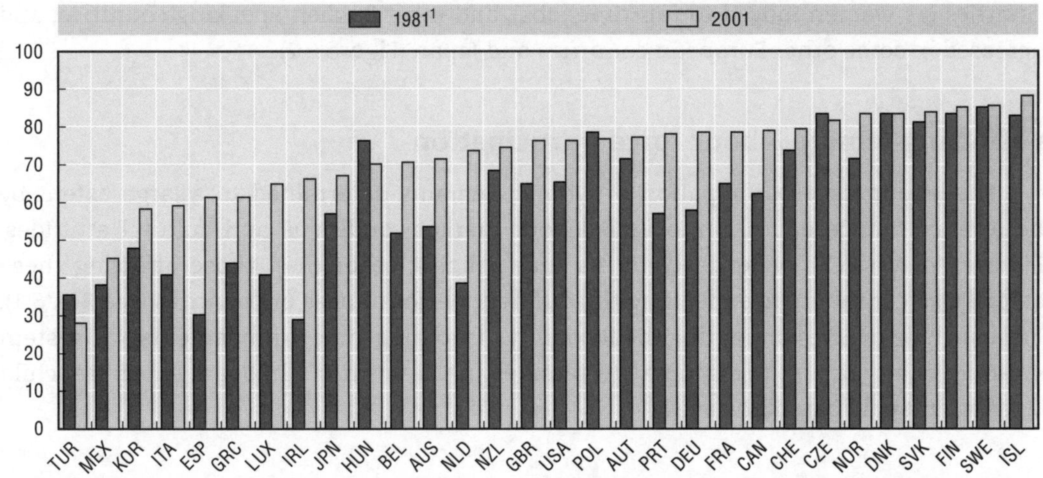

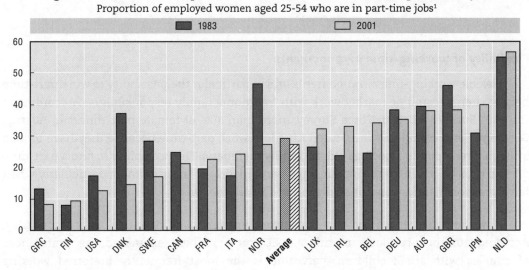

1. 1983 for Greece and Luxembourg, 1986 for New Zealand, 1988 for Turkey, 1991 for Switzerland, Iceland, and Mexico, 1992 for Hungary and Poland, 1993 for the Czech Republic, 1994 for Austria and the Slovak Republic.

Source: OECD Labour Market Statistics.

the traditional male-breadwinner model is the preferred model only in Central European countries (Czech Republic, Hungary and Poland).

There are large differences across countries in the share of women working part-time. On average in the OECD, about one-quarter of female workers at age 25-54 have part-time jobs. Countries where this share is higher include most Northern European countries (excluding most Nordic countries) and Pacific countries (Australia, Japan, New Zealand). On the other hand, the prevalence of part-time is relatively low in Central Europe, most Nordic

Figure 6.2. **About one-quarter of female workers have a part-time job**

Proportion of employed women aged 25-54 who are in part-time jobs[1]

1. Part-time employment refers to persons who usually work less than 30 hours per week in their main job. Data include only persons declaring usual hours.
For Australia, part-time data are based on actual hours worked, and include hours worked at all jobs.
For Japan, part-time data are based on actual hours worked and defined as less than 35 hours per week.
For the USA, the share of part-time in employment is for wage and salary workers only.

Source: OECD Labour Market Statistics.

countries, Southern Europe, and the United States. While average proportions of part-time work barely changed over the past two decades, it declined significantly in Scandinavian countries (as women moved to full-time jobs), and most English-speaking countries, and increased in some other European countries and Japan (Figure 6.2).

Policies affecting female labour force participation

The labour force participation of women remains determined to a large extent by the level of female education, overall labour market conditions and cultural attitudes. However, new OECD evidence confirms that policies, other than those affecting these factors, also contribute to explaining the different performances of countries (see Box 6.1). These include policies promoting the flexibility of working-time arrangements, the system of family taxation, and the support to families in the form of childcare subsidies, child benefits, and paid parental leaves.

Box 6.1. **Empirical analysis of the determinants of prime-age female labour-force participation**

The empirical analysis of the determinants of prime-age female participation is based on panel data regressions for 17 OECD countries over the period 1985-1999. The potential determinants include measures of the flexibility of working-time arrangements, the taxation of second earners, childcare subsidies, child benefits, and paid parental leaves. Other potential determinants of the rate of female participation, such as the level of female education, the proportion of married women, the number of children, and overall labour market conditions are controlled for. Finally, country-specific effects are allowed to capture differences across countries in cultural attitudes and institutions. The model is further refined to allow a different impact of the explanatory variables on full-time and part-time participation. The text builds on the significant results of this analysis. See Jaumotte (2003) for further details.

Flexibility of working-time arrangements

Flexible working-time arrangements and in particular the possibility to work part-time help women to combine market work with traditional family responsibilities. According to the 2001 European Labour Force Survey, more than 40% of female part-timers in Austria, Germany, Switzerland and the United Kingdom work part-time because they have to look after children or adults (such as elderly family members). The possibility to find a part-time job can thus be crucial to the labour-force participation of these women, particularly when family responsibilities can not be discharged in another way.[3]

However, preferences for part-time work appear to differ much across countries. According to the previously mentioned EU survey, which examined the preferences of couples with small children, part-time is the most frequently preferred working arrangement for women in Germany, Ireland, the Netherlands, and the United Kingdom. On the other hand, full-time female participation is preferred in some Nordic countries (Finland, Sweden), Southern Europe, and Belgium and France.[4] Across countries, there is a broad correspondence between preferences for part-time and the actual share of part-time in employment.

Overall, the OECD empirical research shows that countries with a higher share of part-time in female employment tend to have higher female participation, after controlling for other factors. Thus, policies that remove distortions against part-time work will lead to an increase in female participation, though the magnitude of this effect is likely to depend on the extent to which women have a preference for such work.

The OECD evidence also suggests that more part-time opportunities may arise when employers attempt to avoid restrictive employment protection legislation by resorting to part-time work which is often exempted from such legislation. However, a downside of this type of part-time work is that it creates segmented labour markets. Similarly, part-time jobs characterised by poor wages and benefits, asocial or excessively flexible hours, low job tenure, absence of training, or few prospects of promotion tend to marginalise women in the labour market.[5] Some countries have attempted to solve this problem by giving parents greater rights to change hours (including the right to work part-time but also to resume their full-time job). Other countries have helped women turn to full-time jobs with better prospects, for example, through more generous family support (see below).

Family taxation

Taxation influences work incentives in general, but may have a particularly strong impact on the decision of married women to work. This is because typically their choice is not only between leisure and market work, but between home production (and leisure) and market work. Indeed, traditionally home production has been regarded as a closer alternative to market production for women than for men. This makes the (market) labour supply of married women more sensitive to the changes in the net wage. An argument could even be made for taxing married women less than men and single women, because the distorting effects of taxes on their labour supply are larger (Boskin and Sheshinski, 1983). However, this would conflict with the principle of equal taxation for equal income.

In contrast with the theory, married women are effectively taxed more heavily than single individuals in most OECD countries, providing scope for a move to neutrality (Table 6.1). Only in a few countries (Finland, Greece, Hungary, Mexico, Sweden, and Turkey) are second earners and single individuals taxed equally. In some countries the difference in taxation is bigger for lower income earners. The high taxation of married women was traditionally explained by the system of joint household taxation, in which the income of the second earner is subject to higher tax rates because it is pooled with the first-earner's income. While most OECD countries applied joint taxation of couples at the beginning of the 1970s, almost all countries now have separate taxation or at least offer the option of separate taxation for couples. The fact that married women remain more heavily taxed despite the move towards separate taxation results from the dependent spouse allowance which still exists in most systems and which is lost if both spouses work, and from the introduction in some countries of a number of family-based tax measures. Over the past two decades, relative tax rates of second earners declined in most Nordic countries and the United States, while they increased significantly in some Western European countries and Canada. Nordic countries (excluding Iceland), Austria, France, and the United Kingdom have a relatively favourable tax treatment of second earners.

Table 6.1. **Comparison of tax rates of single persons and second earners, 2000-2001[1]**

	Women earning 67 per cent of APW, 2001			Women earning 100 per cent of APW, 2000			Type of taxation system, 1999[2]
	Second earner	Single	Ratio second earner/single	Second earner	Single	Ratio second earner/single	
Australia	27	19	1.4	32	23	1.4	Separate
Austria	25	22	1.1	29	28	1.1	Separate
Belgium	51	34	1.5	53	42	1.3	Separate
Canada	32	21	1.5	36	27	1.4	Separate
Czech Republic	40	21	1.9	39	23	1.7	Separate
Denmark	50	41	1.2	51	44	1.2	Separate
Finland	26	26	1.0	34	34	1.0	Separate
France	26	21	1.2	26	27	1.0	Joint
Germany	50	34	1.5	53	42	1.3	Joint
Greece	16	16	1.0	18	18	1.0	Separate
Hungary	29	29	1.0	..	..	..	Separate
Iceland	42	15	2.8	42	21	2.0	Separate
Ireland	24	10	2.3	31	20	1.5	Optional/Joint
Italy	38	24	1.6	39	29	1.4	Separate
Japan	18	15	1.2	18	16	1.1	Separate
Korea	8	8	1.1	10	9	1.0	Separate
Luxembourg	20	19	1.0	28	27	1.1	Joint
Mexico	-4	-4	1.0	3	3	1.0	Separate
Netherlands	33	27	1.2	41	36	1.1	Separate
New Zealand	23	19	1.2	23	19	1.2	Separate
Norway	30	26	1.2	32	29	1.1	Optional
Poland	39	30	1.3	37	31	1.2	Optional
Portugal	17	13	1.3	20	18	1.1	Joint
Slovak Republic	27	18	1.5	35	20	1.7	n.a.
Spain	21	13	1.6	23	18	1.3	Separate/Joint
Sweden	30	30	1.0	28	33	0.9	Separate
Switzerland	24	19	1.3	26	21	1.2	Joint
Turkey	29	29	1.0	29	29	1.0	Separate/Joint
United Kingdom	24	19	1.3	26	24	1.1	Separate
United States	29	22	1.3	30	26	1.2	Optional/Joint
Unweighted average	28	21	1.4	31	25	1.2	

1. The relevant "marginal" tax rate for a married woman's decision to participate or not in the labour market is the average tax rate on the second earner's earnings, defined as the proportion of these earnings that goes into paying increased household taxes. The husband is assumed to earn 100 per cent of Average Production Worker earnings (APW) and the couple is assumed to have two children. This tax rate is compared to the average tax rate for a single individual with the same gross earnings as the second earner. The tax rates include employee's social security contributions and are net of universal cash benefits. They do not include employer's social security contributions, indirect taxes, nor means-tested benefits (except some child benefits that do vary with income).
2. For detailed country notes, see Jaumotte (2003).

Source: OECD database "Taxing Wages"; *OECD Tax Models*; OECD (2001).

Another dimension of the tax influence on female participation is the tax incentive to split income – and thus work hours – between spouses. This can be measured by the increase in household disposable income when a wife takes on a part-time job to substitute for part of her husband's earnings.[6] Like the measure of relative taxation of second earners, the magnitude of this tax incentive will depend on the type of household taxation (joint or separate), the size of the dependent spouse allowance, and the progressivity of the tax schedule. For example, even if the tax treatment of the second earner is perfectly neutral, under a very progressive tax system the total tax paid for a given household income will be larger if the husband earns all the income than if the income is earned equally by the two spouses. In 1999, a shift of earnings of 33% of the APW level from the husband to the wife would have yielded an increase of 3% in the household disposable income on average in OECD countries, and an increase close to 10% in Finland, Mexico, and the United Kingdom. Looking at its evolution over the past two decades, this tax incentive declined in Scandinavian countries and Spain, while it increased slightly in some other Northern European countries and Canada.

The evidence from OECD countries suggests that countries with a high tax wedge between second earners and single individuals tend to have lower female participation rates, after controlling for other factors. The tax incentive to share market income (and hence market work) between spouses also appears to have a large impact on the female supply of part-time labour in OECD countries. For example, based on the analysis reported in Jaumotte (2003), if France were to have the same tax incentive to share market income between spouses as the United Kingdom, its female participation rate would increase by about 6 percentage points.

Support to maintenance and care of children

Governments have various ways in which they can provide support to families with young children: paid parental leaves, childcare subsidies, and child benefits.

First, paid parental leaves (including maternity, parental, and childcare leaves) help mothers of young children reconcile work and family life, and may strengthen their labour market attachment through a job guarantee. In line with existing studies,[7] the OECD research finds evidence of such a positive effect on female participation. However, beyond a certain length (estimated at the equivalent of 20 weeks of full pay in this study), a further increase in paid parental leave appears to have a negative effect on female participation. This reversal suggests that extended parental leave may weaken labour market skills and damage future career paths and earnings, making it difficult or less interesting for mothers to return to the labour market.

Second, childcare subsidies reduce the relative price of childcare, thereby increasing the return of market work relative to home production (in addition to increasing effective income). They may be seen as a way to reduce tax-induced distortions to the participation of mothers (see above), or as an offset to the otherwise negative participation effects when a highly compressed wage structure raises the relative wages of carers and thus the cost of childcare.[8] Finally, childcare subsidies may also help low-income mothers break away from welfare dependence.[9] There is evidence in OECD countries that more generous childcare subsidies are accompanied by higher female participation, even after all other policy influences have been taken into account.[10] This is mostly true for formal day care subsidies (*i.e.* for infants), while there is no clear relationship between female participation and public spending on pre-primary school. The latter could reflect that inactive mothers also send their children to pre-primary school for educational purposes.

The OECD evidence suggests that more generous childcare subsidies and paid parental leaves translate into higher full-time participation of women, and not higher part-time participation. However, other evidence for Canada and the United States suggests some effect of childcare subsidies on part-time participation, though smaller than on full-time participation (Powell, 1998).

Finally, child benefits (including tax allowances) are essentially transfers for the maintenance of children. By increasing the income of families with children, they are intended to promote equity across different family types and to reduce child poverty. However, the increase in income may lower the incentives to work and, hence, female participation.[11] In contrast with childcare subsidies, the increase in income is not accompanied by an increase in the return to market work. The empirical research finds a depressing effect of child benefits on part-time female participation. It is indeed for women working part-time that the income effect from child benefits is likely to be large enough to induce a reduction in participation. Thus, from the point of view of stimulating female participation, childcare subsidies appear preferable to child benefits.

Although the three types of family support could to some extent be seen as substitutes, countries which provide more of one type actually tend to provide more of the other types, and the level of support varies significantly across countries (Figure 6.3). Countries in which it is relatively high include, by decreasing order, most Nordic countries, France, Austria, Germany and, to a lesser extent, Belgium. It tends to be below the OECD average in the English-speaking countries, Japan, Mexico, Portugal, Spain, and Turkey. Childcare subsidies (usually targeted at formal day care and pre-primary school) averaged 0.7% of GDP in 1999, but reached levels between 1.5 and 2.7% of GDP in the Scandinavian countries.[12] The average length of paid parental leave was 26 weeks, with the longest paid leaves found in Finland and France. There was no paid leave entitlement in Australia, New Zealand, and the United States in 1999 (New Zealand recently introduced paid leave). Finally, child benefits increased on average the disposable income of two-children families by 7.5%, with the highest increases recorded in Austria and Belgium.

In all countries for which data are available, childcare subsidies per child increased in real terms between 1985 and 1999. However, the Scandinavian countries, which started with a higher level of spending, recorded much larger increases than the other countries, thereby widening the cross-country dispersion in the level of support. Provisions for paid parental leaves also became more generous in almost all countries between 1981 and 1999, leading to a doubling of the average length of paid parental leave. However, again, the largest increases were recorded in a number of countries which had among the longest paid leaves at the beginning of the 1980s, most strikingly France, Germany and most Nordic countries. Finally, despite a slight increase in their average level, child benefits underwent a mixed evolution, increasing in a number of countries, but decreasing in others.

Figure 6.3. **The generosity of family support varies across countries**[1, 2]

OECD indicators of generosity of provision, 1999[3]

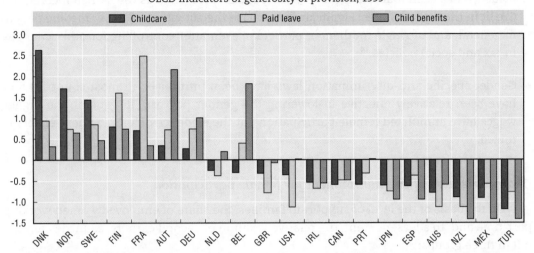

1. Childcare subsidies per child (in 1995 PPP-US$) are calculated as total government spending on formal day care and pre-primary school in 1999, divided by the number of children of age lower than the age of entry to primary school. Non-refundable tax allowances and credits for private formal daycare expenses are not included. However they constitute a relatively small part of total spending. Paid leave refers to the maximum number of paid leave weeks a woman is entitled to by the national legislation on account of maternity, parental and childcare leaves for the birth of a first child. The number of paid leave weeks is the sum of leave weeks, each multiplied by the corresponding statutory income replacement rate. Means-tests are not taken into account. Child benefits denote the percentage increase in household disposable income between a family with two children and a childless couple, where the husband has gross earnings of 100% of APW, and the wife 33% of APW.
2. For countries for which data were not available for 1999, the closest available year was used. See Jaumotte (2003) for country notes.
3. Each indicator is calculated as the deviation from its OECD mean and is expressed in multiple of its OECD standard deviation.

Sources: For government spending on childcare (*i.e.* formal day care and pre-primary school): OECD Education database; OECD Social Expenditures database; Eurostat; various other sources. For parental leave: Gauthier and Bortnik (2001) and *Social Security Programmes Throughout the World* from the United States Social Security Administration. For child benefits: OECD database *Taxing Wages*. See Jaumotte (2003) for details.

Other policies

The analysis has focused on policy instruments which affect directly the participation of married women and mothers. However, several other policies have an impact on female participation, albeit sometimes indirectly:

- Excessive regulations of the service market tend to hinder the development of the service sector, which is the predominant employer of women (Pissarides *et al.*, 2003). They also tend to restrict the supply and drive up the prices of services such as childcare and household services. This problem is straightforward (but possibly not easy) to deal with through policy reform – which is likely to have positive effects beyond those on female participation.[13]

- In some countries, less restrictive immigration policies have permitted an increase in the supply of labour employed in household services, including childcare and care for elderly family members.

- High welfare and other income support payments relative to wages tend to discourage employment and activity. In some countries, single mothers are particularly affected due to the fact that a large fraction of them are low-skilled and have low potential earnings. Evidence has been found that make-work-pay schemes (such as the Earned Income Tax Credit in the United States) significantly increase the activity rate of low-income people in general, and of single mothers in particular, even after controlling for other changes in tax and social policies.[14]

● Gender-specific anti-discrimination laws have been introduced in most countries and have been relatively effective in lowering the gender pay gap. In general, the higher wages have stimulated female participation but the evidence on employment effects is mixed.

Characterisation of the environment for female participation

On the basis of the level of support to families, the share of employed women working part-time and, to a lesser extent, the relative taxation of second earners, countries tend to fall in three groups:[15]

● High childcare subsidies, low part-time incidence, and favourable taxation: countries which share these features include most Nordic countries, France, and (to a lesser extent) Austria. Participation rates of prime-age women are very high, close to or higher than 80%.

● Low childcare subsidies, high part-time incidence: countries in this group include most other Northern European countries and Pacific countries. The tax treatment of second earners does not show a clear pattern across these countries and is in general close to average. Female participation rates range from close to 80% in Switzerland to about 65% in Ireland and Japan.

● Low childcare subsidies, low part-time incidence: this category groups countries with very different income levels. It includes Canada and the United States, on the one hand, and the Czech Republic, Korea, Mexico, Portugal, Spain, and Turkey, on the other hand. Female participation rates differ tremendously across these countries, ranging from very high levels in Canada, the Czech Republic, Portugal, and the United States (close to 80%) to significantly lower levels in the remaining countries (60% and below), despite a favourable tax treatment of second earners in some of the latter countries.

The potential for reforms to increase female labour force participation

This section presents some simulations to illustrate that the policies examined in this chapter can have a significant impact on female participation. The simulations, presented in detail in Burniaux et al. (2003), are based on empirical estimates of the models of female participation behaviour summarised in Box 6.1. The simulated policy measures are by necessity stylised and in some countries they may imply radical departures from current policies. They may thus not be feasible policy options in some countries. With this caveat in mind, an illustrative scenario was simulated which assumes for all countries a neutral tax treatment of second earners, high tax incentives to share market work between spouses (highest value observed), and an increase in public childcare spending per child to the highest level in the OECD. Under such a scenario, the prime-age female participation rate would increase on average by 10 percentage points across OECD countries (Figure 6.4).

The scope for reforms however differs across countries, depending on their current policies. Countries which stand to gain the most from a neutral tax treatment of second earners include the Czech Republic, Ireland, Italy, and Spain. On the other hand, the increase in childcare spending yields particularly large participation gains in Australia, Canada, the Czech Republic, Korea, New Zealand, and Southern European countries. Finally, the largest predicted gains from tax incentives to share market work between spouses are found in Germany, Japan, and the Netherlands.

Increases in childcare subsidies and cuts in tax rates will most likely impose a net budgetary cost, even though they may be partially self-financing.[16] In turn, this may require an increase in tax rates creating other distortions in the economy, or a cut in other budgetary expenditures. Such effects have not been taken into account in the simulations. Beyond the budgetary cost, childcare subsidies may encourage excessive use of childcare (both in quantity and quality). For example, it has been argued that childcare subsidies in Sweden are too large, in the sense that a reduction in the subsidies accompanied by a budget-balancing reduction in marginal income taxes would increase efficiency, not least by reducing the excessive production of household services.[17]

In order to keep the costs of reforms down, and at the same time increase the efficiency of reforms, the receipt of childcare subsidies can be conditioned on the employment of the mother, or at least on active job search by the mother. Furthermore, tax cuts and childcare subsidies can be targeted to low-income mothers whose labour supply is more responsive to the net wage.[18] However, greater targeting implies higher marginal effective tax rates as income rises, and a careful design of the tax cuts and childcare subsidies is needed to limit the negative impact on the supply of hours. Finally, the effectiveness of childcare subsidies and tax cuts in raising female participation hinges on the responsiveness of the childcare supply. A priori, the supply of childcare should be very responsive because of the low capital requirement for home-based childcare arrangements, and evidence of high responsiveness has been found for the United States (Blau, 2001). As discussed earlier, policies which may enhance this responsiveness include less restrictive product market regulation and immigration policies.

In some instances, the policies which promote female participation may imply a cost in terms of reduced equity. For example, separate household taxation and, more generally, greater neutrality of the tax treatment of second earners, imply less equity between families of different types. Indeed, under separate taxation, the tax paid by families with a same gross household income varies with the split of this income between the two spouses. Likewise, although childcare subsidies are preferable to child benefits from the angle of raising female participation, child benefits may be justified on grounds of equity across different family types and reducing child poverty. A careful balancing of policies is thus needed.

Figure 6.4. **Policy reforms could increase female participation**[1]

Increase in the participation rate of prime-age women (percentage points)

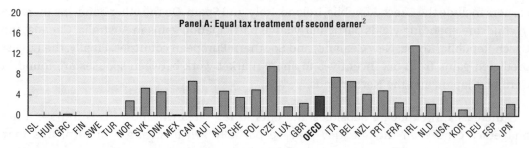

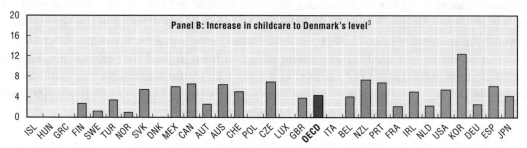

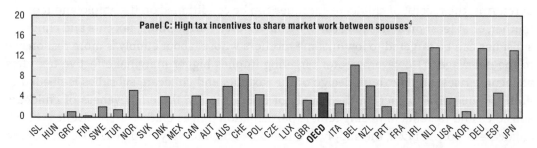

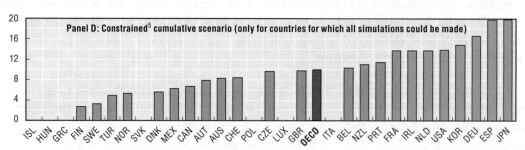

1. The baseline participation rates are the projected female participation rates for 2025 based on cohort effects and are taken from Burniaux *et al.* (2003); OECD refers to the unweighted OECD average.
2. Panel A assumes an equal tax treatment of second earners and single individuals (at 67 per cent of APW), as is already the case in Finland, Sweden, Hungary, Mexico, and Turkey.
3. Panel B assumes that public childcare spending per child converges in all countries to the OECD maximum of US$8009 observed in Denmark. No simulation could be made for Greece, Hungary, Italy, Luxembourg, and Poland due to lack of data on public childcare spending in these countries.
4. Panel C assumes that the increase in household disposable income between a situation where husband and wife share market work (100 per cent and 33 per cent of APW respectively) and a situation where the husband earns all the market income (133 per cent of APW) is 11 per cent, *i.e.* the maximum value observed in Finland and Mexico. No simulation could be made for the Slovak Republic, due to lack of data.
5. The constrained cumulative scenario combines the policy measures simulated in Panels A to C, under the constraint that the resulting female participation rate can not exceed the male participation rate projected for 2025 in the baseline. This constraint is also applied to Panels A to C, though to a lesser extent. The constrained cumulative scenario was only calculated for countries for which all individual policy measures could be simulated. It is thus not calculated for Greece, Hungary, Italy, Luxembourg, Poland, and the Slovak Republic.

Source: OECD estimates.

Notes

1. This chapter is based on recent, more detailed OECD research (Jaumotte, 2003).

2. See Jaumotte (2003) for further references on these surveys.

3. Even in the Netherlands, where part-time working is fairly common, the flexibility of working hours appears to be low and women who want to reduce substantially their working hours have a higher propensity to leave the labour market (Euwals, 2001).

4. The high preferences for full-time participation of women in Nordic countries may reflect the fact that childcare is more readily available in these countries. In Southern Europe, on the other hand, these preferences may arise from cultural attitudes towards the role of women, implying an all or nothing choice with respect to the participation of women.

5. Note that this does not necessarily imply that part-time work is second best. Making such a case would require assessing the consumption and production benefits of parental care.

6. Specifically, the wife is assumed to earn 33% of APW, and her husband 100% of APW. This situation is compared to the case where the husband earns 133% of APW and his wife does not work. This measure of the tax incentive to split income may be theoretical in some cases because the shift of work hours between spouses may be difficult in practice. Where this shift of work hours is feasible, the increase in female participation could in principle be offset by a reduced labour supply from men, leaving total participation unchanged. However, this is not very likely to happen as men's labour supply is quite stable. The tax indicator used here is more a proxy for the tax treatment of second earners working part-time than for the incentives to share market work between spouses per se.

7. For example, Ruhm (1998) found that paid parental leaves increased employment rates in nine OECD countries. A portion of the positive relationship between paid leave duration and the employment-population ratio reflects the fact that mothers on parental leave are counted as employed (but absent from work), rather than not employed.

8. This argument refers to an excessive compression of the wage structure (i.e. beyond the distribution of marginal productivities), such as those potentially produced by centralised wage-setting and minimum wage laws. The wages of carers (who tend to be concentrated at the bottom of the wage distribution) rise relative to those of mothers, reducing the access of mothers to childcare. There are other policy instruments to tackle the distortion, including a more general one which some countries have tried, namely reduced employer's social security contributions for low-skilled workers.

9. Other justifications that have been suggested for childcare subsidies, but which are beyond the scope of this study, include child development and social integration, as well as gender equity.

10. This confirms most of the abundant single-country evidence. See Jaumotte (2003) for futher references.

11. On the other hand, if liquidity constraints prevented the mother from working because she was unable to pay for childcare, the increase in income could lead to an increase in labour supply.

12. In addition to childcare subsidies, governments also grant tax allowances for private childcare expenses. These expenditures are not included due to a lack of data for most countries. However, even in the United States and Canada, where they are a more important component of childcare support, they only account for about 10% of public spending on childcare (including pre-primary school).

13. This recommendation does not have as its focus regulations which ensure a minimum quality of childcare, which are clearly necessary. Rather, it is concerned with excessive regulations and administrative burden which tend to discourage the supply of valuable childcare services.

14. Note that the predicted effects of the EITC have an ambiguous effect on overall labour supply. The literature provides consistent evidence that the EITC positively affects labour force participation. However, it also finds smaller, negative effects on hours of work for people already in the labour market and for secondary earners.

15. A country is defined as having a high value for an indicator if it is higher than the average value for all countries. Iceland, with relatively high child support, a relatively high share of part-time in female employment, and an unfavourable tax treatment of second earners, does not fit in any of the groups.

16. They are partially self-financing because the resulting increase in female labour supply leads to higher government revenues. See Burniaux *et al.* (2003).

17. See Rosen (1996). Of course, a full evaluation of the costs and benefits of childcare subsidies would have to take into account positive externalities on child development and socialisation, as well as considerations of equity (including gender equity).

18. It has been argued that the case for conditioning and targeting childcare subsidies has to be weighted against the potential benefits of childcare for the children's future development and their integration into society.

Bibliography

BLAU, D.M. (2001), *The child care problem: an economic analysis*, New York: Russell Sage Foundation.

BOSKIN, M.J., and E. SHESHINSKI (1983), "Optimal tax treatment of the family: married couples", *Journal of Public Economics*, Vol. 20.

BURNIAUX, J.-M., R. DUVAL and F. JAUMOTTE (2003), "Coping with ageing: a dynamic approach to quantify the impact of alternative policy options on future labour supply in OECD countries", *OECD Economics Department Working Papers*, No. 371.

EUWALS, R. (2001), "Female labour supply, flexibility of working hours, and job mobility", *Economic Journal*, Vol. 111.

GAUTHIER, A.H. and A. BORTNIK (2001), "Comparative maternity, parental, and childcare database", preliminary version (February), University of Calgary.

JAUMOTTE, F. (2003), "Female labour force participation: past trends and main determinants in OECD countries", *OECD Economics Department Working Papers*, No. 376.

PISSARIDES, C., P. GARIBALDI, C. OLIVETTI, B. PETRONGOLO and E. WASMER (2003), "Women in the labour force: how well is Europe doing?", Fondazione Rodolfo De Benedetti.

POWELL, L.M. (1998), "Part-time versus full-time work and child care costs: evidence for married mothers", *Applied Economics*, Vol. 30.

ROSEN, S. (1996), "Public employment and the welfare state in Sweden", *Journal of Economic Literature*, Vol. 34.

RUHM, C.J. (1998), "The economic consequences of parental leave mandates: lessons from Europe", *The Quarterly Journal of Economics*, Vol. 113.

ISBN 92-64-00836-5
Economic Policy Reforms
© OECD 2005

Chapter 7

Long-term Budgetary Implications of Tax-favoured Retirement Saving Plans[1]

In most OECD countries, governments promote private pensions by means of tax incentives, most commonly in the form of a tax exemption on contributions and investment income, with taxation applying instead on pension benefits. This Chapter provides a projection over the next 45 years of the budgetary impact of tax-favoured private pension plans in 17 OECD countries. The findings suggest that aside from leading to a deferral of tax revenues, such tax treatment of private pensions represents a net cost for public finances, largely because the taxes foregone on contributions and asset accumulation exceed taxes collected on pension benefits. Going forward, as larger cohorts reach retirement age and pay taxes on pensions, the net budgetary cost is expected to diminish in the majority of countries, but the impact on public finances will likely remain negative in most cases. The reason is that tax-favoured private pension plans tend to be used mostly by upper-income individuals who would most likely have saved equivalent amounts even without incentives. The Chapter discusses a number of alternative policy options that may help to broaden participation among lower-income earners so as to raise the impact on private savings and diminish the budgetary cost. Compulsion is one option. Another is to change the design of occupational retirement plans so that enrolment is the default option. The value of the tax incentives to participate could also be re-balanced in favour of lower-income earners by replacing the tax deduction for contributions by a non-wastable tax credit.

Introduction

In most OECD countries, governments promote the development of private pensions by means of tax incentives.[2] In the most common regime, private pension contributions are exempt from income tax, as are the accrued returns on investment of the pension fund, but pension benefits are taxed on withdrawal. Apart from providing a tax incentive to pension saving, this tax treatment also creates an implicit fiscal asset in the form of deferred tax revenues. So far, little work has been done to assess such implicit fiscal assets or, more generally, to examine the budgetary implications of tax breaks for private pension plans.[3] What follows is an analysis of these fiscal assets and of the evolution over time of the budgetary impact arising from tax-favoured pension regimes in 17 OECD countries.

The chapter first presents the data and methodology used to project the budget impact of private pension schemes and then discusses the main findings, that are summarised here:

- In all the countries examined, tax-favoured private pension schemes currently represent a net cost for public finances. This is because taxes foregone on contributions and accumulation exceed those collected on pensions. Going forward, the impact on government budgets is expected to remain negative in most countries. However, the net budgetary cost will in many cases diminish over time, as larger cohorts reach retirement age and pay taxes on pension benefits from such plans.

- The main reason why budget impacts are projected to remain negative is that tax-favoured pension plans are unlikely to generate significant amounts of additional private saving. Instead, pension contributions to a large extent substitute for other private saving vehicles, which accumulate out of taxed income and where the return is taxable. Such substitution is particularly prevalent because private pension schemes tend to be used mostly by upper-income individuals who would most likely have saved equivalent amounts even without incentives.

- The relatively weak participation rates in tax-favoured schemes among lower-income earners can be explained by a number of factors. One is that because the tax incentive often takes the form of a deduction from taxable income, the value of the incentive depends on the marginal tax rate and therefore is diminished at lower income levels. Another is that the design of public pension systems is such that the incentive for making additional private saving is often limited for lower-income individuals. Finally, lower-income earners are less likely to work for a firm that sponsors a pension plan as compared with highly-skilled workers.

- A number of policy options may help to widen participation across the income distribution and thereby reduce the net cost of tax-favoured plans. One is to make membership in an occupational plan compulsory, as is currently done in a number of countries. Mandatory participation in private pension plans may not, however, be desirable in countries where several layers of mandatory pension regimes already exist.

- Broader participation of lower-income earners in voluntary occupational retirement plans could be enhanced by designing the plans so that enrolment is the default option and/or by having employees to join at low contribution rates but with a pre-commitment to gradually raise them. For these measures to be most effective, however, governments should ensure that access to occupational schemes is widespread, including among small- and medium-sized firms.

- Another option consists in re-balancing the value of the tax incentive in favour of the lower-income earners. This could be done by replacing the tax deduction for contributions with a non-wastable tax credit (or subsidy) set at a uniform rate.

- Finally, rather than reforming the schemes with a view to broaden participation rates and stimulating private saving, another approach to lowering the cost of tax-favoured pension plans is to reduce the size of the tax incentive altogether. This can be achieved, for instance, by imposing a flat tax on accrued investment income, albeit at a preferential rate, as is currently done in a number of countries.

Private pensions in OECD countries

While several forms of long-term saving could be viewed as pension plans, the latter are narrowly defined in this study so as to include only privately-managed pension plans that accumulate assets specifically to pay for retirement, *i.e.* where the retirement objective is formally specified on a contractual and/or legal basis. Hence, certain types of long-term saving instrument that are close substitutes for formal retirement savings vehicles (*e.g.* life insurance) are not included in the definition of private pension assets. Furthermore, only pension plans that are privately-managed and, in principle, fully-funded are included.[4] In a number of countries, mandatory pension plans operating on a *pay-as-you-go* (PAYG) basis are partly funded, to the extent that they have associated reserves which in some cases can be quite large (for instance in the United States, Japan, Canada and Finland). These plans are not covered. On the other hand, the analysis does include private plans that may be under-funded with respect to future liabilities. In several countries, large funding gaps in occupational defined-benefit schemes have emerged since 2000, partly as a result of the stock market collapse, but also reflecting the decline in expected future rates of return.

Nearly all countries have at least one, and more often several private retirement saving schemes that benefit from favourable tax treatment relative to alternative savings vehicles. Thus, among the privately-managed and fully-funded pension schemes, the study focuses in each country on those that share the same tax treatment, independent of whether they are mandatory or voluntary, occupational or personal.[5]

Tax treatment of private pensions

A savings vehicle is usually considered as being taxed favourably when its tax treatment deviates from a regime that treats all sources of income equally (the so-called *comprehensive income tax* regime). In a pure comprehensive income tax system, pension contributions are made out of taxed earnings and the return on assets accumulated in the fund is also subject to income tax. In return, withdrawals from such savings vehicles are exempted from tax. Such arrangements are known as "taxed-taxed-exempt" (TTE) schemes. One alternative, more commonly adopted, regime exempts the portion of income that is saved in pension schemes.

When both the funds contributed and the investment returns on accumulated funds are exempted from taxation while the benefits are treated as taxable income upon withdrawal, such arrangements are commonly referred to as "exempt-exempt-taxed" (EET) schemes.

Table 7.1 summarises the current tax treatment of private pension plans in OECD countries. Twelve countries (Canada, Finland, Greece, Iceland, Luxembourg, Netherlands,

Table 7.1. **Tax treatment of private pensions in 2003**[1]

	Contributions[2]	Investment income	Pension benefits[3]
Australia[4]	T	pT	T/PE
Austria[4]	T(PE)	E	T/PE
Belgium[4]	E(TC)	E	T/PE
Canada	E	E	T
Czech Republic[4]	T(S)	E	T/PE
Denmark	E	pT(15%)	T
Finland	E	E	T
France	E	E	T/PE
Germany	E	E	T/PE
Greece	E	E	T
Hungary[4,5]	T	E	E
Iceland	E	E	T
Ireland	E	E	T/PE
Italy	E	pT(12.5%)	T/PE
Japan	E	E	T/PE
Korea	E	E	T/PE
Luxembourg[4]	E	E	T
Mexico	E	E	T/PE
Netherlands	E	E	T
New Zealand[4]	T	T	E
Norway	E	E	T
Poland	E	E	T
Portugal[4]	E(TC)	E	T/PE
Slovak Republic	E	E	T(15%)
Spain	E	E	T
Sweden	E	pT(15%)	T
Switzerland	E	E	T
Turkey	E	E	E
United Kingdom	E	E	T
United States	E	E	T

Abbreviations: E (exempt), T (taxed under personal income tax), TC (tax credit), PE (partial exemption or deduction from taxation), S (state subsidy), pT (partial taxation).
1. Private pension refers to mandatory or voluntary funded privately-managed pension schemes.
2. Tax-deductible contributions are subject to a certain limit in most countries.
3. This generally concerns the tax treatment in the case of annuities. Many countries allow pension benefits to be withdrawn in the form of lump-sums, in which case a partial exemption is granted so as to preserve tax neutrality with annuities.
4. The tax treatment of the employer's contributions is different from those of the employee's.
5. Mandatory contributions are fully taxed, but voluntary contributions receive tax credits.
Source: Yoo and de Serres (2004).

Figure 7.1. **Net tax cost per dollar of contribution in tax-favoured private pension plans**

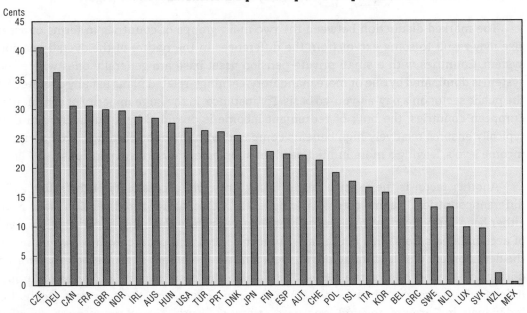

Cents

Source: Yoo and de Serres, 2004.

Norway, Poland, Spain, Switzerland, United Kingdom and the United States) come close to the pure EET regime. Another ten countries (Austria, Belgium, France, Germany, Ireland, Japan, Korea, Mexico, Portugal, and the Slovak Republic) also apply an EET regime, but one where withdrawals are taxed more leniently or where contributions are granted a tax credit rather than a full deduction. The practice in other OECD countries differs from the EET regime to the extent that contributions and/or accrued income are taxed, albeit partially.

A rough estimate of the size of the tax incentive provided by governments to stimulate the development of private pension savings can be obtained by comparing the tax treatment of private pension schemes with that of alternative savings vehicles which usually do not benefit from preferential tax treatment. More specifically, the tax favours granted to pension saving relative to other vehicles can be synthesised as an implicit subsidy per unit of contribution. Such calculations have been made for all OECD countries and the results are shown in Figure 7.1.[6] The size of the subsidy varies significantly across countries, ranging from around 40 cents per dollar or euro of contribution in private pensions (Czech Republic) to around zero (Mexico, New Zealand). Despite the differences in tax treatment of private pension savings across OECD countries, most provide a sizeable incentive, amounting to at least 10 cents per dollar of pre-tax contribution.

Importance of tax-favoured private pension schemes

The significance of tax-favoured private retirement saving schemes in terms of asset size, participation and share of total retirement income varies largely across countries. With respect to the importance of private pension assets, most OECD countries fall into one of two broad groups: one where assets (as defined in this study) represent at least 40% of GDP (the Netherlands, Denmark, Switzerland, Canada, United States, Iceland, United Kingdom, Australia, Sweden and Ireland) and one where accumulated assets remain, at 15% or less

(Portugal, Germany, Finland, France, Belgium, Italy, Mexico, Spain, Hungary, Austria, Poland and the Slovakia Republic). Japan and Norway are intermediate cases (Figure 7.2).

The marked distinction between the two main groups of countries in terms of asset size may result to some extent from the differences in the nature of the overall pension system. Countries with a small private-pension asset base are generally ones where the system is dominated by one or more mandatory, earnings-related plans usually operated by the public sector on a pay-as-you-go basis. For instance, in the large majority of continental European countries, the bulk of retirement income is provided by a public system that typically ensures relatively high benefits compared with previous earnings, even at upper income levels, leaving a more limited need for supplementary private pensions.

Another factor is the relative degree of maturity and accessibility of the schemes in different countries. In some cases, it is only recently that tax-favoured pension plans have either been introduced or made more broadly accessible, explaining in part the low level of accumulated assets. This is the case in most Central European countries, which made the development of fully-funded private pensions a key element of social security reforms during the second half of the 1990s. This is also the case in parts of Western Europe. Indeed, life insurance, which is not covered in this study, was the only real means for individuals in Germany to fund long-term saving on a private and voluntary basis until the pension reforms of 2001, which saw the introduction of tax relief for both occupational and individual pension schemes. With tax-favoured pension schemes restricted to specific categories of workers, life insurance has also been the favourite long-term private saving vehicle in France, Austria and, to some extent, Norway. Life insurance often represents a more flexible form of long-term saving and, at least in the case of France, it also benefits from a favourable tax status, albeit not as generous as an EET scheme.

Figure 7.2. **Assets in tax-favoured retirement saving plans**

Percentage of GDP

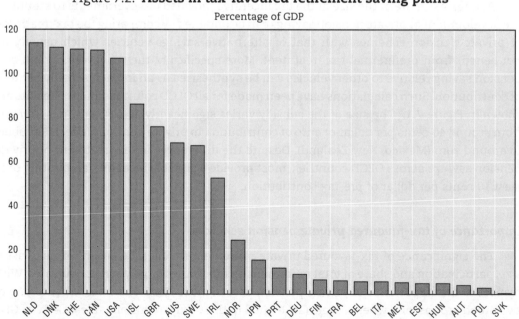

Source: International Pension Funds and their advisors, National sources and Antolin P., A. de Serres and C. de la Maisonneuve (2004).

Conversely, the large proportion of assets accumulated in the Netherlands, Denmark, Switzerland, Iceland and, to a lesser extent, Australia can largely be explained by the quasi-universal nature of their occupational schemes. In all five countries, the main occupational pension plan is not only mandatory (or quasi-mandatory), but it is also privately managed and fully funded. It should be noted, however, that at least in the case of Switzerland and Australia, the high proportion of assets also reflects the significance of voluntary contributions above the compulsory component. In Sweden as well, the coverage of the fully-funded occupational plan is extended to a large share of the workforce, owing to the centralised nature of wage contract agreements. However, given that this funded scheme provides coverage that supplements the unfunded mandatory plan, contribution rates are lower than in the Netherlands or Switzerland.

In all other countries with a large asset base, participation in private pension schemes is essentially voluntary.[7] Even so, participation is relatively high in part because the pension income provided by the public system in those countries is low in proportion to earned income, especially for middle and upper wage groups. In the United States, the United Kingdom, Canada and Ireland participation in private pension plans exceeds 50% of the workforce (Figure 7.3). Furthermore, in these countries private schemes have been in existence for many years, allowing the accumulation of substantial assets. Finally, participation in these schemes is influenced by the particularly generous incentives offered, as shown earlier.

Figure 7.3. **Participation in tax-favoured retirement saving plans**
Percentage of total employment

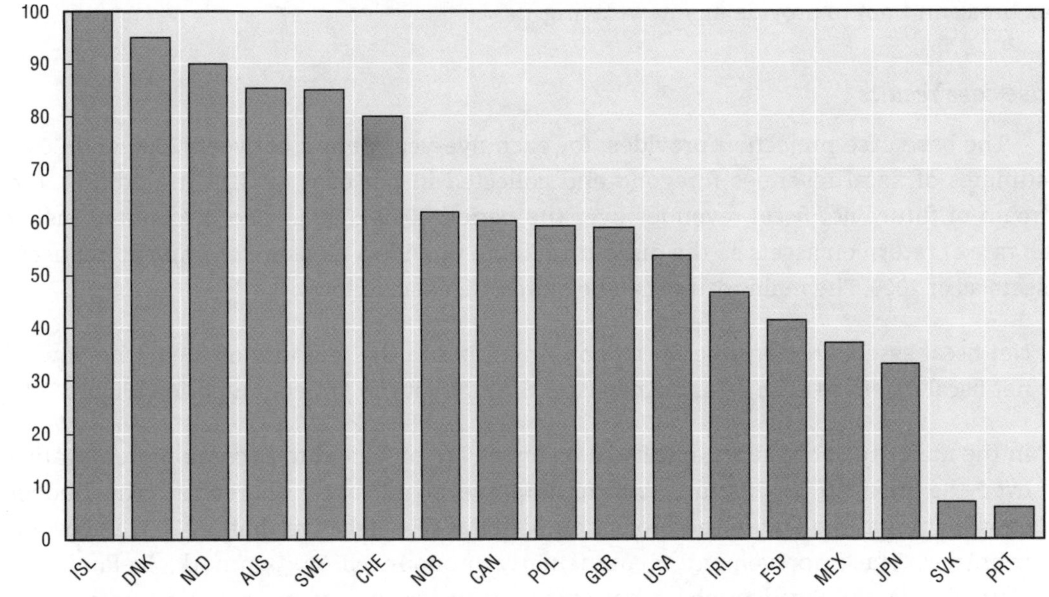

Source: National sources and Antolin P., A. de Serres and C. de la Maisonneuve (2004).

Future net fiscal revenues associated with tax-favoured pension plans

Methodology

In order to generate estimates of future costs and benefits of tax-favoured saving plans, total contributions and withdrawals are projected for five-year age groups over a period going from 2000 to 2050. The projections of contributions and withdrawals take into account differences in characteristics across age-groups such as the average income, the average rate of participation in pension plans and the average amount contributed per participant. In addition to the average characteristics of individuals belonging to a specific age group, estimates of total contributions and withdrawals depend also on the size of each group, which is allowed to evolve over time according to demographic projections. Once future profiles of contributions and withdrawals are estimated, net fiscal revenues in each period are calculated as taxes collected on withdrawals less revenues foregone due to the non-taxation of both contributions and (in the case of EET schemes) investment income. Revenues foregone are measured as those that would have been collected if participants to private pension plans had put their funds in a regular savings vehicle which are generally treated less favourably from a tax point of view.[8] Details concerning the overall methodology as well as the assumptions made to derive the relevant tax parameters used to calculate tax revenues collected and foregone are provided in the Appendix.

Results

Current and future net fiscal revenues and assets were estimated for 17 OECD countries for which sufficient information was available and in which accumulated assets in tax-favoured retirement saving schemes were equivalent to at least 20% of GDP.[9] The baseline projections were based on the assumption that contributions to private pension plans do not affect the overall level of national savings. In other words, private consumption was assumed to remain unchanged following the introduction of a tax-favoured scheme. Hence, contributors were assumed to save the amount corresponding to the value of the tax break and not to provide any new saving.

Base case results

The base case projection provides, for each five-year period between 2000 and 2050, estimates of fiscal revenues foregone and collected in per cent of GDP. In addition, the stream of future net fiscal revenues over the period 2005-2050 is also discounted (using the rate of return on assets as the discount rate) to provide a measure of implicit net fiscal assets as of 2000. The main results can be summarised as follows:

- Net fiscal assets are negative for all countries, and in the majority of them, the flow of net fiscal revenues even remains negative throughout the projection period (Figure 7.4).

- In the majority of countries, net fiscal revenues are projected to become more negative over the next 10 to 20 years, but to improve significantly thereafter. The budget contribution at the end of the projection period is less negative than in 2005 in several countries. The improvement is particularly pronounced in Denmark, Iceland, the Netherlands and Sweden where net revenues approach zero or even turn positive. In contrast, net fiscal revenues are expected to remain below their 2005 level at the end of the projection period in Ireland, Japan, Poland, Portugal, Slovak Republic, Switzerland and the United Kingdom.

- In Denmark and Sweden, the low initial drain on revenue and eventual positive budget contribution reflects the fact that accrued income on investment is at least partly taxed (ETT treatment) whereas in the case of Iceland the similar profile of net revenues results from the low tax rate imposed on regular savings vehicles used as a benchmark.

Figure 7.4. **Projected net fiscal revenues 2000-2050**
Percentage of GDP

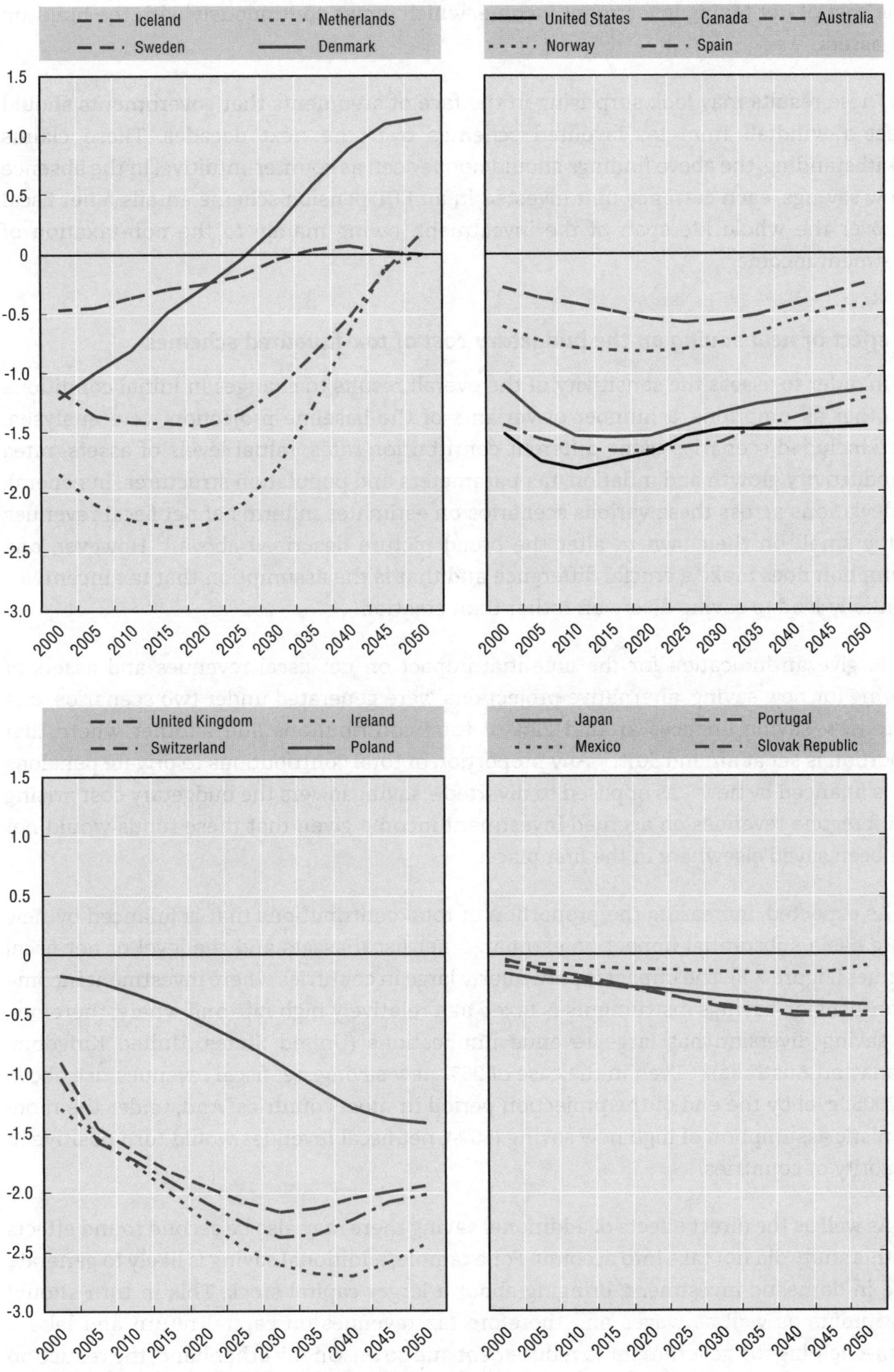

Source: Antolin P., A. de Serres and C. de la Maisonneuve (2004).

- In the case of Japan, Poland, Portugal and Slovak Republic, the flow of net fiscal revenues continues to decline throughout the projection period, as the results are dominated by the cost of not taxing investment income, which grows continuously with the build-up of assets.

These results may look surprising in the face of arguments that governments should expect a windfall from tax-favoured schemes over the next decades. These claims notwithstanding, the above findings should not be seen as counter-intuitive. In the absence of new savings, each currency unit invested in an EET pension scheme entails a net fiscal cost over the whole life span of the investment, owing mainly to the non-taxation of investment income.

The effect of new saving on the budgetary cost of tax-favoured schemes

In order to assess the sensitivity of the overall results to changes in initial conditions and other assumptions, a number of variants of the baseline projection were analysed. These included scenarios using different contribution rates, initial levels of assets, rates of productivity growth and inflation, tax parameters and population structures. In general, the deviations across these various scenarios on estimates in terms of net fiscal revenues are too small on their own to alter the broad picture described above.[10] However, one assumption does make a crucial difference and that is the assumption that tax incentives essentially lead to saving diversion rather than creation.

To give an indication for the potential impact on net fiscal revenues and assets of allowing for new saving, alternative projections were generated under two scenarios, one where new saving finances around 25% of total contributions and another where that proportion is set at around 50%.[11] Any proportion of total contributions to private pensions that is financed by new – as opposed to diverted – saving lowers the budgetary cost arising from foregone revenues on accrued investment income given that these funds would not have been saved elsewhere in the first place.

As expected, increasing the proportion of total contributions that is financed by new saving has a substantial impact on estimated net fiscal assets and the level of net fiscal revenues (Figure 7.5). The impact is particularly large in countries where investment income in non-pension savings instruments is taxed at a relatively high rate and where, therefore, less saving diversion has large revenue implications (United States, United Kingdom, Canada and Australia).[12] Even in the case of 25% new saving, net fiscal revenues rise above the 2005 level by the end of the projection period in most countries. And, under the more optimistic assumption of high new saving (50%), net fiscal revenues would turn positive in a majority of countries.

As well as the direct effects of additional saving there may also be second round effects that this study did not take into account. For example, additional saving is likely to generate a rise in domestic investment, bringing about a larger capital stock. This in turn should boost profits as well as wages and therefore tax revenues on capital return and labour income, helping the government to reduce debt and so on. On the other hand, the reduction in consumption in the short run would entail a loss of indirect tax revenues. Furthermore, an increased supply of saving may well have an impact on investment returns.

Figure 7.5. **Net fiscal revenues under alternative assumptions on new savings: selected countries**

Percentage of GDP

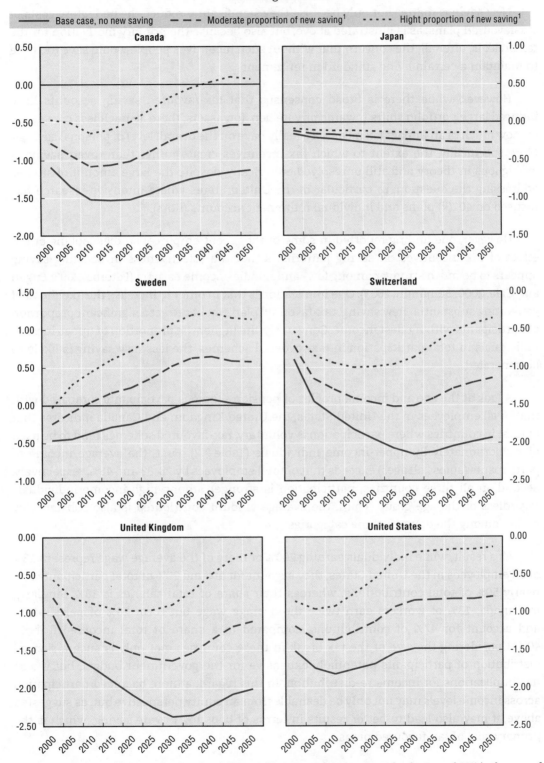

1. The proportion of total contribution that is financed by new savings is assumed to be around 25% in the case of moderate new saving and around 50% in the case of high new saving.

Source: Antolin P., A. de Serres and C. de la Maisonneuve (2004).

Policy issues

Distribution across income levels and effectiveness of tax-favoured plans

New savings matter not only because they significantly reduce the budgetary costs of tax-favoured plans, as is illustrated above, but also because the primary motivation for the tax break is, after all, the concern that without such incentives people would save too little to maintain a certain living standard in retirement.

However, while there is broad consensus that tax-favoured saving accounts have induced large portfolio shifts towards private pension assets, there is much less consensus on how much of an impact tax incentives really have on the overall level of personal savings. More specifically, the extent to which tax incentives create rather than divert saving is ambiguous in theory and still unresolved empirically, despite the large amount of studies addressing the question, in particular in the United States where intensive research has focused on 401(k) plans and individual retirement accounts (IRAs).[13]

However, one finding reported in some of the recent empirical studies looking at the effect of tax incentives on saving patterns is that the effectiveness in boosting saving appears to be much stronger among low- and middle-income earners (Poterba, 2003; Engen and Gale, 2000; Benjamin, 2003). One implication is that in order to increase the likelihood of generating substantial new saving, tax-favoured plans must attract a significant proportion of participants with modest income. Conversely, the higher the proportion of upper-income individuals in total participation in tax-favoured schemes, the less new saving is likely to be generated.

A look at the age and income profiles of pension schemes participants compared with that of all employees in the United States, the United Kingdom and Canada indicates that at least in countries where participation is voluntary, tax-favoured schemes tend to be used disproportionately by upper-income individuals (Table 7.2). First, the average income of participants (across all ages) exceeds that of total employees by 28, 33 and 45%, respectively. Second, in all three countries, participation is stronger among high-income individuals regardless of the age group. Third, the average amount contributed is also substantially higher among the upper-income categories.

As a result, while individuals earning 200% or more of the average wage represent 13% of all employees in the United States, they account for around 20% of total participants and nearly 50% of total contributions, whereas their share of total salaries is 38%. Similarly, in Canada, 13% of workers earn twice the average wage but form 26% of participants and account for 47% of contributions, compared to a share of total income of about 40%. Considering the size of the tax break in these countries, not only is such a skewed distribution of participants potentially expensive for the government budget, but it also has implications for income re-distribution. In this regard, a more balanced participation across income levels may not only be desirable from an equity perspective but, as suggested above, it may also lead to better results in terms of boosting private saving, which is the primary goal of tax-favoured plans.

Table 7.2. **Age and income profile of participants in private pension plans**

United States, 1997	Under 30	30 to 44	45 to 59	60 +	All ages		
Average income per employee ('000 $)	23.1	44.5	52.7	41.6	39.7		
In % of average income across all employees	58.3	112.1	132.7	104.7	100.0		
Average income per contributor ('000 $)	32.9	52.9	60.6	51.7	51.0		
In % of average income across all contributors	64.6	103.8	118.9	101.3	100.0		
In % of average income of employees in same age group	142.4	118.8	115.0	124.2	128.4		
United Kingdom, 2001	Under 30	30 to 39	40 to 49	50 to 59	60 +	All ages	
Average income per employee ('000 £)	13.8	19.9	21.3	17.8	10.3	17.7	
In % of average income across all employees	77.8	112.4	120.2	100.4	58.1	100.0	
Average income per contributor ('000 £)	19.7	24.6	25.6	22.2	19.0	23.5	
In % of average income across all contributors	83.9	104.6	109.0	94.5	81.1	100.0	
In % of average income of employees in same age group	143.2	123.5	120.4	124.9	185.0	132.7	
Canada, 2001	Under 25	25 to 34	35 to 44	45 to 54	55 to 64	65 +	All ages
Average income per employee ('000 C$)	11.0	28.4	35.9	39.9	36.9	35.7	31.3
In % of average income across all employees	35.1	90.8	114.9	127.5	118.0	114.1	100.0
Average income per contributor ('000 C$)	21.1	39.2	47.4	50.6	49.5	48.3	45.4
In % of average income across all contributors	46.6	86.4	104.5	111.5	109.1	106.5	100.0
In % of average income of employees in same age group	192.5	138.0	132.0	126.8	134.1	135.3	145.0

Source: US Congressional Budget Office, UK Department for Work and Pensions, Family Resources Survey, and Statistics Canada.

Factors affecting the distribution of participants across income levels

Possible explanations for the weaker participation and contribution rates from low and middle-income groups focus on two aspects: variations in workers' access to occupational pension plan membership and differences in the set of incentives and options faced by eligible employees. An important driver of eligibility is that when plan membership is available within a firm, non-discrimination rules usually ensure that the offer is extended to all categories of workers and, partly as a result, employee participation is often automatic. In fact, data on sponsorship of pension plans by US firms indicate that, for various reasons, lower-income workers are less likely to be employed by a firm that offers membership (Copeland, 2003). In the United States, less than 50% of workers with an annual income below $50 000 are employed by a firm that sponsors a plan, whereas the sponsorship rate rises to 75% for workers with earnings above that level.

One possible reason is that low-skilled, low-paid jobs may be more highly concentrated among small and medium-sized firms that cannot as easily absorb the administrative costs of sponsoring a pension plan. Figures for 2002 indicate that while the sponsorship rate is around 68% in large US firms (over 100 employees), it falls to 28% among smaller firms (less than 100 employees).[14]

Variations in eligibility to occupational pension plans can only go so far in explaining the uneven distribution of participants across income levels. After all, tax-favoured personal pension plans are available in many countries, in part to give workers with no access to an occupational scheme an opportunity to accumulate retirement saving under similar tax rules. However, it appears that where eligible workers do have a choice of whether to join or not, as is the case with personal pension plans and many occupational schemes (such as the 401(k) plans in the United States), participation is also weaker at lower income levels. One basic reason is that for individuals living on very low income, saving may be neither possible nor optimal, in particular for those whose income prospects have clear chances of improving over time.

Perhaps more important, given that in most countries the tax relief on contributions takes the form of a deduction, the value of the incentive diminishes at lower income levels and may be of little value for workers with low taxable incomes. In addition, since in many countries the basic state pension and other transfers are often incomes-tested, the marginal effective tax rate on benefit withdrawals may be very high for individuals whose pension income is expected to hover around the incomes-testing threshold. In contrast, one factor contributing to the generosity of the tax incentive for high-income individual is that tax-deferred schemes are often designed in a way that creates the scope for significant tax smoothing, especially in countries with very progressive tax schedules.

Some options to raise participation of low- and middle-income workers

Several countries have achieved rates of participation in tax-favoured private pension plans that are both high and uniformly distributed across income levels, but they have done so by means of compulsion, either *de jure* or *de facto*. For instance, membership in an occupational private pension plan is mandatory in Australia, Hungary, Iceland, Mexico, Poland and Switzerland. Denmark, the Netherlands and Sweden have also reached a quasi-universal degree of private pension coverage, but this has been achieved *via* broad collective agreements between social partners, whereby most firms are bound by industry-wide commitments to sponsor membership. Such a widespread degree of commitment may not be easily replicated, however, in countries where collective bargaining is much less coordinated.

As well, some countries may find it difficult to justify compulsion in the case of private pensions, not least when those are supplementary to mandatory public schemes. In such cases, the discussion above suggests that in order to maximise the creation of new saving, the value of incentives may need to be strengthened for low and middle-income workers. One way to do so – in the context of EET or ETT schemes and without considering more wide-ranging changes in pension and tax systems – would be to replace the deduction from taxable income with a non-wastable tax credit (or a subsidy) that would be set at a flat rate. Currently, only a few countries apply a tax credit (Austria, Belgium and Portugal) or a subsidy (Czech Republic, Germany and Mexico).

Incentives can only be effective, however, if potential participants are given relatively easy access to a pension plan. One question is whether such access is most efficiently provided by personal pension plans (such as IRAs in the United States) or occupational schemes. Since they are not based on an employment relationship, one advantage of personal pension schemes is that they largely avoid the problem of portability of pension plans. They may also facilitate access to private pension saving for part-time workers or for those whose labour market participation is not continuous. Furthermore, considering the limited capacity of many small and medium-sized firms to bear the administrative costs and responsibilities of sponsoring a pension plan, it is probably easier to achieve broad eligibility with personal plans. Indeed, the recent problems experienced by many large firms in funding their pension plans suggest that the difficulties may not be confined to small firms only.

However, an advantage of employment-based schemes is that matching contributions by employers can create an additional incentive for the employee to join. Investment fees are also generally lower in the case of occupational plans. In addition, occupational schemes may be better at overcoming inertia or procrastination over the decision to participate in a retirement saving plan (Mitchell and Utkus, 2003). In particular, a number of studies have shown that by making enrolment in a plan the default option and by having participants pre-commit to rises in contribution rates that are linked to wage increases, membership in voluntary schemes can be boosted substantially.[15] Such arrangements are essentially designed to help individuals to discipline themselves to save.

Tax-favoured plans may help achieve other objectives

The existence of tax-favoured pension arrangements does not seem to be questioned even though these schemes may appear costly from a public finance point of view. In fact, more and more countries are either introducing them or extending their coverage. A question that arises is whether tax-favoured arrangements could be justified even in the case where they fail to raise private and national saving. Three factors could help motivate their existence. One is that the shift towards long-term retirement saving may be an objective worth pursuing, not least to stimulate the demand for long-term financial instruments.

Another is the need to establish a framework for encouraging private pension in order to ease the impact of future reductions in public pension benefits on the income level of future retirees. The latter concerns primarily countries where the pension system rests essentially on a public pay-as-you-go pillar and who are under pressure to reform the system so as to cope with ageing population. Several of these countries, including Germany, France and Spain have implemented or extended EET-type private arrangements in recent years to promote the development of private pensions. However, promoting private pension as a substitute for public pensions raises issues regarding risk bearing and administrative costs which need to be carefully examined.

Finally, it could be argued that tax-favoured retirement-saving plans have played a useful role in allowing governments to shift important fiscal revenues to a period in the future when the fiscal impact of ageing will peak. As mentioned earlier, even in the case where little new saving is created, future net revenues are being projected to improve significantly relative to 2005 in many countries, allowing governments to partly recoup revenues foregone in earlier periods. Without such a shift, it is not clear that governments would have resisted political pressures to spend these revenues rather than using them to build assets so as to meet the future cost of populations ageing.

Notes

1. This chapter is based on recent, more detailed OECD research (Antolin *et al.*, 2004 and Yoo and de Serres, 2004).

2. Throughout this chapter, private pension schemes and retirement saving plans are used interchangeably.

3. Studies addressing this issue include CBO (2004), Boskin (2003), Auerbach *et al.* (2003) and Feldstein (1995) for the United States as well as Mérette (2002) and Finance Canada (2003) for Canada.

4. For the purpose of this study, fully-funded plans are loosely defined as those where the benefits are entirely financed by previously accumulated pension assets, without any implication or requirement in terms of degrees of actuarial fairness. Hence, the study includes plans that operate either on a defined-contribution or defined-benefit basis or any combination of the two.

5. Occupational pension plans are defined as those where access is linked to an employment relationship between the plan member and the sponsor. In contrast, access to personal plans is not linked to an employment relationship. In the latter case, individuals independently purchase and select material aspects of the arrangements without intervention of their employers (ISSA-INPRS, 2003). In both cases, the plans can take the form of individual accounts.

6. The numbers shown in Figure 7.1 represent an average of the cost per dollar of contribution across different age groups and are based on the same basic assumptions as those used for the projection exercise reported later in the chapter. A detailed exposition of the methodology and assumptions used to make the calculations as well as results from sensitivity analysis can be found in Yoo and de Serres, 2004.

7. In the case of occupational pensions, they are voluntary to the extent that employers are not obliged to offer a plan to their employees. However, when firms do offer such plans, employees may not have the choice whether or not to participate.

8 In most cases, the tax treatment of the alternative savings vehicle is TTE.

9. The countries included are Australia, Canada, Denmark, Iceland, Ireland, Japan, Mexico, the Netherlands, Norway, Poland, Portugal, Slovak Republic, Spain, Sweden, Switzerland, United Kingdom and United States.

10. A detailed sensitivity analysis can be found in Antolin, de Serres and de la Maisonneuve (2004).

11. More specifically, the assumption made is that the proportion of personal savings (*i.e.* total contributions *excluding* the tax subsidy) that is financed by new saving is ⅓ and ⅔, respectively, as compared to zero in the baseline. What this implies in terms of the proportion of new saving in total contributions (*i.e. including* the tax subsidy) actually varies slightly across countries as it depends on the marginal tax rate used to calculate revenues foregone on contributions. In most cases, the proportion of new saving (*i.e.* financed by a reduction in private consumption) is approximately 25 and 50%, respectively.

12. For reasons of parsimony, the results are shown for only a subset of countries.

13. The range of estimates found can vary from almost one extreme to the other. Nevertheless, the weight of evidence would suggest a proportion of new saving in total contributions of between 25 to 40% at most.

14. Another possible contributing factor, at least based on some evidence from Canada and the United States, is the relative decline in manufacturing jobs – and along with it the decline in unionisation.

15. See in particular, Madrian and Shea (2001) and Thaler and Bernatzi (2004).

APPENDIX

Methodological details and key assumptions

General framework[1]

Generating estimates of future costs and benefits of tax-favoured saving plans requires projecting forward a number of key variables including the number of contributors, total contributions, assets, accrued income from assets, and withdrawals. In each case, the total figure is obtained by aggregating across 13 five-year age groups from ages 20 to 85, calculated for each of the eleven five-year periods from 2000 to 2050. The projections also require estimates of relevant tax rates associated with each component of net fiscal revenues. Net fiscal revenues in each period are obtained as the net sum over all age groups of revenues collected on withdrawals, revenues foregone on contributions and revenues foregone on accrued income.

Withdrawals were modelled on the assumption that the total amount of assets accumulated until the age of 65 is run down according to a constant annuity formula until full exhaustion at the age of 85. In those cases where sufficient information was available, early withdrawals between the age of 55 and 65 were allowed, using the withdrawal rates per age category observed in recent years.

As contributions can generally be fully deducted from taxable income, *revenues foregone on contributions* made by each age group were calculated as the product of the age-specific marginal income tax rate on contributions and the total amount contributed by each age-group. The age-specific rates of participation in tax-favoured schemes used in the calculations were based on current rates of participation, which were assumed to remain constant in all cases except Mexico, Poland and the Slovak Republic (where schemes have only been in place for a short time). In these cases participation was assumed to rise gradually over time to reach full participation in the cases of the former two countries, consistent with the mandatory nature of their schemes, and to around 50% in the case of the Slovak Republic. In most countries where private pension schemes are voluntary, participation rates generally increase with age until the mid- or late-50s after which participation declines. In cases where participation is mandatory or quasi-mandatory (Australia, Denmark, Iceland, Netherlands, Sweden and Switzerland), the participation rates used were the same across both age-groups and time.

Foregone tax revenues on accrued income from investment measures taxes that would have been collected on investment income if private savings had instead been invested in a benchmark savings vehicle. This is the net present value of taxes paid on a stream of investment earnings, and is thus dependent on the tax rate on accrued income from alternative savings, the nominal rate of return on assets and the amount of assets accumulated. Note that in contrast to the calculation of revenues collected on withdrawals, the relevant stock of assets in this case is not total assets invested in the scheme but only those accumulated from diverted savings. The reason for including only a subcomponent of total assets is that contributions to tax-favoured pension plans comprise the tax subsidy plus personal saving. The latter can in turn be split into diverted saving and new saving. Since neither the new saving nor the tax subsidy components would have generated investment income in the absence of the scheme, they need to be excluded from the calculation of tax revenue losses.

Key parameters

The relevant tax rates used to estimate revenues foregone on contributions and accrued investment income, as well as revenues collected on withdrawals, were calculated based on a number of assumptions. First, the current tax treatment of standard savings vehicles in each country was taken as the benchmark. Second, marginal tax rates corresponding to different levels of income and family status were derived from a tax model reflecting the current tax code in each country. Third, as concerns taxation of investment income, detailed information on the tax treatment of specific non-pension savings vehicles included in the benchmark portfolio (i.e. a mix of interest-bearing instruments and shares, see below) was used to derive implicit tax rates on the return to investment. Furthermore, the following assumptions were made concerning the allocation of assets and returns in the benchmark and private pension portfolio:

- The portfolio was composed of 60% interest-bearing assets (bank deposits or bonds) and 40% equities. Hence, the benchmark considered only financial assets and excluded real estate or housing

- The pre-tax nominal rate of return on assets (both bonds and equity) was set at 6.5% per annum, including 2% inflation.

For tax purposes in the case of the benchmark portfolio, the return on equity was assumed to be one-third dividends and two-thirds capital gains. Shares were assumed to be held for 6.7 years on average and to be subject to capital gains tax.[2] The time horizon was allowed to vary from 1 to 40 years, depending on the age of the investor at the time the contribution was made.

Fourth, given the lack of sufficient information about the overall income of private pension beneficiaries, the general rule was to set the tax rate applied to benefit withdrawals at 5 percentage points below the average tax rate (across age-groups) used to calculate revenues foregone on contributions. The motivation for having a lower tax rate on withdrawals is that tax deferral often creates the scope for tax smoothing, suggesting that the effective tax rate is most likely to lie somewhere between the marginal and the average tax rate corresponding to the amount of pension benefits. However, a proper calculation would require adequate information about the level and the various sources of *taxable* income of pensioners who have participated in a tax-favoured scheme.

Notes

1. A more complete exposition of the methodology can be found in Antolin, de Serres and de la Maisonneuve (2004).

2. This is equivalent to assuming that 15% of the shares held in the portfolio are sold every year. Admittedly, this is based exclusively on US observations (Burman and Ricoy, 1997).

References

ANTOLIN, P., A. DE SERRES and C. DE LA MAISONNEUVE (2004), "Long-term budgetary implications of tax-favoured retirement plans", *OECD Economics Department Working Papers*, No. 393.

AUERBACH, A.J., W.G. GALE and P.R. ORSZAG (2003), "Reassessing the fiscal gap: Why tax-deferred saving will not solve the problem", *Tax Notes*, July 2003.

BENJAMIN, D.J. (2003), "Does 401(k) eligibility increase saving? Evidence from propensity score subclassification", *Journal of Public Economics*, Vol. 87.

BOSKIN, M.J. (2003), "Deferred taxes in public finance and macroeconomics", Hoover Institution, Stanford University.

BURMAN, L.E. and P.D. RICOY (1997), "Capital gains and the people who realize them", *National Tax Journal*, Vol. 50.

CBO (2004), *Tax-deferred retirement savings in long-term revenue projections*, Washington D.C.

COPELAND, C. (2003), "Employment-based retirement and pension plan participation: declining levels and geographic differences", *EBRI Issue Brief*, No. 262

ENGEN, E.M., and W.G. GALE (2000), "The Effects of 401(k) Plans on Household Wealth: Differences Across Earnings Groups", *National Bureau of Economic Research*, Working Paper No. 8032.

FELDSTEIN, M. (1995), "The effects of tax-based saving incentives on government revenue and national saving", *Quarterly Journal of Economics*, Vol. 110.

FINANCE CANADA (2003), *Tax expenditure and evaluations*, Ottawa.

ISSA-INPRS (2003), "Complementary & Private Pensions throughout the World", in *International Social Security Association and International Network of Pension Regulators and Supervisors*, Geneva.

MADRIAN, B.C. and D.F. SHEA (2001), "The Power of Suggestion: Inertia in 401(k) participation and Saving Behaviour", *Quarterly Journal of Economics*, Vol. 116.

MÉRETTE, M. (2002), "The bright side: A positive view on the economics of ageing", *Institute for Research on Public Policy*, Vol. 8.

MITCHELL, O. and S. UTKUS (2003), "Lessons from behavioral finance for retirement plan design", *Pension Research Council Working Paper 2003-6*, University of Pennsylvania.

POTERBA, J. (2003), Government policy and private retirement saving, CES-Munich Prize lecture.

THALER, R.H. and S. BENARTZI (2004), "Save more tomorrow: using behavioural economics to increase employee saving", *Journal of Political Economy*, Vol. 112.

YOO, K.Y. and A. DE SERRES (2004), "The Tax Treatment of Private Pension Savings in OECD Countries and the Net Tax Cost per Unit of Contribution to Tax Favoured Schemes", *OECD Economics Department Working Papers*, No. 406.

OECD PUBLICATIONS, 2, rue André-Pascal, 75775 PARIS CEDEX 16
PRINTED IN FRANCE
(12 2005 03 1 P) ISBN 92-64-00836-5 – No. 53825 2005